Flourishing a Nation and Enriching the People

Chongyang Institute for Financial Studies,
Renmin University of China

Flourishing a Nation and Enriching the People

PETER LANG
New York - Berlin - Bruxelles - Chennai - Lausanne - Oxford

Library of Congress Cataloging-in-Publication Control Number: 2024007470

Bibliographic information published by the Deutsche Nationalbibliothek.
The German National Library lists this publication in the German National Bibliography; detailed bibliographic data is available on the Internet at http://dnb.d-nb.de.

Cover design by Peter Lang Group AG

ISBN 9781433185908 (hardback)
ISBN 9781433185915 (ebook)
ISBN 9781433185922 (epub)
DOI 10.3726/b18039

Published by Peter Lang Publishing Inc., New York, USA
info@peterlang.com - www.peterlang.com

Contents

Foreword

The *In Dialogues with Masters Series Lectures*, a brand activity organized by Chongyang Institute for Financial Studies, Renmin University of China (RDCY), has been receiving extensive attention from all fields including governmental departments, colleges and universities, research institutions and the media. Since the first lecture, an audience of about 6,000 has been attracted to the lecturing rooms of the Renmin University of China by the profound thoughts and insightful opinions of renowned experts and scholars in different fields, immersing themselves in a sea of wisdom that those experts and scholars have accumulated over the long years. More than a million people have learned about their interpretation of China's development through the Internet and other media. There is no denying that the lectures are highly influential in society. The enthusiastic responses from the audience are undoubtedly the best support for the *In Dialogues with Masters Series Lectures* organized by RDCY.

To intensively display the insightful thoughts and opinions of these renowned masters, we publish a new edition, Flourishing a Nation and Enriching the People*: Interpretation of China's Development—RDCY Master Lectures*, of the RDCY Think Tank Series, following the *To Lectures by Renowned Professors at the Renmin University of China.*, First Volume of the RDCY Think Tank Series. In this new volume, the thoughts and opinions regarding the interpretation of China's development were offered by 16 well-known experts and scholars including Zheng Xinli, former deputy director of the Policy Research Center of the CPC Central Committee and executive chairman of the China Association of Policy Science, Zhao Suisheng, professor of the School of International Relations and director of the Center for China-U.S. Cooperation at University of Denver, Wu Xiaoqiu, vice president of Renmin University of China, Yang Guangbin, director of the

School of International Studies at Renmin University of China, Shi Yinhong, second-level professor of the School of International Studies and director of the Center for American Studies at Renmin University of China, Nie Huihua, executive vice president of the National Academy of Development and Strategy at Renmin University of China, etc. They review, sort out, and summarize the paths China has taken, the remarkable attainments China has achieved, and the difficulties China has been facing in its course of development from the aspects of "a stronger nation" and "an affluent people". By comparing China and Western countries, they explore the rationality and innovation embodied in China's path of development to outline China's future path of development. Relying on their profound academic knowledge, long-term field research experience, and abundant work experiences both at home and abroad, they make, with the help of both theories and examples, understandable and vivid descriptions of the path of development and its future. With their proposals of practically feasible policies and recommendations, this book is highly readable for its profound ideas and knowledge. As a book full of vivid and detailed information, it will help scholars, governmental personnel, and ordinary readers to understand the path of China as well as Chinese society.

The *In Dialogues with Masters Series Lectures* have achieved desirable social effects and are popular among people from all fields. All the topics of the lectures are closely associated with hot and hard issues of great strategic significance for the people in the course of development in contemporary China, such as the advancement of the Belt and Road Initiative and building a community with a shared future for mankind, the significance of expanding domestic demand for China's economic development, how to deal with China-US trade frictions, the history of the United States' changing policies about China, China's surrounding environment and security strategies, China's financial reforms, China's political reforms, China's fiscal and taxation reforms and other critical frontier issues. Taking advantage of their profound fascinating speeches in plain words and inspiring thoughts and wisdom, famous scholars and masters communicate with the public and audience face to face. Therefore, the lectures have shortened the distance between the audience and cutting-edge knowledge, the latest ideas, and the pulse of China's development in this era. This kind of university spirit featuring inclusiveness and academic freedom, and the fervent scenes of people crowding the lecturing halls will remain the same at the RDCY lectures.

As a new type of think tank with Chinese characteristics, RDCY has always been committed to bringing the functions of the think tank into full play in political consultation, human enlightenment, provision of suggestions, and cultivation of talented people. To build a bridge between the academic world and society, ideas and the public, and policies and research, we wish to introduce the thoughts and academic achievements accumulated over a long period in various cutting-edge fields to more people and help them to learn from and exchange ideas with each other. Above all else, we sincerely hope that accomplishments in thoughts as a result of such exchanges and communications can be timely submitted to relevant decision-making departments for the making of greater decisions that are more influential in society.

Welcome to the *In Dialogues with Masters Series Lectures* of RDCY. We will continue to share the feast of thoughts in the future.

Wang Wen
Executive dean of the Chongyang
Institute for Financial Studies,
Renmin University of China
Beijing

I. Flourishing a Nation

1. *The Belt and Road Initiative: Any Practice Pursuing Fast Success is Inappropriate*

YANG SHU

China has made remarkable achievements since its proposal of the Belt and Road Initiative. However, there are still fields that leave much room for improvement. In the face of such an unprecedentedly innovative undertaking, the academic world remains exactly the field with the slightest endeavor—no effort is dedicated to research. For the achievements and problems that we have had over the past six years, we shall analyze and summarize them carefully. For the Belt and Road Initiative, a colossal project in collaboration with other countries, six years is just the beginning of a plan that would last at least 20 to 30 years. Any ideas and practices that pursue fast success and go against reality are inappropriate. Only by facing the problems head-on can we solve them successfully. That's the self-confidence in the true sense.

This book mainly focuses on the Silk Road Economic Belt. In fact, the Silk Road Economic Belt and the 21st-Century Maritime Silk Road cannot be separated. As a result, some chapters in the book talk about the Belt and Road as a whole. When it comes to certain specific issues, the main attention is usually on the Silk Road Economic Belt.

Major Countries and Regions Not Participating in the Belt and Road Initiative

The Belt and Road Initiative is the first large-space and full-economic cooperation proposal that China has offered to the world. According to the *Vision and Actions on Jointly Building Silk Road Economic Belt and 21st-Century Maritime Silk Road* (hereinafter referred to as the *Vision and Actions*), jointly issued by the National Development and Reform Commission, the Ministry of Foreign Affairs and the Ministry of Commerce, the Belt and Road Initiative mainly focus on Europe, Asia and Africa, but is not confined to these regions. Therefore, China proposed the Belt and Road Initiative, a cooperation scheme involving a vast area as well as all sectors of the economy to the whole world. It has boosted China's economic development, put forward industrial restructuring, promoted cooperation with developing countries (which are major collaborators of the Belt and Road Initiative), accelerated the infrastructure constructions both at home and abroad, reinforced the foundation to cooperate with countries and regions along the Belt and Road routes in the future, and augmented China's export of technology and high-tech products, all of which have, to a large extent, helped the world view China from a different angle.

Countries and regions not participating in the Belt and Road Initiative include North America (the United States and Canada, which refuse to participate with a determined attitude), Australia, Japan, South Korea, most of Europe (mainly Central and Western Europe), and India.

North America is not the topic of this book for its non-participation in the Belt and Road Initiative when it was proposed. Among all the countries and regions refusing to participate, India is the most controversial country and thus worthy of special attention. As a neighbor of China, India accounts for half of the population and more than 1/4 of the GDP throughout the entire Maritime Silk Road region. Therefore, there would be a problem if India does not take part.

Due to our scarce attention to India at present, we are short of even the minimum understanding of it. I repeatedly called for attention to this issue at various important academic conferences, hoping that the research on India could be strengthened.

Table 1.1 presents the trade between China and several countries and regions that refuse the Belt and Road Initiative. In 2017, the trade volumes between China and such countries and regions accounted for approximately half of China's total foreign trade. Some of these countries and regions do not fall into the cooperation scope of the Belt and Road Initiative, while others, especially the European Union and India, do.

Table 1.1. Bilateral trade between China and some countries and regions in 2017

Country (Region)	US	Korea	Japan	EU	India	Total
Total trade volume with China ($100 million)	6,359.7	2,399.7	2,972.8	6,444.6	845.4	19,022.2
Share of China's total foreign trade (China's foreign trade totaled $4,104.504 billion in 2017)	15.49 %	5.85 %	7.24 %	15.70 %	2.06 %	46.34 %

Data source: The Ministry of Commerce of the People's Republic of China.

The Silk Road Economic Belt and the Four Economic Corridors

There are four major economic corridors within the scope of the Silk Road Economic Belt, namely the China-Mongolia-Russia Economic Corridor, the New Eurasian Land Bridge Economic Corridor, the China-Central Asia-West Asia Economic Corridor, and the China-Pakistan Economic Corridor. Some may question whether it is appropriate to integrate the China-Pakistan Economic Corridor into the Silk Road Economic Belt. It is considered part of the Silk Road Economic Belt because this economic corridor stretches from the southern part of China's Xinjiang Uygur Autonomous Region to Pakistan, serving as one of the important passages of the ancient Silk Road. "Belt and Road countries with a dual identity" is a concept I put forward two years ago. With a dual identity, a country is believed to be along both the Silk Road Economic Belt route and the Maritime Silk Road route. Therefore, Pakistan is one of such countries.

Transport arteries serve as the main body of the economic corridors. The China-Mongolia-Russia Economic Corridor was established in the 1950s. In 1951, some socialist countries signed a railway transportation agreement applicable to socialist countries in Warsaw, which is known as the Warsaw Agreement. The agreement stipulated a wide range of convenience in taxation, transit fees and import and export procedures. In a later period, although the increasingly strained relationship between China and the Soviet Union had caused the amount of transportation via this corridor to drop sharply, the transportation has never ceased. Over the years, this corridor has already regained its former function in transportation and even reached a higher level in this regard.

The New Eurasian Land Bridge is a hybrid of old and new infrastructure facilities. One of its sections in China, from Lianyungang to Urumqi, was open to service as early as 1962. The section from Urumqi to Alashankou, built in 1990, was officially put into operation and connected to the existing railways in Central Asia in 1992. This means that both the eastern and western sections of the New Eurasian Land Bridge are worn-out while the part in the middle is newly built. The New Eurasian Land Bridge has been in service for many years with a rising volume of transport.

The China-Central Asia-West Asia Economic Corridor faces huge problems since it is not yet open to service by now. This corridor was originally called the China-Kyrgyzstan Railway, with planned terminals at Aksu Prefecture in China and Osh in Kyrgyzstan. A plan in a later period attempted to extend it to Uzbekistan and further westward. However, no progress has been registered over the years since the proposal of the plan, nor a clear attitude has been expressed on the side of Kyrgyzstan. Of the four corridors, this one is the slowest in progress.

Most extensively publicized in China, the China-Pakistan Economic Corridor is believed to be the most successful one in the eyes of the public and media. As far as I'm concerned, however, the negative effects of this corridor have been ignored. This corridor has, somehow, a close connection with India's refusal of the Belt and Road Initiative. As a conception of economic cooperation, the Belt and Road Initiative involves no military purposes at all. However, the China-Pakistan Economic Corridor has been endowed with some implications beyond economic cooperation, causing India to worry about the reason for a national strategy.

First of all, can railways be constructed along the way? The northern section of the Karakoram Highway passes through the Jammu and Kashmir region, which is located at the Pamirs Plateau. A few years back, several Chinese geological research institutions spotted 17 typically serious geological disasters in this region, such as landslides, earthquakes, and mudslides, after their investigations and studies. In terms of geological engineering conditions, this region is not suitable for railway construction, not to mention high-speed railways.

Secondly, can a pipeline be laid from Gwadar Port to Kashgar? This segment rises from 0 meters to nearly 5,000 meters in elevation. To transport oil up the mountainous region, a great number of booster stations should be built along the way in addition to the measures that should be taken for heating up—sometimes the temperature at night in summer drops to -10 ℃. Despite all the necessary measures, a power transmission line in parallel with the pipeline is also indispensable in such a place where electricity is the only source of power. Considering all these costs, the construction of the pipeline would be extremely high.

If neither railways nor pipelines can be constructed, does it mean that we can do nothing at all? Of course not. Renovating the existing Karakoram Highway is our priority because parts of the Karakoram Highway are so steep and narrow with sharp turns that they are in urgent need of improvement.

Achievements of the Silk Road Economic Belt

Positive International Responses and Reinforced Global Consensus

Since the proposal of the Belt and Road Initiative in 2013, the number of countries and regions that have shown positive responses, especially in Latin America the Caribbean, and the South Pacific, has been on the rise. Among all of them, Italy is worthy of special attention. Currently, Italy is the only one among the major EU member states that has expressed a willingness to participate in the cooperation. However, with only the intention expressed by a deputy prime minister, such a declaration has not yet gained the affirmative support of the government.

In addition to the governments, more responses come from the companies. In countries like the United Kingdom, Switzerland, Germany, and Japan, although the government has not demonstrated a clear commitment to join the Belt and Road Initiative, some sectors, a great number of companies in particular, have shown positive responses.

Organizations and initiatives aimed at strategic coordination include EEU, AU, and ASEAN, the Bright Road Initiative of Kazakhstan, the Middle Corridor Initiative of Türkiye (a corridor between Europe and West Asia, which is highly consistent with the China-Central Asia-West Asia Economic Corridor), the Development Road Initiative of Mongolia, and the Two Economic Corridors and One Economic Circle Initiative of Vietnam.

The Belt and Road Forum for International Cooperation stands out as a remarkable achievement. The first Belt and Road Forum for International Cooperation was successfully held in Beijing in 2017, in which the heads of states and governments from 29 countries and 1,600 representatives of more than 140 countries (regions) and over 80 international organizations attended. 279 programs have been agreed upon at the forum, and 265 of them have been completed or implemented at a normal pace till now, with the remaining 14 ones in continuous progress and an implementation rate of 95 %.

Demonstration Effects of the Cooperation Projects

Since the proposal of the Belt and Road Initiative, China has, focusing on a framework consisting of "six economic corridors, six roads and numerous ports of various countries", achieved substantial progress in many cooperation projects.

1. Construction of corridors: smooth progress has been achieved in the construction of the China-Pakistan Economic Corridor and the China-Mongolia-Russia Economic Corridor.
2. Construction of railways: the Addis Ababa–Djibouti Railway (from Addis Ababa in Ethiopia to the Republic of Djibouti) and the Mombasa–Nairobi Standard Gauge Railway (from Mombasa to Nairobi) have already been completed and put into service; the China-Laos Railway, the China-Thailand Railway, the Hungary-Serbia Railway (from Budapest to Belgrade) are under steady construction for the time being; and the construction of parts of the Jakarta-Bandung High-speed Railway (from Jakarta to Bandung) has begun.
3. Construction of ports: Hambantota Port and Colombo Harbor of Sri Lanka, Gwadar Port of Pakistan, and Piraeus Port of Greece have been under smooth progress; significant steps have been taken in the collaborated strategic construction of Khalifa Port in the UAE; the negotiation over the Kyaukpyu Special Economic Zone Project in Myanmar is carried on with continued efforts.
4. Cooperation in aviation: China has opened direct flights with 45 countries (regions) along the Belt and Road routes, with a total of 90 airlines from 37 of these countries (regions) operating regular flights to 52 cities in China.
5. China-Europe Express: with numerous more than 10,000 trips in the aggregate, the China-Europe Express trains have visited 43 cities in 15 European countries. It is already a common phenomenon that two of the three trains sent to Europe usually return with 85 % of their containers crammed with goods.
6. Construction of industrial parks: the China-Belarus Industrial Park, the Sihanoukville Special Economic Zone in Cambodia, and the Suez Economic and Trade Cooperation Zone in Egypt have become good examples of industrial cooperation between the countries along the Belt and Road routes.
7. Cooperation in energy: the Sino-Myanmar crude oil pipeline and the bidirectional Sino-Russian crude oil pipelines have been put into service, and the construction of the eastern section of the Sino-Russian natural gas pipeline has proceeded as planned.

Expanding Cooperation in Trade and Investment

Since the proposal of the Belt and Road Initiative, the joint efforts for its goals have dramatically boosted the level of liberalization in trade and investment in China, helping extend China's open space from coastal regions and regions along the Yangtze River to the inland and border areas, which has facilitated a new pattern of opening up featured with internal and external linkage between the coastal and inland areas as well as complementary advantages between the east and the west. The trade and investment cooperation between China and the countries (regions) along the Belt and Road routes has kept expanding, leading to a positive situation of mutual progress and win-win benefits.

Enlarging Financial Cooperation

China proactively cooperates with the countries along the Belt and Road routes in the sector of investment and financing to reinforce financial integration and advance the establishment of a diversified financing system. China has signed the *Guiding Principles on Financing the Development of the Belt and Road* with 17 countries, intending to accelerate the overseas deployment of domestic financial institutions. As of June 2018, China has opened RMB clearing services in 7 countries along the Belt and Road routes, with the RMB cross-border payment system covering 41 countries (regions) along the Belt and Road routes. 11 Chinese banks have set up 71 first-level institutions in 27 countries (regions) along the Belt and Road routes to carry out financing cooperation jointly with the African Development Bank, the Inter-American Development Bank, the European Bank for Reconstruction and Development and other multilateral development banks. In addition, China has strengthened the prevention and control of legal risks by initiating and establishing international settlement mechanisms and institutions for commercial disputes concerning the Belt and Road issues.

Increasing Cultural Exchanges

Since the proposal of the Belt and Road Initiative, China has proactively cooperated with the countries (regions) along the Belt and Road routes in fields such as education, science and technology, and culture, and has formulated and issued special-purpose cooperation plans in education, technology, finance, energy, agriculture, inspection and quarantine, standard interconnection and other sectors. Through the implementation of the Silk Road Scholarship Program and the set-up of educational institutions overseas,

China has helped to train numerous technical management talents for the countries (regions) along the Belt and Road routes.

Problems in the Advancement of the Belt and Road Initiative

Misgivings of the EU, South Korea and Japan

Because of different values, systems, cultures and other divergences, European countries—countries in Central and Western Europe in particular—hold doubtful or adverse attitudes to China's rapid development. Therefore, no countries from Central and Western Europe have ever officially declared to participate in the Belt and Road Initiative. They usually view the initiative from the perspective of geopolitics. China proposed the Belt and Road Initiative as a plan for regional economic development. On the contrary, the countries in Central and Western Europe regard it as an intention of geopolitical expansion rather than a conception of regional economic development beneficial to a vast stretch of land and, therefore, have expressed various negative opinions. Envoys of more than 20 EU member states to China drafted a report in April 2018, in which they raised many questions and expressed misgivings about the Belt and Road Initiative. In fact, the report elaborated on why these countries refused to participate in the Belt and Road Initiative. Under such circumstances, the western end of the Silk Road Economic Belt is kept apart from the Belt and Road Initiative.

South Korea and Japan refused to join the Belt and Road Initiative because of issues of bilateral relations. Since the territorial dispute over Diaoyu Islands in 2007, the relationship between China and Japan had deteriorated to a freezing point until it clearly thawed after Shinzo Abe's visit to China in October 2018, which is considered a turning point for the Sino-Japan relationship. Time is needed, however, to prove whether it is a turning point or not. China and South Korea enjoyed a good relationship when the Belt and Road Initiative was put forward, but it began to sour after 2015. Therefore, it can be inferred that South Korea and Japan show no intention of joining in the Belt and Road Initiative because of the issues of bilateral relations.

The "Threat of China" in Central Asia (Mainly in Kazakhstan)

The "traditional friendship" along the Silk Road shall be interpreted from an objective perspective. In terms of the Silk Road, it is widely believed that "it came into being in the Han Dynasty, prospered in the Tang Dynasty, and gradually declined in the Song Dynasty". The nations in the current Central Asia (except for the Tajik), whose ancestors did not live there when the Silk

Road was in it prime, came to Central Asia with the Mongolian expeditionary armies into the west. In other words, most nations that had a connection with ancient Chinese people at the height of the Silk Road have migrated from Central Asia.

The former Deputy Director of the Institute of Presidential Strategy of Kazakhstan authored a book entitled *Does Kazakhstan Need to Be Afraid of China*, in which he concluded that "Kazakhstan does not need to be afraid of China." He wrote this book because the conception of the Threat of China is still prevailing in Kazakhstan.

The exchanges between China and countries in Central Asia have only lasted for no more than 30 years. Efforts are still in need for the cultivation of a sincere friendship between the two sides, so mutual understanding is the first step. At present, our understanding of Central Asia is limited to some studies on its economy and foreign policies, with much less effort dedicated to its history and culture. Among the researchers of Central Asia, few people understand Central Asian languages, a sign that we still have much to do in this regard. In Russia, however, there was a scholar who, renowned for his research on Central Asia, could speak seven languages and have published the *Twelve Lectures on Central Asia*. The fact is that our knowledge about the culture and history of Central Asia is very limited, which allows for room for deeper mutual understanding between us. Closing that gap in mutual understanding is the first challenge we need to address.

A major medium in Kyrgyzstan has surveyed the influences of Russia, the United States and China on Kyrgyzstan in its political, military, and cultural sectors. The results of the survey are as follows: politically, 67 % of the people believe that Russia has exerted the greatest influence on Kyrgyzstan, followed by the United States (35.6 %) and China (14.8 %) respectively. When it comes to military affairs, 86.8 % of the people think that Russia influences Kyrgyzstan the most, with the United States ranking second (30 %) and China third (6.5 %). In terms of culture, 56.7 % of the people believe that Russia is the most influential in Kyrgyzstan, followed by the United States (35.5 %) and China (6.9 %).[1] There is probably not a big difference in other Central Asian countries.

Disharmonious Relations between Central Asian Countries (Regions)

Due to such factors as history, water resources, territories, the issue of drugs, labor immigration, terrorist activities and extremism, the countries (regions) in Central Asia have shared a low sense of identity with each other since their independence led to contradictions and even conflicts with each other.

As a result, the cooperation across this region remains at a low level, which directly affects the development of Central Asia as well as the regional cooperation of the Shanghai Cooperation Organization and the development of the Silk Road Economic Belt.

The China-Kyrgyzstan-Uzbekistan Railway hasn't been constructed mainly because of Kyrgyzstan's belief that it is Uzbekistan, rather than Kyrgyzstan, that will benefit the most from the railway. As a result, Kyrgyzstan is unwilling to push forward the program in an active manner. The relations between Central Asian countries (regions) have already exerted a negative impact upon the development of the Silk Road Economic Belt, with some of such issues even standing out as acute challenges. After taking office, the new president of Uzbekistan has done a lot to ameliorate the relations between Uzbekistan and its neighboring countries, which has improved the relations among Central Asian countries (regions) to some degree.

Unstable Situations in West Asia

Over the years, instability features a considerable number of countries (regions) in West Asia, where various forces are still racing for power and interests. For the time being, since the countries in West Asia are more concerned about whether China will play a role in the reconstruction of Syria, they pay much less attention to the China-Central Asia-West Asia Economic Corridor. Should China take part? Can it take part? And how can it take part?—They are all realistic issues.

Bleak Economic and Trade Exchanges between Central Asia and West Asia

It is generally believed that Central Asia and West Asia are closely linked in space because the people in the two regions believe in Islam and share various connections in history. It seems to be a matter of course that a corridor between Central Asia and West Asia would be built, but this is actually not the case in reality. The fact is that Central Asia and West Asia are not closely bound in connections, exchanges, economy and trade. Among all the countries in this region, Türkiye is the major country with which Kazakhstan has established a comparatively close relationship. However, its trade with Türkiye only accounts for less than 2 % of its total foreign trade. As for other Central Asian countries, their trade with Kazakhstan is no more than 1 % of Kazakhstan's total foreign trade. However, the situation of Turkmenistan is quite different as it exports tremendous natural gas to other countries.

In history, Central Asia was once conquered by Russia whereas West Asia used to be part of the territory of Britain and France, an apparent proof of loose connections between the two regions. Their relations remained nearly unchanged in the times of the Soviet Union. Now, with a low level of economic and trade cooperation, few direct transportation lines have ever been built between the two regions, not to mention the infeasible proposal of constructing a bridge over the Caspian Sea.

If we draw a straight line between Urumqi and Cairo, the capitals of the countries along the line will include Cairo, Jerusalem, Damascus, Baghdad, Tehran, Tashkent, Dushanbe, etc. I prefer to call this straight line as the Central Asia-Western Asia Transportation Development Axis. As we know, a straight line indicates the shortest distance between two points. If there is an opportunity to build a road in the future, it will likely be constructed along this straight line as it courses through or around most of the metropolises and economic centers involved. Off this line, the construction would certainly cost a higher price with less desirable outcomes.

Insufficient Capacity of the Xinjiang Uygur Autonomous Region

The *Vision and Actions* clearly points out that the Xinjiang Uygur Autonomous Region shall develop into an important transportation hub, a center of trade and logistics, culture, science and education, and the heart of the Silk Road Economic Belt. Due to its weak capacity, however, Xinjiang is dramatically restricted to that end. Xinjiang accounts for only 1.3 % of the total GDP of China, with a share of only 0.5 % in China's overall foreign trade. Irrationally structured in industries, Xinjiang falls behind in both production and technology. In terms of the power of economic radiation, Xinjiang is only feebly influential to its trading partners overseas owing to its dependence on transit trade in foreign trade. Therefore, it is difficult for Xinjiang to take advantage of its superior geographic conditions. Moreover, Xinjiang is also in dire need of funds, technology, and talent to boost its economic development.

Bordering eight of China's neighboring countries, Xinjiang has 17 border ports which only maintain a low level of import and export trade due to their poor natural conditions. I once visited Bakhty Border Port in Tarbagatay Prefecture and spent three hours there, during which I only saw 4 trucks pass to and fro. I also went to two border ports between China and Kyrgyzstan, both at an altitude of about 3,000 meters, where people from the mainland may feel out of breath. Only a scarce amount of goods is transported across the two ports. What is discussed here evidences the prominently insufficient capacity of Xinjiang.

The Maritime Silk Road: An Attraction for Chinese Economically Developed Areas

At present, the "four regions" and "eight cities" are designed as focuses of the national economic development of China. The "four districts" refer to the Beijing-Tianjin-Hebei Economic Circle, the Xiong'an New Area, the Yangtze River Economic Belt, and the Guangdong-Hong Kong-Macao Greater Bay Area, while the "eight cities" cover Beijing, Tianjin, Zhengzhou, Shanghai, Wuhan, Chongqing, Chengdu, and Guangzhou. But northwest China, part of the Silk Road Economic Belt, is not included in the aforementioned key regions, revealing that regional gaps will keep expanding because of limited national investment and resources. Within the Belt and Road framework, this means that the gaps between the Silk Road Economic Belt regions and the Maritime Silk Road regions will further widen, which is an issue we need to pay special attention to. Widened regional gaps would absolutely cause adverse consequences in China which has a vast territory and a huge population.

The eastern part of China houses all the "four regions", which means that China has set the east as its center of economic development as well as a key investee. It is undoubtedly unreasonable that despite a massive land, the northwest shares none of the key cities for development, and this is the same in the northeast. Xi'an has a population of over 5 million in its urban area and a GDP slightly lower than that of Wuhan. In terms of strategic layout, Xi'an should be considered as a key city for development as well.

Relations with the Shanghai Cooperation Organization

Except for India, all member states of the Shanghai Cooperation Organization (hereafter referred to as SCO) are covered by the Silk Road Economic Belt. India and Pakistan joined the SCO in 2015, and Pakistan is the country with a dual identity.

Economic and trade cooperation has always been the weakness of the SCO since its establishment. The SCO has two wheels: security and economy. One of the wheels is considered larger than the other, namely the wheel of security is more important than the wheel of economy. A cart with a larger wheel and a smaller one will certainly run in circles. This is a problem that the SCO hasn't addressed in the long run. There is still no clear answer as regards how to cope with the relations between the SCO member states and the Silk Road Economic Belt and help them supplement each other. Some people raised this question when the concept of the Silk Road Economic Belt was first proposed. The strategic issue is so important that the central government has also taken it into consideration. India's refusal of the Belt and Road Initiative serves as an example that is to the disadvantage of both the development of the SCO and the advancement of the Belt and Road Initiative. What role does the China-Pakistan Economic Corridor play in the Belt and Road Initiative? And what is its role in the SCO? The SCO may encounter more difficulties in the formulation and implementation of some schemes in the future. Therefore, the relationship between the SCO and the Belt and Road Initiative should be explored from a more profound perspective.

Suggestions and the Future

Strengthen the Research on the Relationship between the Silk Road Economic Belt and the Maritime Silk Road

Domestic and international issues that involve both the Silk Road Economic Belt and the Maritime Silk Road are of great significance. However, the Chinese academic circle has only seen limited attainments in this regard, which haven't been pondered over profoundly.

Strengthen the Research on the Relations between the Six Economic Corridors

China should strengthen the research on relations between the six economic corridors. For example, what is the status of the six economic corridors in the Belt and Road Initiative? What influence they will exert on the countries and regions involved? What spinoff effect will be generated because of their influence upon each other?

Strengthen the Research on the China-Kyrgyzstan-Uzbekistan Railway

Existing studies of the China-Kyrgyzstan-Uzbekistan Railway are comparatively limited, but fortunately, I'm one of the first researchers engaged in this research. It was first proposed by the Asian Infrastructure Investment Bank (hereinafter referred to as AIIB) in 2000 to build a railway from Aksu Prefecture in China to Kyrgyzstan, supposed to link only China and Kyrgyzstan with no part of Uzbekistan involved. As a short railway, it would only be over 400 kilometers in length. AIIB planned to invest $4.5 billion in it, a cost of approximately $10 million per kilometer, with a basic requirement of an annual freight volume of no less than 1.8 million tons. However, no matter how it was calculated, it was proven impossible for the railway to achieve such an annual freight volume of 1.8 million tons, indicating that the revenue generated through the railway would be less than the cost. As a commercial bank, the AIIB would not provide financial assistance for free. If the China-Kyrgyzstan Railway was granted substantial financial support, what about the railway between Kyrgyzstan and Uzbekistan? What consensus has Kyrgyzstan and Uzbekistan reached on this issue? And what contradictions have remained?

Strengthen the Research on the China-Central Asia-West Asia Economic Corridor

According to the statistics about the number of academic papers on the six major economic corridors, those on the China-Pakistan Economic Corridor have amounted to several hundred, while those on the China-Central Asia-West Asia Economic Corridor are comparatively limited and only reach about a dozen. The disproportionate gap reveals an extremely abnormal phenomenon. It can be seen that we should deepen our research on the China-Central Asia-West Asia Economic Corridor.

Deepen the Research on Increasing the Economic Benefits Generated by China-Europe Express Trains

Most of the China-Europe Express trains (along the Chongqing-Xinjiang-Europe International Railway) are at a loss economically. Economic losses mean no possibility of further operations over a long period of time. The *Vision and Actions* explicitly indicates that by relying on governmental subsidies alone, no market-oriented operations could be sustained in the long run. We need to deepen our research on increasing the economic benefits generated by the China-Europe Express trains, to turn losses into profits and guarantee the long-term operations of the China-Europe Express trains.

Deepen the Research on the Silk Road, Especially on the Culture and History of the Silk Road

It is Richthofen, a German geographer, who coined the term "Silk Road". While publicizing the Silk Road, especially in foreign-oriented publicity, we should give more priority to the cultural connotations of the Silk Road. If it is less highlighted, various problems might occur when the Belt and Road Initiative is introduced and publicized overseas.

The following are two examples. *Why Did the Europe Conquer the World?* is a work authored by American scholar Philip Hoffman, who concluded in the book that Europe conquered the world with the help of gunpowder—with the gunpowder invented by the Chinese, Europe conquered the whole world, including China. But it is known to all that gunpowder was spread to Europe through the Silk Road.

James A. Millward, another American scholar, authored *The Silk Road: A Very Short Introduction*. The Oxford University Press has very demanding requirements for its books: first of all, the author of the book shall be an authoritative scholar widely recognized in this field; secondly, the language of the book should, instead of being in an academic style, cater to the public for their reading habits. The contents of the book in question are as follows: Chapter One "Environment and Empires", Chapter two "Eras of Silk Road Fluorescence", Chapter three "The Biological Silk Road", Chapter four "The Technological Silk Road", and Chapter five "The Arts on the Silk Road". By introducing the Silk Road from the aspects mentioned above, James A. Millward deepened the scientific, technological and cultural connotations of the Silk Road.

In pursuit of answers, we need new perspectives and new materials as we cannot rely on ancient Chinese literature as the only source. We can't always confine ourselves to the conception that the Silk Road was forged by the Chinese people. On the contrary, we should pay attention to its culture as well as history to deepen our research of the Belt and Road Initiative.

Conclusion

We have achieved remarkable achievements since the Belt and Road Initiative was proposed, but there are still many problems we need to address. In the face of such an unprecedented innovative undertaking, we haven't been fully prepared in all aspects. It is in the academic circle that the greatest problem occurs—no effort has been made to explore the issues. For the achievements and problems that we have had during the past six years, the academic world should analyze and summarize them with a serious and meticulous attitude. For the future of the Belt and Road Initiative, a colossal project in collaboration with other countries, six years is just the beginning of a plan that would last at least 20 years. Any ideas and practices that pursue hasty successes and go against reality are inappropriate. Only by facing the problems head-on can we solve them successfully. That's the self-confidence in the true sense.

(This article is compiled and edited based on Professor Yang Shu's lecture, part of the RDCY Master Series Lectures, on November 20, 2018)

Note

1 It is a multiple-choice survey, in which the sum of the three numerical values doesn't amount to 100 %.

2. *Expansion of Domestic Demand: The Key to Current Economic Development*

ZHENG XINLI

The real estate market has become the hub of financial risks. A prevailing opinion in the field of economics holds that too much cash in circulation boosts housing prices, so it is advised to curb housing prices through tightened monetary policies. The analysis in this article from the macroscopic perspective reveals that the root cause of excessively soaring housing prices lies in the lack of an integrated urban-rural real estate market in China. Expanding domestic demand is a fundamental strategy in the face of the trade war between China and the United States. For the goal of financial reform, China should give priority to monetary policy, direct financing, restraint of housing price appreciation, rural revitalization, and the internationalization of RMB.

Bring the Role of Monetary Policy in Expanding Domestic Demand into Full Play

Hindered export growth is the biggest pressure that the China-US trade war, triggered by the former U.S. President Donald Trump, has exerted on China's economy. Expanding domestic demand is a fundamental strategy in the face of the trade war. The per capita GDP of China is only more than \$8,000 whereas that of the globe and the United States stand at over \$10,000 and \$50,000 respectively. Apparently, China hasn't reached the global average standard and is much less than the United States in terms of per capita GDP. If China could maintain a high-quality economic development at a medium-to-high rate for 10 years, the impact of the trade sanctions launched by Donald Trump on China's macro economy would almost be negligible. In other words, expanding domestic demand could offset the impact of the China-US trade war on China.[1]

The Political Bureau of the Central Committee of the CPC convened a meeting on July 31, 2018, to analyze the economic situation in the first half of the year and plan economic goals for the second half of the year. The communiqué of the meeting revealed an important message: expand domestic demand. As far as I'm concerned, the decision to expand domestic demand was made based on accurate judgment and analysis of the actual economic situation in China because the central government had fully taken into consideration the impact the China-US trade war would exert on China. In a nutshell, inadequate demand has become the principal contradiction in the course of China's economic development. Why is inadequate demand considered as the principal contradiction? Four economic phenomena contribute to this conclusion:

> Firstly, downward pressure on the economy has increased. The economy has been under downturn pressure for six or seven consecutive years, with the economic growth rate dropping from a double-digit to 6.7 % in the first half of 2008. In my opinion, with its economic growth potential, China can boost its economic growth again and maintain it at a medium-to-high rate. In the first half of 2018, China's GDP grew at a rate of 6.7 %, compared with a rate of 4.2 % in the United States in the same period. However, a calculation based on the absolute amount of incremental GDP reveals that the total amount of China's incremental GDP is less than that of the United States, proving that the gap between China and the United States has, instead of being narrowed, further widened. One of the primary intentions of the Trump administration in launching the China-US trade war is to intervene in China's development using all resources accessible to the American government. As we know, American think tanks have divided the interests of the United States into four layers several years earlier: trade, allies, military affairs, and currency (the status as the global reserve currency). In the hierarchy of interests, the United States gives the least priority to trade whereas the most to U.S. dollar as the global reserve currency. The trade war was launched to maintain the status of the U.S. dollar in the global reserve currency system. Therefore, if China could maintain a sustained and sound economic development and gradually narrow its economic gap with the United States through the expansion of domestic demand, the United States' goal of launching the China-US trade war would evaporate like bubbles.

Secondly, the M2 growth rate is lower than the nominal economic growth rate. In the first half of 2018, M2 grew at a rate of 8 % while an economic growth rate of only 6.7 % was maintained. Considering the influence of inflation, however, the economic growth rate would be higher than 8 %. Apparently lower than the nominal economic growth rate, such a growth rate of M2 couldn't meet the demand of economic development.

Thirdly, the sluggish growth rate of private investment. There was no private investment in the initial stage of reform and opening up. Over more than 30 years, private investment has kept rising at an average rate of more than 20 %. Its share in overall social investment, once hitting a record of 65 %, has gradually dropped to 60 % in the last several years with a tendency of further falling. Unlike its lowest rate of slightly over 2 % a few years ago, private investment has regained an average growth rate of 5 % to 6 % in recent years. In comparison to the growth rate of state-owned investment (10 %) and that of overall social investment (8 %), however, the growth rate of private investment remains the lowest. Private investment functions as an indicator of economic vitality, and usually generates comparatively better returns because individual investors, afraid of making mistakes, are prudent in putting their money into investment. Sluggish private investment with a declining growth rate clearly reveals that economic growth requires driving forces and vitality.

Finally, according to the statistics of the International Monetary Fund, 17 % of the Chinese listed companies have business revenues lower than their repayments of capital and interest, which means that 17 % of the listed companies in China have gotten into severe financial losses and interruption of business, leading to financial turbulence if such a situation were not properly handled. Listed companies usually hire tens of thousands of employees and owe banks loans of hundreds of millions of Yuan. Once these companies go bankrupt, numerous social contradictions will burst out as a result.

As indicated by the four phenomena, inadequate demand has become the principal contradiction in the course of China's economic development. Insufficient investment, under-consumption and inadequate exports are prominent evidence of the inadequate aggregate demand in China.

At the aforementioned meeting, the Political Bureau of the Central Committee of the CPC designed the task of expanding domestic demand as a fiscal issue, in order to guarantee the role of fiscal policy in this regard.

Finance has a function of structural optimization whereas monetary policies serve to regulate economic aggregate. As for the task of expanding domestic demand closely related to economic aggregate, the central government has comprehensively profound strategies that come as the result of our reflection on some misunderstandings of finance in the past, in which our excessive attention to monetization ratio in the field of economy—the aggregate amount of M2 has accounted for more than 200 % of GDP—was the most typical. In fact, while analyzing whether the entire financial supply system could meet the needs of economic development or not, the securitization ratio (the ratio of the total stock market value to GDP) is also a factor we should take into consideration in addition to the monetization ratio. The fact absolutely dominating position of the monetization ratio over the securitization ratio in the world of economics in the past deviated from the existing financial structure of China. Because of the current financing structure of China, in which indirect financing plays a major role in combination with the auxiliary effect of direct financing, direct financing has never undergone a mature development, resulting in a relatively low securitization ratio. In comparison to a securitization ratio of 170 % in the United States and that of 160 % in Japan, it is maintained only at 49 % in China. In terms of total stock market value, China used to be the second largest stock market, only next to the United States. Surpassed by Japan in recent years, however, China has slipped to third place in the ranking. In an environment featured by underdeveloped direct financing and blocked financing channels in the stock market, the entire social and economic development will fall short of funding sources if indirect financing is under stringent control. This is a root cause for the current inadequate demand in aggregate. In consideration of such a situation, we need to deal with the current monetary supply comprehensively. There is a connection between the growth rate of M2 and economy. I visited the United States twice to get advice from Milton Friedman, a Nobel Prize winner in economics and founder of numismatics and expert in financial statistics. When he studied the laws of economic growth and M2 growth in Japan, South Korea, and China Taiwan, he found that during a period of rapid economic growth, a M2 growth rate as approximately twice as the GDP growth rate is reasonable, a M2 growth rate higher than twice of the economic growth rate in the long run will result in inflation, and a long-term M2 growth rate lower than the economic growth rate will lead to deflation. From 1990 to 2010, the M2 growth rate of China had been maintained at exactly twice the rate of economic growth. After 2010, the M2 growth rate gradually declined from double-digit to single-digit growth, which dropped to a level lower than the nominal economic growth rate in the first half of 2018. Economic growth on the downside is the most fundamental reason for the passive situation that China is facing at present.

Excessive monetary control is disadvantageous to both the macro economy and the expansion of domestic neither demand nor is it beneficial to the China-US trade war. The People's Bank of China cut down the required reserve ratio by 1 point just within half a month since its last seminar, a sign of further gradual release of monetary liquidity in line with economic performance.

The inadequate aggregate demand resulting from the economic slowdown for six or seven consecutive years and the lack of good investment programs are so challenging that even the People's Bank of China finds no appropriate measures to ease monetary liquidity. Judging from what happened in the last two years, M1 has been growing at a much higher rate than M2. Covering an additional index of time deposit, the growth rate of M2 used to differ from that of M1 by 1 or 2 percentage points. Because of the economic slowdown over the past years, companies can't find glistening spots of business nor promising investment opportunities in the market; they have no access to investment even if they successfully borrow money from the bank. As a result, the companies save the money as current deposits in their bank accounts or charge the money on the financial management accounts of their companies. That's the reason why current deposits seem to grow relatively faster than time deposits. The fact is that we have fallen into the trap of monetary liquidity.

Speaking of supply weaknesses, a considerable number of examples are worth mentioning. Currently, China imports chips and fine chemical products, both worth more than $200 billion, each year from overseas. We are aware of our weaknesses but are unable to improve them despite available funds owing to our inferior technologies. For such a predicament, fiscal policies are needed for coordination: under the guidance of fiscal and development policies, the National Development and Reform Commission can screen and decide some key projects requiring significant breakthroughs and spot promising investment projects in the fields less developed (Some of such projects can be invested through the public-private-partnership model featured by government-enterprise cooperation), which, coupled with the support of financial subsidies or discounts and the provision of bank loans under guidance, can help channel vigor into economy in a step-by-step manner. The formulation of development policies, fiscal policies and monetary policies in close coordination should be relied on for the shattering of the current bottleneck.

Expansion of Direct Financing: A Major Historical Task Faced by the Financial Reform and Development

It hasn't been long since China established its stock market, during which two dramatic fluctuations occurred, both frustrating the confidence of a great number of stockholders and leading to the downturn of the stock market at present. The stock market is believed to have the following three major functions:

1. A channel to discover the value of companies. The stock market is the only place where the value of individual companies can be discovered.
2. Allocation of funds. The capital market can allocate and channel funds to companies with great potential for development.
3. Distribution of profits (incomes). By absorbing investment funds from numerous individual investors, the stock market offers them an opportunity to share the profits of the companies.

In order to restore the normal functions of the stock market, we should motivate institutional investors with greater efforts to shift individual-investor investment, haphazard investment, and follow-up investment to rational investment and institutional investment managed by professionals. China should foster a great number of investors like Buffett to invest funds in companies with tremendous potential for development. For today's China, the following measures should be adopted to reform and develop its capital market:

> Firstly, replace the existing examination and approval system for listed companies with the register and record system. The current situation is: Approving a company for going public is to grant it an opportunity to make a fortune. As a result, all companies try every conceivable means to get listed on the stock market. A variety of unseen bribery and corruption may occur during this whole process and eventually pave the way for the jailing of some officials in charge of examination and approval. That's why the existing examination and approval system needs to be replaced with the register and record system.
>
> Secondly, strengthen supervision of the stock market. Over the years, the Chinese stock market has witnessed numerous cases of violations of laws and regulations, including manipulation of the stock market and "rat trading" etc., the majority of which were discovered and

exposed by the regulatory authorities of Hong Kong, indicating how immature the supervision system in the mainland is for the time being.

Thirdly, advance asset securitization. The debt-to-equity swap was first carried out in the 1990s during the reform of state-owned enterprises (hereinafter referred to as SOE) that has facilitated the establishment of four financial asset management companies and the divestiture of debts of more than ¥2 trillion. During the reform, some companies charged against their non-performing assets with the bank and some converted them into shares. Despite the tremendous progress that SOEs have registered over the past 20 years from the 1990s to the present, they develop on a foundation laid by bank loans, in other words, their capital has not increased at all. A development depending on loans without incremental capital over more than 20 years will inevitably lead to a high debt ratio. Therefore, it is badly necessary to establish a mechanism for the replenishment of corporate capital as soon as possible and cut down the corporate debt ratio through asset securitization. Over the past 20 years, both the government and SOEs have gained a great number of superior assets, which can go public on the capital market to raise capital if they could strip these assets off and enhance their credit (not value).

South Korea was one of the countries with an extremely high debt ratio at the end of the 20th century, ranking second worldwide for its total debt, because South Korea developed its economy mainly through debt. How did South Korea shake off such an unfavorable situation? Asset securitization is the answer to the question. Now is the time for asset securitization.

Take the high-speed rail as an example. China has a considerable number of attractive assets in high-speed rail, for example, the Beijing-Shanghai High-speed Rail, which earned a profit of more than ¥6 billion in 2016, and the Beijing-Guangzhou High-speed Rail, which has already started to yield returns. If asset securitization could offer a chance for the Beijing-Shanghai High-speed Rail and the Beijing-Guangzhou High-speed Rail to go public on the capital market, they would certainly raise hundreds of billions of yuan, with which the enterprises behind them can pull through their difficulties by repaying their due debt services.

The Dalian Steel Plant used to be a profitable manufacturer of special material steel. Taking advantage of its relocation to the suburbs, it borrowed a large sum of money from the bank to update its equipment. Despite its well-managed operations, the plant was stuck in business dilemmas and was unable to repay the debt and interests anymore due to external changes in the market and the falling of steel prices. It went bankrupt for lack of assistance with asset securitization but was fortunately granted a chance of restructuring and reorganization under the guidance of the State Council.

Asset securitization is the most fundamental way for the reduction of debt ratio and also a task of historic significance, which calls for solutions by means of market and asset securitization. Generally speaking, a corporate debt ratio of 60 % to 70 % is reasonable. Any company with a debt ratio higher than it requires help and encouragement to take their profitable assets for asset securitization so that they can raise funds and come through the difficult periods for debt service.

In summary, expanding direct financing is a major historical task faced by the community of finance in China. To accomplish this task, joint efforts of the academic world and the financial community are required.

Tightened Monetary Policy: An Inappropriate Measure against the Rising Housing Prices

The excessively soaring housing prices in first-tier cities have turned the real estate market into a hub of financial risks. A prevailing opinion in the field of economics holds that too much cash in circulation boosts housing prices, so it is advised to curb housing prices through tightened monetary policies. In terms of the real estate market, I have a different opinion because the root cause of excessively soaring housing prices in China, I believe, is the lack of an integrated urban-rural real estate market. Housing prices in Beijing are three times higher than those in New York, Washington, Los Angeles, and San Francisco, but Americans earn an income five or six times higher than ours. To observe this issue, I conducted investigations and studies in the suburbs of Los Angeles, San Francisco and New York, and concluded that the integrated urban-rural market is the key to their comparatively lower housing prices.

Silicon Valley is a typical example. There are more than 200 characteristic towns in the vicinity of San Francisco. How did these small towns take shape? Due to high housing prices in the core areas of Silicon Valley, new stretches of land were designated in the suburbs for the construction of characteristic towns, which have eventually developed into small cities. In addition to lower prices, the houses in the small towns provide a better environment and larger living spaces compared with those in the downtown. As a result, characteristic small towns effectively inhibit the rising housing prices in the downtown. Despite the continuous sprawl of the city in this manner, the modern transportation system linking the downtown and suburbs is convenient enough for people to reach their life circles in half an hour and their business circles in one hour. Especially thanks to the developed expressways in the United States, people can get to their workplaces with only an hour's drive or even half an hour sometimes. Moreover, inter-city rapid rail transit can provide fast and punctual commuter services with large capacity for commuters during rush hour.

But the situations in China are quite different. There are distinct administrative and policy barriers between urban and rural areas as well as between different provinces and cities, resulting in unimaginably high housing prices in central cities while low housing prices in areas around them. Within half an hour's drive from Beijing's Fourth Ring Road, the housing prices drop from tens of thousands of Yuan per square meter to several thousand Yuan. In the United States, the newly built communities and small cities are all well-equipped with educational facilities. As a dwelling place for wealthy people, such communities and small cities are capable of creating favorable educational conditions and superior medical services.

In China, however, the supply side is blocked by administrative and policy barriers, which apparently goes against the laws of the market economy. As far as I'm concerned, establishing an integrated urban-rural real estate market is the most fundamental way to curb the excessively soaring housing prices in a few first-tier cities. As mentioned at the Third Plenary Session of the Eighteenth Central Committee of the CPC, the market should play a decisive role in the allocation of resources, including the decisive role in the allocation of land resources as well as real estate resources. The Nineteenth National Congress of the CPC proposed to set up a sound mechanism of integrated urban-rural development to realize integrated development between urban and rural areas, in which the integration of both urban and rural real estate markets should be involved.

To that end, the spirits and guidelines decided at the Third Plenary Session of the Eighteenth Central Committee of the CPC and the Nineteenth National Congress of the CPC should be advocated to reshape the real estate system in China and establish a new system that meets the requirements of the market economy. At the same time, the commercial residential housing and affordable housing should be combined as well. Sharing housing in some cities is an example worth mentioning. The government should consider the needs of people who cannot afford a dwelling place and ensure residence for all people.

I believe that it is possible to solve the problem of excessive housing prices through the means mentioned above. If we pin all our hopes on tightened monetary policies and count on them as the solution to cut down the excessive housing prices, they would continue to rise even if the economy collapsed under the adverse effects of such policies. In a word, tightened monetary policies are inappropriate measures against the rising housing prices in cities. To solve this problem, the methods of increasing house supply, shattering the urban-rural dual structure, and integrating urban and rural real estate markets should be taken into consideration.

Activation of Rural Land Capital: A Necessary Measure for Rural Revitalization

As mentioned at the Nineteenth National Congress of the CPC, the principal contradiction facing Chinese society has become the contradiction between people's ever-growing needs for a better life and an unbalanced and inadequate development. In addition, the strategic goals of rural revitalization and the development strategy of urban-rural integration were also proposed at this important meeting. With the three proposals, a closely linked strategy profile that covers strategic basis, strategic objectives and strategic measures have come into being.

The problem of unbalanced and inadequate development is mainly embodied in the unbalanced development between urban and rural areas and the inadequate development of rural areas. The imbalanced development between regions reflects, in essence, the imbalanced development between urban and rural areas as well. Public services far inferior to those in cities is a major manifestation of the imbalance of economic and social development between urban and rural areas. The imbalance of ecological environment and economic development between urban and rural areas is mainly featured by non-point source pollution, unguaranteed food quality and safety, and dirty, chaotic and untidy environmental conditions in rural areas. In a word, the gap between urban and rural development has manifested the principal contradiction in society to a large extent. It is based on the aforesaid analysis that the Nineteenth National Congress of the CPC proposed the strategy of rural revitalization.

Urban-rural integration should be relied on to realize rural revitalization. Since the reform and opening up, it has been continuous reforms that promote China's economic restructuring, unleashing fresh driving forces for economic growth. Over the past 40 years, China has witnessed four major transformations in its economic structure.

The first economic restructuring occurred in the 1980s, by which a rural reform helped to bring about the rapid development in agriculture and the rise of township and village enterprises, solved the problem of commodity shortage, and met people's demands for light industrial and textile products and food.

The second economic restructuring, happening in the 1990s, boosted the heavy chemical industry and construction industry by establishing the socialist market economy system and modern corporate mechanism and revitalizing the four pillar industries (including electronic machinery, petrochemical industry, automobile manufacturing, and construction industry).

It was in the first decade of the 21st century that the third economic restructuring was carried out, during which government bonds were issued to raise funds for infrastructure construction. After barely ten years, China became the first worldwide for its high-speed railway network, highway network, and communication network, along with its continuous progress in infrastructure facilities.

The second decade of the 21st century witnessed China's fourth economic restructuring, which, centering on the transformation of economic development mode, facilitated the adjustment of the investment-consumption ratio to make consumption the most powerful driving force for economic growth. In terms of industrial structure, the economic growth model, featured by excessive dependence on the secondary industry, was shifted to a pattern based on vigorous development of the tertiary industry, which has become an economic growth point at present. As for the adjustment of the factor structure, great progress was registered by strengthening technological innovation, improving management and enhancing the quality of workers. Although we have achieved major breakthroughs in the transformation of economic development mode, we still need to carry on this task with continued efforts.

China is embracing the fifth decade since its first structural transformation. From the perspective of national economic structure, the light and textile industry, heavy chemical industry, real estate and infrastructure in China are all well-structured, and the tertiary industry is also in prosperity. Then what are the other major problems in economic structure? For this question, the answer is the distinct gap between urban and rural areas as a result of the urban-rural dual structure, which is the last hard issue in the structural transformation we need to address. In the following ten or even twenty years, we should, in accordance with the spirits and guidelines of the Nineteenth National Congress of the CPC, solve this last structural problem with all the efforts we can rally, and revitalize rural areas to shrink the income inequality between farmers and urban residents, guarantee an agricultural labor productivity close to the average social labor productivity, and build rural areas as beautifully as cities. If all the goals could be accomplished, China would be a high-income country in terms of per capita GDP and the largest economy with a higher economic aggregate than that of the United States.

By establishing a new mechanism for urban-rural integration, China can guide and channel social funds to revitalize rural areas and accelerate the development of both agriculture and rural areas. In the past, many people always relied on fiscal policies for rural issues, while at present, the fiscal expenditure on agriculture, rural areas and farmers has accounted for 10 % of the total national budget. Fiscal support of more than ¥2 trillion each year in this regard is the best effort of the Chinese government. The key to rural revitalization lies in finance, and capitalization of rural land is the best way we can resort to. Detailed reports were published in the *People's Daily* in succession to introduce the experience of the rural residence land system reform carried out in Jinzhai County of Anhui Province, Yujiang County of Jiangxi Province, and Jinjiang City, Fujian Province. In Jinjiang City, residence land was capitalized to attract funds from cities, which were subsequently used to build some joint ventures. With this measure, a large sum of urban capital was introduced to the countryside, bringing impetus for rural revitalization. Making flexible use of land resources to activate the dormant potential of land as a form of capital in rural areas is a major task faced by the financial community in China. The State Council designated 13 pilot counties for rural residence land system reform. Over the past five years, all the pilot counties have succeeded in the reform with remarkable achievements. Their experience should be publicized and promoted as soon as possible for earlier positive effects on a national scale.

Jinzhai County cleaned up more than 20,000 mu (1 mu = 0.0667 hectares) of vacant construction land after rectification of its rural residence land and the new rural construction, 10,000 mu of which were auctioned on the provincial construction land market. At a land price of ¥500,000 per mu on average, the county generated an income of ¥5 billion, with which the local government built new houses for farmers who chose to stay or offered economic compensations to those who gave up their own residence land and migrated elsewhere. The reform satisfied all the farmers whether they chose to stay or leave. With the residence land as a means to absorb and channel capital from cities to rural areas, why should we worry about the funds needed for rural revitalization?

As reported by the *People's Daily*, the collapsed houses, dilapidated houses and vacant houses, in aggregate, in the rural areas of Yujiang County, Jiangxi Province, account for 52 % of the total houses in the countryside. In other words, more than half of the houses in rural areas are vacant without dwellers, some of which are abandoned so that the grasses in the yards are as high as a person's. It is a great loss if rural land resources are wasted to such an extent.

If we combine agricultural modernization, new rural construction, citizenization of rural migrant workers, and the construction of characteristic towns together, push forward them as a whole, make flexible use of idle land resources and further explore sources of financing, China will witness faster progress in its agricultural and rural modernization. Currently, we are facing the significant task of the fifth economic restructuring—solving the problem of the urban-rural dual structure. We need to identify the driving force as well as the source of capital for the fifth economic restructuring.

Explorations of the Establishment of an International Monetary System with the Three Pillars of U.S. Dollar, Euro, and RMB

A low saving rate and the status of the U.S. dollar as an international reserve currency are the major reasons for America's trade deficit over the years. Because of four times of quantitative easing policies implemented in history and the transfer of its domestic crises to the rest of the world by issuing a large sum of U.S. dollars, the United States was the first to shake off the impact of the international financial crisis. 67 % of the U.S. dollars issued by the United States circulate in overseas markets. To maintain a stable international financial system in the future, an international monetary system with the three pillars of the U.S. dollar, euro, and RMB should be established. People would sell a currency and purchase the one appreciating if it depreciated because of over-issuance. It is due to such a mechanism that the governments of the issuing countries of international reserve currencies are forced to guarantee a stable value of the currencies they issue. Only in this way can a stable international financial environment be maintained after the U.S. dollar is delinked with gold. Therefore, China should accelerate the internationalization of RMB, and gradually forge it into one of the international reserve currencies. The internationalization of the RMB will generate tremendous dividends, which can offset the impact of the China-US trade war to some extent. Once RMB is given the status of international reserve currency, instead of trading iron ore and oil with our labor-intensive and resource-intensive products, we can import them with any piece of paper printed with certain currency symbols. In a word, we should create favorable conditions for the era to come, in which RMB, as an international currency, will generate dividends for every one of us.

(This article is compiled and edited based on Zheng Xinli's lecture, part of the RDCY Series Lectures, on October 11, 2018)

Note

1 The author published *Expanding Domestic Demand Is the Fundamental Strategy in the Face of the US-China Trade War* in the *Study Times* of the Party School of the Central Committee of CPC.

3. *U.S. Strategy to China and China's Responses*

SHI YINHONG

China and the United States have seen frequent frictions in their trade relations ever since the beginning of 2018 as Donald Trump, the former President of the United States, started to "confront" China in the fields of national strategy and economy and trade. As a response, China needs to adopt new strategies of "keeping a low profile" and "achieving something" at the same time to abate or even eliminate the possibility of a dichotomy in the world economy, thus guaranteeing China's smooth development in the long run. China should stick to this strategy with great determination as well as great patience. As a great power in the world, China, with every move and decision, will have a significant impact on the whole world.

Frequent frictions have been common in the trade between China and the United States ever since the beginning of 2018 as Donald Trump, the former President of the United States, started to "confront" China in the fields of national strategy and economy and trade. In addition to the speech that the U.S. Vice President Pence delivered on October 4, 2018, the U.S. has, in general, summed up the following "five crimes" of China in recent years: firstly, economic aggression, especially against developed economies. Secondly, military expansion, namely the so-called military strategic issues in the narrow sense. Thirdly, Rex Tillerson, the former Secretary of America, used the word "predatory" to comment on China in 2017, which immediately became a standard adjective to describe China's economic activities in developing countries in the opinion of the U.S. government and the public. This time in Pence's speech, he put forward a new term—"China's debt diplomacy". Fourthly, Donald Trump is never an advocator of human rights and democracy. Sarcastically in Pence's speech, however, he devoted the majority part of his talk to a severe criticism of the so-called human rights issues in China. The fifth and last accusation is relatively a new one. Donald Trump once mentioned on his Twitter account and at the UN Security Council meetings in advance that as a response to the China-US trade war he launched, China would have to mainly target at the white grassroots voters in support of him and plan necessary trade retaliation aimed at America's agriculture. In the bulk of his discourse, Mike Pence accused China of intervening in, both secretly and publicly, the American social system and the opinion of the public through a wide range of activities. In a word, all kinds of fundamental contradictions between China and the United States are getting worse and worse.

Therefore, for the profound revelations we can learn from the China-US trade confrontations and the countermeasures China needs to take, I will share my opinions in the following discussions. For China, improving our basic understanding and optimizing our fundamental strategies are of great significance. As far as I'm concerned, distinguishing between the most important issues and the less important issues and making according adjustments are the most urgent issues China needs to tackle at present.

Six Problems with China's Economy and Trade

Some developed and developing countries believe that they're faced with six problems in association with China's foreign trade and economic activities. In my opinion, some of the problems are fabricated stories, some are exaggerated, and some are absolutely misunderstandings. The six problems are as follows:

> Firstly, China has a surplus in free trade, which means that many of China's trading partners suffer a huge deficit in their trade with China.
>
> Secondly, the market in China is typical with strict access and an unfavorable environment for foreign investment. More specifically, China had long suspended relaxing access to its capital market and even tightened regulations in some respects until not long ago.
>
> Thirdly, there are some negative opinions and criticisms about China's economic cooperation both at home and abroad. Compared with most countries in the world, China takes stricter control of its economic activities both at home and abroad at a more extensive range than other countries. In recent years, however, such control has even been intensified in both the scope and degree.
>
> Fourthly, in comparison to foreign companies in China and Chinese private companies, Chinese SOEs are granted a variety of

preferential policies, including substantial subsidies, by the Chinese government.

Fifthly, the problem of loaning transparency is related to the hot issue of the debt crisis recently.

Finally, China's outward foreign direct investment usually, or at least sometimes, fails to fully alleviate the problems of employment, economic development, and ecological protection in local societies with tangible effects.

Additionally, the most urgent and important issue at present is that the Chinese government advocates economic globalization and has, over the years, played a due part within its capacity to that end. We believe that the global economic and trade order or globalization is beneficial to both China and the people of all countries worldwide, but reforms are still required to make it more beneficial to developing countries. Only in this way can an impartial, reasonable, and sustainable global economic and trade order be maintained. We now understand that it is not a principal issue for maintaining and improving globalization, but an issue of less importance or even one we should not pay much attention to.

China's Needs of Reinforced Responsiveness and Faster Action to Principal Issues

It should be noted that influenced by the trend of reverse globalization in some major countries, a large number of voters in developed countries have begun to resist or even "resent" globalization. Such an environment, full of discontent and complaints, allows no room for the globalization advocated by China all the time.

Under the guidance of "common prosperity", a concept proposed at the times of Deng Xiaoping and pursued by China as a constant belief, China has achieved considerable progress in its development and rendered its people a much better life. Globally, however, "common prosperity" is not yet a norm and basis for China to deal with its relations with other countries of the world. Over the decades of economic globalization, the conception of "common prosperity" should have led to a consensus about common prosperity between developed and developing countries, which is the only appropriate philosophy in line with the development demands and situations of all countries across the world.

In the past, common prosperity did not stand out as an issue between developed countries and developing countries as developed countries are too affluent whereas developing countries are too poor. Now, we should be aware that common prosperity is an issue between China and all the other countries. What are all the other countries? More than 200 countries (regions) on earth except for China, including both developed countries and developing countries, are "all the other countries". As a big country with a vast territory and a huge population, China's economy keeps growing at such a rapid pace that its influence worldwide increases sharply as a result. Since China's decisions and actions will exert an increasingly tremendous impact on the international community, we need to consider the issue of common prosperity between China and the rest of the world.

To sum up, China should make appropriate adjustments as regards its conceptions and perceptions. For issues of significant importance, China should reinforce its capacity to deal with them and make faster responses. Moreover, China also needs to deepen and expand domestic reforms in the long run, and further implement and strengthen measures for foreign exchanges and mutual understanding.

Donald Trump: A "Cruel" Strategist But Smart Tactician

I am reluctant to hear people define Donald Trump as a businessman. It implies that people can make a deal with him, and it seems to be an easy job to make a deal with him. I think opinions like these are ridiculous. Speaking of his attitude toward China, Donald Trump is a "cruel" strategist but a smart tactician. He is a strategist because, in terms of relations with China, he has never dragged himself into a two-line battle, let alone fought his opponent over a wide range of issues; instead, he always rallies all his bullets for a single campaign during a particular period. In addition to the concentrated strategies, he always takes the initiative to attack. At least, he launches whatever campaigns he plans to. He launches campaigns periodically and, after a period of truce, focuses all his attention on another campaign he launches. In terms of specific strategies, he likes to impose unprecedented pressure on and threaten his opponent, but will also occasionally console it with petty favors. In a word, he squeezes out as many benefits as possible in each campaign.

Resorting to the same strategies, Donald Trump puts unprecedented pressure on China and threatens it at the same time when it comes to China-US economic and trade frictions, in an attempt to extract maximum interests. In addition to the China-US economic and trade relation, he even resorts to the same logic in affairs of strategic front and political ideological front.

Regardless of the temporary gains or losses, China would, after a period of tense confrontation, have to make some concessions in its trade with the United States at an appropriate moment, given a negotiation based on fair and mutual respect and no compromise of China's core interests when it comes to issues about China's sovereignty and dignity. The major concession is about a substantial increase of imported products from the United States to China and a substantial relaxation of market access for the U.S. funds to the Chinese market. Without such a compromise, the war of economy and trade will never end, nor will a comparatively long period of truce be reached. We require a comparatively long period of truce or, more precisely, a truce for some areas in our economy and trade. Likely, the war of economy and trade can only be temporarily suspended if the two sides start to impose high tariffs on each other's exported products in turn. Judging from what happened in the past, the Trump administration has never given up the strategy of short-term truce. After several rounds of the China-US trade war, I believe that China needs to make timely adjustments in the China-US trade relationship to win peace for some of its areas involved in the China-US trade war, thus creating a favorable environment for the optimization of its pattern of economy and financial technology.

Countermeasures with Both "Palliative Effects" and "Permanent Effects": China's Proper Response to the Trade War

I hold that comprehensive countermeasures are required to end "palliative effects". In the face of the high-pressure and unreasonable tariff policies of the United States, we should plan resolute and powerful measures of trade retaliation to express our determined threats of trade retaliation on the one hand and demonstrate our willingness to negotiate and make concessions on the other. The stance of the Chinese government has been clear over the past several months: China is willing to negotiate on the premise that the United States treats China on a fair footing with an honest and trustworthy attitude. The willingness for a negotiation doesn't embody the outcomes of the negotiation, and the stances and strategies adopted in negotiation have nothing to do with the willingness for a negotiation.

Speaking of "permanent effects", I think we should, first of all, have a deep understanding of the nature of the so-called "permanent effects" to further strengthen our determination. In an important keynote speech at the opening ceremony of the Boao Forum For Asia on April 10, 2018, President Xi Jinping declared, in a clearer and more specific manner than in the past, a series of significant decisions with permanent effects that the Chinese government has planned to adopt, which include: substantial relaxation of market access, creation of a more attractive environment for investment, strengthening of intellectual property protection, and expansion of imports in a more active manner. Now the whole world and all the Chinese people are watching how these decisions are implemented and how long they will be in effect. China indeed needs to make some appropriate adjustments that will be truly put into practice in a later period. This is an indispensable foundation for the safeguarding of economic globalization.

Current international and domestic situations indicate that China needs to deepen comprehensive reform through vigorous and long-lasting structural adjustments and strive for substantially extensive development. China still has great potential in both the domestic market and internal resources. At the same time, China should accordingly reduce its dependence on external markets, external resources, and external technologies to further advance our technological independence and innovation. In a word, China should carry out and deepen comprehensive reforms through long-term structural adjustments and strive for a substantive in-depth opening up.

China's Needs of New Strategies to "Keep a Low Profile" and "Achieve Something" at the Same Time

Over the past five or six years, China has registered unprecedented achievements in foreign relations. Since the G20 Hangzhou Summit in September 2016, especially from early 2017 to Kim Jong-un's visit to Beijing in March 2018, China has accomplished goals it failed to accomplish for over one decade. Ever since George Walker Bush took office for the second time, problems from the peripheries of China have emerged increasingly as more and more neighboring countries started to contend with each other over disputes. In just over a year, China's diplomatic relations with neighboring countries has improved dramatically, a very good sign for China's development. China's diplomatic strategy is based on the principles of coordination, reconciliation, consultation or winning as many friends and neutrals as possible, which will certainly be attached great importance to and be further optimized so that the relations between China and its neighboring countries in an all-around way will be further improved.

In the future, China needs to pursue new strategies to "keep a low profile" and "accomplish its goals" at the same time. This means that in the next five or six years, China should abide by a moderately conservative strategy and adjust its trade policies, accordingly, to regain the comparatively relaxed environment before major countries worldwide deepen their misunderstandings of China and become hostile towards us and find the opportunities to accomplish its goals of development.

Since early 2018, the increasingly volatile political and economic environment worldwide has started to reveal a possibility of a dangerous tendency—dichotomy. On the one hand, the U.S. government has substantially eased its economic and trade conflicts with other developed economies through bilateral negotiations and has, therefore, established a close partnership with other economies, which may subsequently lead to separate free trade or quasi-free trade agreements between the United States and its partners respectively. Sooner or later, the United States will abandon the WTO mechanism both practically and nominally. Now let's review the WTO mechanism. Its greatest advantage lies in its globality regardless of its incapability in the current trade in service and labor conditions. When a global mechanism is abandoned practically and nominally, we cannot set aside the fact that global trade is always in need of a system of rules. The United States may seek to establish a new system of economic and trade rules with other advanced economies and its close partners. However, such a new system of economic and trade rules may not be globally applicable but only cover the developed countries and their close partners.

In addition to the trend of dichotomy, a variety of fundamental contradictions between China and the United States have also been exacerbated dramatically, and the U.S. government may implement the negative covenants in the U.S.-Canada-Mexico Free Trade Agreement—the other two countries have the right to veto if one of the countries attempts to negotiate with a non-market economy country for a free trade agreement. According to America's standards, China, of course, falls into the category of non-market economy country. If the U.S. government resorts to the above "group economy and trade" policy, it may drive China into a dilemma where there will be fewer and fewer choices. In the future, China may have to rely on developing countries that are friendly with China, especially the cooperative countries along the Belt and Road routes, for major foreign economic and trade activities.

China should do its utmost to abate or even eliminate the possibility of such dichotomy in the world economy so as to guarantee China's development in the long run. As a great power in the world, China should be both determined and patient for its every move and decision that will exert a significant impact on the world.

(This article is compiled and edited based on Professor Shi Yinhong's lecture, part of the RDCY Series Lectures, on November 12, 2018)

4. *A Pragmatic China Is the Best Countermeasure against the Technological Blockade of the West*

CHEN YAOGUO

Independent research and production of advanced home-made products is a process full of difficulties, and substituting imported products with such home-made products is also a long way to go. As home-made products require long-term improvement in both quality and stability, there is still a huge gap between the current home-made products and internationally representative products. Technological blockade of Western countries, despite its adverse impact on China in the short term, will help and motivate China to take a path of independent technological development. It is just a matter of time for China to become a world-class technological power if its domestic competition mechanism could be further improved and the mechanism for the protection, competition and elimination of independently developed technologies is under control.

This article aims to analyze the problem of industrial "lockdown" in China, which involves the following six major aspects.

Elimination of the IOE Influence

IOE is the short-term for IBM, Oracle and EMC. IBM is a major provider of servers and minicomputers, Oracle focuses on the business of database and data management, and EMC provides solutions to storage problems, all of which have a considerable share in the field of finance. Their products and services, favored by banks in the past for their superb reliability, have earned a lot for their high market share. Of course, this is not only a matter about money, but also about the security of national key information. So shaking off the IOE influence is a key issue that China cannot avoid in its promotion of IT applications nationwide. China should develop advanced products and services of its own to substitute those imported overseas.

However, independent research and production of advanced home-made products is a process full of difficulties. Take the database industry that I engage in as an example, Renmin University of China is one of the first institutions that devote themselves to the independent research and production of databases in this field in China. RUC King Base is currently among the top domestic database companies in China. Substituting imported products with home-made products is also a long way to go. As home-made products need long-term improvements in both quality and stability, there is still a huge gap between the current home-made products and internationally representative products. It is worthy of our attention that some Chinese database companies with an Internet background have developed at a rapid pace in recent years.

The Chip Issue

Another field worthy of our attention is chip manufacturing. From what ZTE suffered, we come to realize how heavily the Chinese chip industry, the sector of CPU and GPU hardware in particular, is dependent on foreign technologies. Mask aligner, a sophisticated machine dedicated to chip manufacturing, for instance, requires a relatively closed environment for its production of high-precision chips. China depends heavily on imported mask aligners as it is extremely difficult for Chinese companies to manufacture such highly sophisticated equipment totally on their own. Even if some mask aligners are successfully manufactured, their quality is far from what's required. Things like this have become a "soft underbelly" of China subject to the technological blockade of the West. The fact that the equipment for the manufacturing of chips does not meet the requirements is one of the key reasons for the less developed situation of Chinese chips in the long run. Additionally, from the perspective of industrial background, the Internet and software industries are more attractive to talents. In the field of equipment manufacturing, however, the investment in its research has not yet been given too much attention, which subsequently leads to a severe outflow of talent from this industry. Brain drain plays a key factor behind China's lack of breakthroughs in core technology and weak foundation for manufacturing techniques, both of which contribute to the "technological blockade" situation that China is facing. What is talked about here is the problem of hardware.

Gap in System Software

In terms of software, a wide gap exists between home-made system software, such as operating systems, databases, big data software and industrial software, and foreign advanced system software. In the field of industrial software, problems like a shortage of talent and lack of accumulated experience are not uncommon. In the era of big data, open-source software is developed thick and fast, which is definitely to our advantage as we have access to reference objects in our research. However, since the United States takes the leadership in the research and development of big-data system software, such as Hadoop, Spark and other popular software, China has scarcely registered some independent achievements in this regard. Having come to realize this problem, many Chinese companies, including Alibaba, Huawei and others, have started to invest in the development of open-source software as well as independent software with great efforts, and have achieved some progress. However, a distinct gap still remains in talent training and scientific research between China and some foreign countries.

Unseen Apprehensions behind the Rapid Development of Artificial Intelligence

Artificial intelligence (AI) has undergone dramatically rapid progress in recent years. Over the past three to five years, Chinese AI technology has always been a hot topic because of the rapid progress registered in unmanned vehicles, automatic speech and image recognition. In a facial recognition competition famous in the international realm of facial recognition, the top five are all Chinese companies. Currently, China has taken the lead for some of its AI algorithms that are more accurate than those of other countries.

At present, algorithm engineering has emerged as one of the most attractive occupations in China because the algorithm is the key to AI in the field of software. Because of the popularity of machine learning, for example, a great number of students have swarmed to learn it, setting aside basic development of software. They all believe that their study of algorithms will easily bring them an ideal job. It is known that RUC postgraduates of AI, algorithms, or related majors can earn an annual salary of about ¥400,000, and that figure for some excellent doctoral graduates of related majors can hit ¥800,000 per year. In comparison with other majors, the knowledge about algorithms is easy to learn. A sum of tens of thousands of Yuan in training institutions would offer a channel for students to learn it. They will be skillful in algorithms after attending some additional programming courses. Since there are plenty of open training courses on the market, students can easily find access to them. On the contrary, very few people study subjects or engage in jobs related to system software. TensorFlow, systematic software for deep learning for instance, is an intellectual product developed by such large foreign companies as Google and core scientific research teams overseas rather than Chinese companies. When Google first developed it as open-source software, it had actually been at least three to five years inferior to the advanced technologies that Google had mastered—Google can't publish its latest and most advanced technologies immediately after they are developed. The lack of independent research and development of fundamental technologies is indeed an unseen predicament that worries AI research and development in China.

Inevitable Competition for Strategic Resources of Big Data

Why have big data and AI in China kept developing so rapidly? Data resources appear to be one of the key reasons. Big data and AI technology mean a lot to large Internet companies. For colleges and universities, it would be very difficult for them to conduct AI-related research without the help of big data. Because of the privacy protection conceptions and constraints of policies and regulations in the United States, researchers in American universities have no access to big data, which subsequently leads to their relatively conservative research and development in exploring technological breakthroughs. It reveals how important strategic resources of big data are. To illustrate the importance of big data, some media even compare it to a new type of oil. The globe will undoubtedly see an inevitable trend of rivalry over data resources in the future.

Sober Understanding of China's Advantages and Disadvantages in Big Data and Artificial Intelligence

China has achieved rapid progress in the research and development of big data and AI products as well as their applications, which seems to be a great threat in the eyes of Western countries. Considering China's colossal economic scale in particular, the United States will certainly intervene in China's development with every conceivable meas. Then, how can the United States intervene in China's development? Technological lockdown is the very answer to this question. Our prominent technological weaknesses happen to be the core technologies we are in urgent need of for China's industrial development, like the engine of an airplane. The mask aligner and system software mentioned previously also fall into this category of less developed technology, which is prone to be a "soft underbelly" for China's development.

Whether it is the research and development of intelligent manufacturing or big data, they are all conducted to get rid of the "technological blockade" predicament. They are carried out not to improve and perfect a certain product, but to develop and manufacture it from the very beginning. If Oracle refuses to provide products and services to China anymore, it will otherwise offer an opportunity to Chinese database companies. Technological lockdown of the West indeed has adverse effects on China in the short term, but in the long run, it is beneficial for China to develop its own technologies. It is just a matter of time for China to become a world-class technological power if its domestic competition mechanism is further improved and the mechanism for the protection, competition and elimination of independently developed technologies is under control.

Big data and AI industries in China have undergone rapid progress over the past five or six years and may have surpassed the United States. Currently, as an attraction for talents all over the world for its advantages in big data and AI, China has welcomed numerous top professionals to return. The reason for big data and AI enjoy such advantages in China is that we have abundant data resources, countless users, and diversified application scenarios in this regard. That's the core competitiveness of China in the development of big data and AI in the future.

China's major disadvantages are mainly reflected in some basic system technologies like basic system software. To get rid of the "technological blockade" predicament, what China needs is not only application products but also basic technologies, institutional innovations and a solid foundation. After all, only advancement in every aspect could pave the way for breakthroughs. At present, the Internet is under rapid development, and the sector of AI has attracted numerous outstanding talents. On the contrary, the market of basic research and development demonstrates relatively weak vitality so students are unwilling to engage in the development of systems or basic code and construction of basic systems. Instead, they invariably target the study of algorithms in the hope of earning a higher salary. This tendency can only be changed through the means of the market over time. Therefore, we should pay extra attention to the brain drain phenomenon in the research and development of basic system software. Moreover, we should strengthen the protection of intellectual property rights as well. Better protection of intellectual property rights is the only way that guarantees the return of innovations. In a nutshell, laying a solid technological foundation through pragmatic research and development is the single reliable way for China to counter the technological blockade of the West.

(This article is compiled and edited based on Professor Chen Yaoguo's lecture, part of the RDCY Series Lectures, on November 23, 2018)

5. *The Nature and the Root Causes of China-US Trade Frictions*

HE WEIWEN

A trade war, with the largest sum of money involved in history, broke out on July 6, 2018. Donald Trump, who seemed to have changed his mind a few months before its outbreak, has never shifted away from his original plans as confrontations and negotiations are both means for his ultimate goal of the realization of the "America First" policy. Launching a trade war was a plan already established; negotiations serve as campaigns for trade interests at the negotiating table. In this article, thorough analyses are conducted to clarify the root causes of the China-US trade war as well as four widely known misunderstandings. A variety of countermeasures and suggestions are proposed from multiple perspectives.

The United States may have envisaged the following scenario before raising additional tariffs on July 6, 2018: the heads of China and the United States make a phone call to each other to temporarily cease the trade war at the last minute. But that is just an ideal assumption rather than reality. The American government launched the trade war in the end and China took immediate countermeasures as a response, thus kicking off the trade war.

On June 15, 2018, the Trump administration officially approved imposing an additional 25 % tariff against 1,102 Chinese products of $50 billion exported to America, which would be levied in two groups respectively. The tariff of the first group, consisting of 818 products worth $34 billion in total, would be collected starting from July 6; whereas the schedule for the second group of products, with a value of $16 billion, is still undetermined. But America's current tariff plan for only one group of products is by no means a reasonable ground to let us off guard because a new plan for the $16 billion worth of products would come in the near future. In parallel with the American government's announcement of its tariff policy against the first group of Chinese products, the Ministry of Commerce of the People's Republic of China immediately declared similar countermeasures, which are as stringently as its opponent's, against America.

Donald Trump made another statement on June 18 to impose additional tariffs on $200 billion worth of Chinese products and possible additional tariffs on another batch of Chinese products that amount to $200 billion ($400 billion worth of products in total). As far as I'm concerned, such a policy is obviously impractical.

This article will focus on the following four issues about the trade war.

Review, Estimated Prospect and Impact of the Trade War (What Happened? and What Will Happen?)

A Brief Review: Donald Trump Did Not Deviate from His Original Purposes

People believe that Donald Trump has gone back on his words because what his administration has done has deviated from the consensus reached between China and the United States on May 18, 2018. In my opinion, however, Donald Trump has never swerved in his core idea of launching a trade war between China and the USA because not a word was mentioned to avoid a trade war or the taxation of additional tariffs in the China-US Joint Statement reached on May 18—collection of additional tariffs was, instead of being canceled, just postponed. Starting from March 22, the whole process could be divided into five stages: confrontations—negotiations—a new round of confrontations—new round of negotiations — further confrontations.

In the first stage, Donald Trump signed an executive order on March 22 to authorize the Office of the United States Trade Representative (hereinafter referred to as USTR) to announce imposing an additional 25 % tariff on $50 billion worth of Chinese products, against which China declared immediate countermeasures. This is the beginning of confrontations.

The second stage featured two rounds of China-US negotiations from May 3 to 18 that have led to consensuses on a wide range of issues. This is the phase of negotiation, but the so-called negotiations are as good as confrontations judging from the listed requirements of the United States.

During the third stage, the White House declared on May 29 that it will publish a list of $50 billion worth of Chinese products on June 15, against which additional tariffs will be imposed soon. Moreover, it also expressed that other investment and product restrictions will also be adopted against China starting from June 30. This is a new round of confrontations.

The fourth stage started with the visit of Wilbur L. Ross, the U.S. Secretary of Commerce, and his delegation members to China for a trade negotiation from June 2 to 3, a sign of a new round of negotiations.

In the fifth stage, the White House announced an official plan on June 15 to impose additional tariffs on Chinese products starting from July 6, with the first group of products of $34 billion subject to the new tariff policy starting at 0:01 July 6, Washington time while the tariff schedule for the second group, consisting of products of $16 billion, to be implemented in a later period. As a response, the Chinese government declared to charge additional tariffs against $34 billion worth of imported products from America as a countermeasure. This is the stage of further confrontations.

In fact, both confrontation and negotiation are methods for the realization of the "America First" policy, the ultimate goal of the United States. In an attempt to substantially cut down China's trade surplus over America and maintain America's technological advantages, the American government wishes to force China to make concessions in line with the interests and rules of America as well as nullify its national policies and subsidies for its Made in China 2025 program. China is expected to abide by rules established by America rather than those of the WTO in terms of economic and trade issues—this is the real purpose of America, for the realization of which both confrontation and negotiation serve as the approaches. South Korea, for instance, agreed to amend the Korea-US Free Trade Agreement to increase imports of trucks from the United States and reduce related tariffs lest the United States would impose a 25 % tariff on its steel and aluminum products—a typical example to prove that confrontation is just a measure for the United States to implement its trade policies. Just like war is a continuation of politics, negotiation is a trade war by the side of the negotiating table. There is no essential difference between themes. A review of the history reveals that Donald Trump has never changed his core values about China despite his various changing strategies. As Karl Marx said the force of matter can only be destroyed by the force of matter, China should respond to America's tariff policies with resolute countermeasures as stringently as the latter's because negotiations and tolerance will never win us an opportunity to solve the problem.

Estimated Prospect: What Will Be the Trump Administration's Next Move?

Donald Trump will never change his attitude when it comes to the following two aspects: firstly, abandon the multilateral tariff negotiation mechanism within the WTO framework to unilaterally impose additional tariffs. Secondly, restrict China from implementing and subsidizing its national program of Made in China 2025 from the perspective of strategic interest. There are two distinct features in Donald Trump's strategies: firstly, continuously restrict activities in key industries and investments associated with China while maintaining an additional-tariff policy against Chinese products exported to the United States; and secondly, intervene in China's transfer of technology and industrial policies in joint efforts with other countries.

The Trump administration may take the following two moves: levy additional tariffs, and impose more restrictions on high-tech industries in China.

The Trump administration may adopt the following two strategies: negotiate (the Trump administration may demonstrate signals for negotiation, and then China should carry out further negotiations with it), and implement stricter tariff measures. For China, confrontation and negotiation are also means rather than purposes. China pursues two purposes: maintain the authority of the WTO and its regulations, and safeguard China's right to develop, both of which are red lines that no one is allowed to cross.

There might be three possibilities in the future: firstly, the two sides negotiate and reach a quick consensus; secondly, a total trade war breaks out, with the United States imposing additional tariffs on Chinese products of hundreds of billions of U.S. dollars and the trade war spreading to various countries and regions; and thirdly, a consensus is finally reached after rounds of confrontations and hard negotiations. The most unlikely to happen, the first possibility has been proven unrealistic. Though the second situation has a small chance to occur, we should still be cautious and make preparations accordingly. The third scenario is the most possible for the reasons listed below: first of all, since China and the United States differ a lot in a wide range of things as well as in their core interests, the agreement they reach would not be stable; secondly, the United States has overestimated its chances of winning the trade war; and lastly, the United States will find that the trade war would possibly play a limited role in changing China's attitude and its status quo one year after the trade war broke out. The negative effects of the trade war might stand out in America, forcing its government to compromise in pursuit of different solutions.

To predict the impact of the additional tariffs policy, we should first make a comparison of the products of China and the United States. In 2017, computer and electronic products accounted for the largest share among the top ten products exported from China to America, amounting to nearly $200 billion. The total export of China would value more than $300 billion plus transportation equipment and chemical products. According to the Ministry of Commerce of the People's Republic of China, 59 % of the $34 billion worth of products to be tariffed was produced by American companies. All the data indicate how hastily the Trump administration has gotten prepared for the trade war.

It would be a mistake if we believed that the United States was starting to soften by proposing that U.S. companies are entitled to apply for tariff exemptions and consider it a new intention of the United States. The fact is that such a proposal was put forward only based on the protocol of the USTR, apparently not a sign of change in America's attitude toward the trade war. In terms of product categories, automobiles will suffer the most direct influence, China's additional 25 % tariff measure against automobiles imported from America will result in a decrease in the number of such products, which is apparently good news for automobile manufacturers in Europe and Japan.

China and the United States have different estimations of their economic losses. According to the statistics of the Chinese customs authorities, the Chinese mainland's trade surplus over the United States was approximately equivalent to the total of its trade deficits against Japan, South Korea, and China Taiwan in the first quarter of 2018. The figures reveal the flows of products from the perspective of the industrial chain. In fact, Asia houses the bulk of the industrial chain whereas the United States takes control of the two ends of the Smiling Curve, explaining why all these countries and regions will be affected.

The WTO has made a relatively optimistic estimation of world trade, which has started to rebound since 2017 and has grown at a rate of more than 4 % in both 2018 and 2019. But now, the trade war between China and the United States has aggravated to such an extent that the WTO will definitely lower its expectations if it continues like this in the future. A recent prediction from Morgan Stanley indicates that if the trade war continues to expand, the GDP growth rate of both China and America will be 3 % lower than it would be without the trade war; the EU will see an even more dramatic fall, approximately 4 %, in its GDP growth; and Canada, South Korea and other countries may experience a drop of 10 % due to their excessive economic dependence. Therefore, there exists such an opinion: the world is at the most critical moment since the fall of the Berlin Wall. This kind of opinion is worthy of our attention, but we shall never easily believe in it without giving it a thorough thought. We shall not forget to carry out research with a sober mind under the principle of science, nor shall we be off guard to underestimate the severe impact of the trade war.

The Nature and Root Causes of the Trade Frictions and the Trade War between China and the United States

The Nature of the Trade Frictions and the Trade War between China and the United States

There are two key points in the nature of the trade frictions and the trade war between China and the United States: firstly, whether the WTO rules are still in effect. Can the multilateral system be maintained? If the multilateral system were abandoned and the world returned to its former state before World War II, just like in the 1930s, what would the world be like? Secondly, a fundamental issue—whether China has the right to develop emerging and high-tech industries and the right to implement the Made in China 2025 program—is considered an important national strategy related to the great rejuvenation of the Chinese nation. In short, the nature of all the problems is about multilateral rules on the one hand and China's right of development on the other hand.

For the first key point, the principle is that WTO rules cannot be changed or abandoned. The fact that the United States is not allowed to do so is because Articles 22 and 23 of the memorandum concerning the WTO dispute settlement mechanism stipulate that no member states shall be allowed to implement one-side restrictions or tariffs. Twenty years ago, ruling the United States' General Clause 301 Investigation against Europe as illegal, the WTO authorized the latter to take retaliation measures against €2 billion worth of American products, driving the former to give up its General Clause 301 Investigation and promise to comply with the WTO rules. In a later period, the United States has gradually come to realize the effect of tariff as a good weapon. If China "plays safe" like South Korea, its concession would pose challenges to the authority of the WTO rules. The multilateral trading mechanism established through the efforts of several generations after World War II is facing severe challenges arising from the unilateralism and protectionism advocated by the Trump administration. From 1929 to 1933, the United States adopted a high tariff policy against Europe to protect its manufacturing industry and employment, because of which European countries took immediate tariff countermeasures that caused the export and import of the United States to drop by 69 % and 66 % respectively and the world trade to fall by 66 %. The employment rate in the United States slumped rather than rose, bringing a serious impact on the world economy. It was not until the re-establishment of the multilateral rules after the formation of the Three Pillars in 1944 that the world economy started to embrace a boom that lasted for decades after World War II.

For the second key point, the principle is that no one is allowed to damage the right of development and other legitimate rights of China. A comparison of the General Clause 301 Investigation and the list of the $34 billion worth of products to be tariffed reveals that many Chinese high-tech products included in the tariff list this time were not covered in the General Clause 301 Investigation, which is apparently an excuse to conceal the United States' real target—the Made in China 2025 program—and contain China's development in this field. The Made in China 2025 is an internal affair of China, in which the United States has no right to interfere. What everyone should abide by is the common rules of the WTO, not the norms and standards of the United States. But the current situation has clearly shown that Donald Trump has put aside the WTO rules, not allowing the Made in China 2025 program to pose a threat to the United States.

Fundamental Reasons behind the China-US Trade Frictions Triggered by Donald Trump

Fundamental reasons for Donald Trump to trigger the trade frictions between China and the United States are listed below.

1. Political reasons in America. As the midterm election was approaching, Donald Trump needed to repay the voters with significant feedback as regards his achievements. While running for the presidency in the general election in 2016, Donald Trump had promised the voters seven objectives, including terminating the so-called violations of China in trade and substantially diminishing America's trade deficit against China. As the midterm election was drawing on, Donald Trump felt obligatory to repay the voters with some feedback on the promises he had made on the one hand and, making use of populism, achieve something in August and September, a crucial period for the future election, on the other hand. In this sense, the U.S. trade policy is kidnapped by its domestic politics. In fact, the China-US trade deficit is a political problem rather than an economic issue. By denouncing China's trade surplus over America and its impact on the unemployment of Americans, Donald Trump, out of the need for an election, has successfully set China as the biggest target of the United States.
2. Strategic reasons. The United States has positioned China as a strategic opponent. Identifying China and Russia as their strategic opponents is one of the characteristics of the National Security Strategy

of the United States of America that was released in December 2017. Due to China's position as a strategic opponent, it is natural for the United States to obstruct China's development. The United States agreed on China's entry into the WTO in hopes that China would gradually shift to a development mode in Western style, but China's persistence in its development path has disappointed the United States so much that its hostility toward China has grown dramatically stronger. The 2018 Trade Policy Agenda reveals that the U.S. trade policies are formulated on five foundations, among which national security is given the highest priority. When it comes to national security, treating China as a strategic opponent is the focus. National strategies function as a pillar of trade, so it is a matter of course that the trade policies of the Trump administration would target China given China's position as a strategic opponent as is defined by the U.S. national strategy.

3. Historical reasons. What will be talked about here refers to the outdated experience of the 1980s. Donald Trump once mentioned the metaphor of "Prisoner of the 1980's". Then what was the thought in the 1980s? Donald Trump expressed his favor of trade protectionism as early as the 1980s. But the world has completely changed since then, so Donald Trump can't deal with today's world using his obsolete ideas. Before the establishment of the WTO, it was usual for the United States to set tariff barriers against countries that would threaten its industrial advantages, which was suspended only after the WTO was founded. Apart from Donald Trump, Robert Lighthizer, an officer of the USTR, also expressed that the United States has given up an effective measure to protect its industries. Since the two of them are in power now, it's not surprising that they would trigger the trade war.
4. Theoretical reasons. Donald Trump preaches the obsolete mercantilism, prevailing in the 19th century, wherever he goes for its tenet that trade deficit causes unemployment and leads to the gap between the rich and the poor. This is actually an erroneous pseudo-theory we must correct because the conception of attributing unemployment and the gap of wealth to a trade deficit doesn't hold water at all. The fact is that most of the U.S. trade deficit originated in the 1990s. From 1990 to 2000, the U.S. deficit in global merchandise trade had quadrupled from $111 billion to $452.4 billion, of which its trade deficit against China only accounted for a small fraction. But that decade had witnessed the booming of America's industrial production which had

kept growing at an average annual rate of 5.4 % between 1992 and 2000, along with a basically stable number of employees in the manufacturing industry. So it is wrong to hold China fully responsible for the U.S. trade deficit.

According to the statistics of the U.S. Department of Labor, the U.S. global trade deficit had increased by 1.4 % from 2011 to 2016, with an increased employment rate of 7.5 % in the manufacturing industry. In 2017, the U.S. global trade deficit grew by $59.478 billion, and the number of employees in the manufacturing industry increased by 232,000 rather than shrank. It's interesting that among the six major sectors (computers and electronics, transportation equipment, oil and gas, clothing, electrical equipment and appliances, and machinery) that made the greatest contributions to the U.S. global trade deficit, only the sector of clothing experienced a reduced deficit (by $355 million), together with an unexpected decrease of 6,200 employees in this field; all the other five sectors saw an increase in their respective deficits as well as the number of employees, evidence of the absurdity of the so-called causal relationship between unemployment and trade deficit. By contrast, the U.S. global trade deficit significantly dropped by $305.181 billion in 2009, along with an unexpected substantial decrease of 1.38 million workers in the field of manufacturing. Therefore, it is clear that what causes the employment rate to drop is not a trade deficit, but an economic recession.

Nor is the decline in the incomes of the American middle class a consequence resulting from the trade deficit. Statistics from the U.S. Bureau of Economic Analysis show that the U.S. real per capita disposable income had raised by 23 % from 2000 to 2016, but this is just a figure on average as most people saw no increase in their incomes at all. Then where did the money go? A survey reveals that 1 % of Americans possessed 80 % of the wealth in the United States from 2009 to 2013. The United States has no effective social policies that can be relied on to render necessary relief assistance to the poor because of the greedy nature of financial capital and the lack of solid social measures. Such a situation has nothing to do with the trade deficit, as evidenced by the U.S. trade deficit in 2013 which is lower than that in 2008.

5. Policy guidelines and root causes. "Death by China" and "China's economic aggression", proposed by Peter Navarro, are the bases of U.S. policies and guidelines. In the face of such propositions, we need a sober mind and great determination to prove their absurdity.

Incorrect or Questionable Viewpoints

Some of the incorrect or questionable viewpoints are listed below:

> Firstly, the opinions in support of Donald Trump. There is an opinion in support of Donald Trump, which holds that China's requirement of mandatory transfer of technology is in violation of the WTO rules—an opinion holding no water at all. The U.S.-China Business Council conducted a survey on the business environment of its members in 2017, which reveals that only 19 % of the companies reported receiving requirements for the transfer of technology, two-thirds of which were raised by other companies rather than the Chinese government. Even if there indeed exist cases where the government requires the mandatory transfer of technology, all of them can be settled under the WTO dispute settlement mechanism for its mature protocol. Disputes like this are at most confined to some areas, posing no threat in all respects as the United States asserts. The United States has indeed sued China at the WTO because of the so-called mandatory transfer of technology required by China. But the truth will finally come to light after the WTO makes a ruling.

The United States is the country that has violated most of the WTO rules. As of July 9, 2018, a total of 556 cases had been filed and investigated under the WTO dispute settlement mechanism, of which 147 cases, namely 1/4 of the total, were handled with the United States as the defendant whereas only 84 cases and 41 cases were raised against the EU and China respectively. Apparently, the cases involving China are just a fraction of those against the United States. The WTO has filed 21 new cases since 2018, of which 14 cases, accounting for 2/3 of them, sued the United States as the defendant. So it is clear that it is the United States that violates the rules.

The United States repeatedly stresses that its entry to the WTO has caused it to suffer while China has fished for tremendous benefits. But the United States is by no means a sufferer of the WTO rules because it had seen a surplus in cumulative export growth over cumulative import growth from 2002 (the second year after China joined the WTO) to 2017, whether it was against Canada, Mexico or China, a proof of the untenable assertion of the United States' losses.

> Secondly, some empty and overoptimistic opinions, which believe that winning the friendship of the Trump family is enough for China to

harvest a different attitude of America toward it. Isn't the $250 billion worth of imports from America in 2017 a pleasant favor to Donald Trump? The next day after this big order was signed up, however, he spared no effort in criticizing China in Vietnam. Despite all the benefits we had offered to the United States, the USTR did not soften in drafting a schedule, according to which trade suppression measures and a trade war will be rolled out step by step. Any opinions believing in the cooperation between China and the United States at all events are unrealistically empty and overoptimistic.

Thirdly, the opinions influenced by Donald Trump's standpoints, which advocate a substantial increase of imports from the United States by purchasing myriads of American products. In the $250-billion significant import order in 2017, $101 billion worth of products were imported from the United States, much more than the $70-billion agreement we have reached with Russia this time. But has such a pleasant favor made any difference? Of course not. Unlimited imports of products from the United States cannot eradicate the problem. From China's perspective, we still need to take account of national food security and the scheme of natural gas import covered in the Belt and Road Initiative.

And lastly, the opinions that preach a drastic, and even an "epic" trade war between China and the United States. Some people believe that the more vehement the China-US trade war is, the more losses the United States will suffer and the more favorable it is for China. This is a conception without a scientific basis. President Xi Jinping proposed the Two Steps Strategy at the 19th National Congress of the CPC for the goal of the great rejuvenation of the Chinese nation but has never mentioned the trade war as a way to that end. Escalating the trade war, as proposed in numerous articles, is an irresponsible idea taking no consideration of the consequences.

Countermeasures and Suggestions

Judging from the current trend, there is still a possibility of reaching an agreement in the future despite the breakout of the trade war, though probably in the long run. Our general policy should be a comprehensive one that resorts to both negotiations and confrontations with equal priorities. Strategically, despising the opponent should be a general guideline for China to follow. With the formation of the global industrial chain in recent years, a complementary relationship has taken shape in trade between China and the

United States. As a form of ultimate superstructure, economic policy can by no means alter the underlying economic foundation nor can it defeat the laws of economics. Paul A. Samuelson, a Nobel laureate, mentioned, "No great kings can change the currents in the ocean." But when it comes to specific tactics, we should carefully plan and make mid-term schemes that are fully prepared—the more fully prepared the better—not only for the upcoming months. We should stick to the overall guiding principle that there are no voluntary countermeasures unless we are suppressed and fight back with justified reasons to our advantage and controllable measures. Under the guidance of our general strategy that combines confrontation and negotiation, we shall never forget our pursuit of cooperation: cooperation will last if it is won through confrontation but will come to an end if it is the result of concession or compromise; confrontation is a weapon to safeguard cooperation, which renders supportive force for confrontation in turn. We should bear in mind that the more determined we are in the face of America, the better we may cooperate with it in the days to come. We shall not compromise without the bottom line, nor shall we be a follower of American policies.

> The first thing we need is resolute countermeasures, for which we should discard our illusion-like goodwill and the balance because it is useless to discuss trade balance with the Trump administration. For the time being, it is advisable that we should consider suspending some of the major investment projects in America, including the coal shale gas project jointly invested by China Shenhua Energy Company Limited and the West Virginia government, a $83 billion worth of project that accounted for 1/3 of the $250-billion invest program agreed upon in 2017 and can be canceled given its role in the local energy and gas supply system.
>
> Secondly, negotiations with great determination are also necessary. All the negotiations should be carried out based on the WTO rules rather than the so-called General Clause 301 Investigation, compliance with which would otherwise mean our acceptance, in an implicit manner, of the abandonment of the WTO rules.
>
> Thirdly, multilateral mechanisms are the weapon we can rely on. Even if the two sides are willing to negotiate, the WTO rules must play as the foundation. If the United States puts forward a list of requirements, China can also raise its claims to shake off its former humble attitude like how students would behave in front of their teachers in old times. China shall never give in if the United States fails to meet our list of requirements. It is worth our attention that since the U.S.

Secretary of the Treasury has no right to formulate trade policies as is required by the laws of America, our major opponent in the negotiation is Robert Lighthizer, who makes decisions in trade affairs, rather than Steven Terner Mnuchin.

Fourthly, make good use of our allies. I'm honored to be the vice chairman of the Global Alliance of Small and Medium Enterprises (hereinafter referred to as GASME), which co-hosted the World Manufacturing Conference, attracting 109 participants from the Fortune Global 500 companies, with the Anhui Provincial Government of China, the United Nations Industrial Development Organization, and the Chinese People's Association for Friendship with Foreign Countries in May 2018. Whirlpool from the United States declared to establish its global R&D center in Hefei, Volkswagen of Germany announced the successful manufacturing of the Volkswagen-JAC new energy vehicle that had already been off the assembly line, and the German Red Dot Design Museum, renowned for its exhibitions of designs of Red Dot Design Award, the Oscar in the community of industrial design, also decided to set up a branch in Hefei. Do these multinational companies have complaints about China? Of course, they do. Though some multinational companies from the United States or Europe sometimes feel that they are not equally treated in China, they still proactively expand their investment in China. According to the American AmCham Shanghai, a collaborator of the GASME, 62 % of its members are planning to expand their investment in China whereas that figure hit 53 % in 2017. Many trade organizations and associations in America oppose Donald Trump's unilateral tariff policies, among which the National Retail Federation (hereinafter referred to as NRF), the Semiconductor Industry Association, the U.S. Chamber of Commerce, the U.S.-China Business Council, and the AmCham China especially hate the trade war because they are the real victims of it. Moreover, a great number of multinational companies have made it clear that they do not approve of increased tariffs but prefer negotiations as the solution to disputes. Therefore, it can be seen that although many American multinational companies may not support China as they did in the past, they are still our allies.

Fifthly, change our self-oriented publicity. Chinese media report and comment on the opinions of the U.S. business community and the public against the Trump administration's tariff measures from a very one-sided perspective. According to statistics from the U.S.-China

Business Council, when it comes to the attitude towards China, what the U.S. business community differs from the Trump administration is not whether any actions should be taken or not, but whether the tariff measures will be effective. According to the reports of U.S. and British media and the surveys conducted by various American polling agencies, most Americans approve of the Trump administration's measures against China. A poll carried out by the *Washington Examiner* on April 9 revealed that 62 % of the interviewees agreed with the increased tariff policy against China whereas 56 % of them believed it is a measure with a negative impact. The NRF, a powerful organization in the United States, expressed that what it objects to is not the purpose behind the Trump administration's trade policies against China, but the possible negative effects after the additional tariffs are collected. In other words, the mainstream public opinions in the United States are, though opposed to Donald Trump's measures of increased tariffs, in favor of the tenet of their President's trade actions against China.

It is Donald Trump who has a say within the United States. In response to China's countermeasure of cutting down the import of soybeans from America, Trump publicized that China, instead of correcting its unfair measures in this regard, has taken further steps that will harm the interests of American farmers and against which he will render financial subsidies. Therefore, the American farmers will certainly not be on China's side. Now, it is necessary for us to change our old self-oriented publicity strategy, with real examples reported by mainstream media of the United States and other Western countries, the fact that the trade between China and the United States did not affect the American people and it is Donald Trump who triggered frictions for no reason. It must be clearly expounded that China is forced to take such countermeasures and is willing to cancel additional tariffs as long as the Trump administration promises the same thing. Meanwhile, it should also be highlighted how the further deepening of China's opening up will benefit the business community and people in America. The personnel of the Economic and Commercial Office of the Embassy of the People's Republic of China in the United States of America and the staff of Chinese-funded enterprises in America should expand their scope of activities to befriend and communicate with as many Americans as possible.

Sixthly, seek solid cooperation with the underlying grassroots units. According to the objective law of economic complementarity between

China and the United States, a future of infinite possibilities will be laid in front of the two countries if China could join hands with the local, state and grassroots companies in the United States. China will continue to promote its trade and investment cooperation with a good number of companies in a wide range of states, counties, and cities of the United States. The investment from California to the Chinese market reached $175 billion in 2017. Jerry Brown, Governor of California, denounced Donald Trump on May 3, 2018, for his "silly" action of triggering the trade war and announced that California will by no means follow Washington in this regard. The bilateral trade volume had still reached a historical high in spite of a variety of uncertainties in China-US trade relations in 2017 and witnessed a year-on-year increase of 8.5 % in the following year. Since the establishment of 40 years of diplomatic relations between China and the United States, continuous political, economic, and trade frictions have always featured the relationship between the two sides in contrast to an increase of trade volume by 240 times, a rare phenomenon in the history of human civilization. In a word, we must, full of confidence, never forget our pursuit of cooperation amid confrontations on the one hand, and remember to measure potential risks of confrontations in our cooperation on the other hand.

Finally, focus our research on issues that are more strategically important and forward-looking. It is short-sighted if we just focus on what is happening at present but wise if we can have a forward-looking vision. I hope that we can consider more the China-US trade war and its further consequences, making joint efforts to guarantee the stable advancement of trade cooperation and economic relations between China and the United States, the promising future that will bring benefits to all the Chinese people, and the great rejuvenation of the Chinese nation.

(This article is compiled and edited based on He Weiwen's lecture, part of the RDCY Master Series Lectures, on July 10, 2018)

6. *Trade War, Crisis Contagion and China's Strategic Choice*

Bao Jianyun

As one of the oldest inventions of mankind, trade has started to develop and evolve in company with the advancement of human civilization ever since the end of primitive society after human beings were able to hoard a surplus of products, classify their labor and start trading with each other. Therefore, the development patterns of trade, transaction methods and even transaction conflicts stand for some features of the development of mankind. There is a tie between trade and war, as some trade leads to war while some wars promote the development of trade.

This article will explore the following issues in an attempt to offer some possible solutions. Why does a trade war happen? What are the reasons for the current trade war? Who will win and who will lose in the trade war? From the perspective of globalization and the people across the world, what influences will be exerted on global trade, industries, finance, and governance in the wake of the trade war?

Why Did the Trade War Happen and Who Will Be the Winner?

I plan to expound on the following questions: why did the trade war happen? And who will be the winner (Is it true that whoever triggers the trade war will win it in the end?)? — I will give answers from the perspective of economics.

The United States announced on June 15, 2018, that it would levy an additional 25 % tariff on more than 1,100 products, with a total value of $50 billion, imported from China starting from July 6. On June 16, China declared a tariff policy against over 600 imported items of $50 billion from the United States since July 6. It was on June 18, happening to be the traditional Chinese Dragon Boat Festival, that Donald Trump proposed to plan and prepare a measure of an additional 10 % tariff on Chinese products that amounted to $200 billion. Provided no agreement is reached with China, it will take further steps to impose additional tariffs on another $200 billion worth of Chinese products. As a whole, $450 billion worth of traded goods will be levied in total.

According to the statistics of the Chinese customs authorities, Chinese commodities exported to the United States totaled $429.8 billion in 2017. But Donald Trump is planning to tariff $450 billion worth of Chinese products, $20 billion more than the actual trade volume of Chinese goods exported to the United States. According to the statistics of the Chinese customs authorities, such a tariff measure is absolutely infeasible because the object of taxation does not exist at all. Is it possible for a trade war like this to happen? As far as I'm concerned, the chance is comparatively slim. Leaders of major powers usually prefer the strategy of negotiation— "the art of the deal" in Donald Trump's words, which is considered, in our opinions, as a measure of maximum pressure but depicted as an action of "extreme blackmail" by some other scholars, both indicating the same connotation despite different wording.

Will a trader resist and fight back under maximum pressure? If it is a weak economy, neither its resistance nor compromise will make a difference to its weak position. However, if it is an opponent of equal strength or a smarter and stronger one with a variety of tactics, then what kind of counter strategies will it adopt? It may resort to countermeasures leading to extreme punishment against its opponents. There is no denying that measures of maximum pressure will give rise to ultra-extreme punishment or ultra-extreme anti-blackmail countermeasures. In the trade war, the key is to figure out who the opponent is and how it is measured in competence, knowledge, structure, and patience.

Why Global Trade Wars Happen?

Trade is a great invention of mankind. Its evolution and even the forms of trade war manifest different historical stages of the development of mankind. How did the current trade war, especially the trade conflicts between China and the United States, happen? We must understand the fundamental background for its happening: firstly, it is the result of the big-power game; secondly, it is the product of the game between the East and the West; and finally, it is the consequence of the model game. In this article, the reasons will be analyzed mainly from the perspective of big-power games.

Why does the trade game exist between big powers? With limited space and markets on earth, superpowers are closely related in interests and play their due part in the linked web of cooperation. Under such circumstances, it is natural that conflicts and frictions occur between major countries—it would be abnormal if no conflicts or frictions existed between them. As for how intensely, in what forms, and when the conflicts and frictions happen, they are manifested with different features, which will be observed and considered from the following five perspectives:

> Firstly, the elite communities of the major powers. There is no denying that the United States and China have become the two largest and most influential economies in the world. For such a dramatic change in the international landscape, the elite communities hold different opinions. Changes have taken place in international patterns with the rapid development of emerging BRICS countries such as China, India, Brazil, and Russia. As a result, the global dominant position of Western societies over the past 300 years has been affected, along with the changes in structures of international trade, power, economy, discourse and even culture. Although I do not fully agree with the opinion that it is a change that took place in the past millennium as is advocated by some scholars, an important transformation has been taking shape in human history at least over the past 300 years. New structural layers have emerged in the balanced system of economic as well as scientific and technological power between the East and the West due to the rise of the East and the comparatively declined position of the West. Such a change, independent of human wills, has caused the major countries, especially their elites and the elites of America in particular, to worry and fidget. In the face of unprecedented changes, the elite decision-makers have grown more and more anxious over the uncertainty of the future.

Then what are their worries? What should they do had any changes taken place in their statuses of power, trade and culture and even in ideological structure over the past 300 years? Will they lose their original status as a result? Such problems give rise to their anxiety. Of course, the same feeling of worry keeps upsetting emerging powers as well. For instance, emerging countries like China and India tend to reposition their statuses as they are quite different from what they used to be and to reposition themselves will be a journey full of uncertainties leading to worries and anxieties. In 2017, the United States, the largest economy worldwide, had a GDP of more than $19 trillion while China, the world's second-largest economy, created a GDP of over $12 trillion calculated according to the exchange rate, accounting for approximately 60 % of that of the former. In 2017, the US GDP accounted for about 25 % of the global total, and China contributed approximately 15 %. Since the end of World War II, the proportion of US GDP to the global total has kept declining in contrast to the rising share of China with an unstoppable upward trend. This happens as a matter of course. Since China's reform and opening up, its GDP has kept growing at a rate of over 6.5 % even in the most unsatisfactory years—especially since 2000—and exceeded 10 % in the best times. The United States failed to maintain a GDP growth rate of over 3 % in none of the years since 2012 and could only sustain it between 1.6 % and 2.6 % most of the years. Apparently, China's GDP grew at a rate nearly twice of that of the United States even in the worst years.

Some scholars speculate that if such a trend continues, China's total GDP will have exceeded that of the United States by 2027 (it may be earlier in my opinion). The United States accounted for more than 45 %, the largest share, of the global GDP during World War II, and is still the largest economy worldwide regardless of its declined GDP share to the current 25 %. Starting from an extremely small scale, China has made a miracle by developing its economy to the current level. Surpassing the United Kingdom in the economic aggregate, the United States leaped to the largest economy worldwide in 1894 and has maintained that laurel without peers for more than 100 years. In the future (probably in the upcoming ten or even five years), however, a dramatic transformation might occur because the United States may have to face the rise of an emerging economy that is economically equal to it. What does such a dramatic transformation mean? The production of global wealth—the abilities to create wealth, markets and technologies and the ways of cultural expression will all be changed without being noticed, leading to a dramatic transformation that spawns the worries and anxieties of the elites. Under such circumstances, it is natural that some frictions occur in the field of trade.

> Secondly, the decision-makers of major powers. The leaders of China and the United States govern the country in different ways. Abiding by the mechanism of partisan competition for the selection of leaders, the U.S. decision-makers rely on campaign strategies to win the election, which leads to the interweaving of the decision-makers trade policies, foreign policies and campaign strategies. Unlike the United

States, Chinese leaders are advocates of the philosophy of credit and honesty in foreign affairs. China is credible and trustworthy to its people. Leaders of major powers usually make different choices in the face of the ancient philosophy of credit and honesty of the East and the campaign strategy of the West. Because of such differences, Donald Trump chose the trade war as one of his campaign strategies when the midterm election was approaching. The Chinese people attach too much importance to credit and honesty, evidenced by the old philosophical motto "A dishonest man can achieve nothing." Chinese ruling elites or decision-makers should be credible and honest, a quality for them to maintain national stability and development, safeguard China's core interests and defend China's trade interests. In such a context, it is not surprising that trade disputes come as a result of the disparities between the decision-makers of the two countries.

Thirdly, the social strata of the great powers. Squeezed between the pressure from the elite community and the bottom of society, the middle class in Western society—especially that in the United States which constitutes the stable source of this community—has started to experience structural publication since the outbreak of the financial crisis in 2008, resulting in negative impacts on the distribution of social wealth and the stability of social structure. With the rapid economic development of emerging countries represented by China, a huge emerging middle class has taken shape in these countries. They attach great importance to their own interests as well as trade interests and cannot be ignored for their influence on national decision-making. Under such circumstances, reverse transformations have emerged in both China and the United States: the middle class in the United States has been undergoing structural publication gradually, while that in China has been growing for the better. Populism has sprouted among the people at the bottom of American society that is featured by emotions of anger and resistance; in China, on the contrary, with the development of the middle class, people have raised higher requirements for the safeguarding of national interests—a positive demand for Chinese leaders to consider while formulating trade policies—after the number of impoverished people has dropped and the stability of social structure has been further reinforced. Chinese policymakers can't ignore such a change in social structure, and they will respond effectively to and formulate trade policies in line with the people's demands.

> Fourthly, the cluster of friendly major powers. The biggest difference between Chinese culture and Western culture is as follows: traditional Chinese culture holds the conception of "the world as a family", which, the "one-world doctrine" as I call it, means that the world is shared by everyone and all people are akin to each other like family members; Western culture, however, is under the influence of ancient Greece and Rome cultures, especially the influence of Athens and Sparta, two city-state societies that are typical of the gains and losses and rivalry for interests between each other. There is a significant difference between the "one-world doctrine" vision represented by the Chinese culture and the world view of the city-state represented by the Western culture. Different conceptions give rise to certain contradictions and conflicts, which will subsequently be manifested in the form of trade wars across the global society.

And finally, the cluster of trade opponents. In addition to the alliance and partnership between great powers, they also need to face a vying relationship with their opponents. Donald Trump once compared China to the reviser that altered the China-US trade system. So the formation or establishment of a cluster of trade opponents is another important reason for trade frictions and conflicts.

Judging from the aforementioned five perspectives, it is normal for a trade war to happen. China and the United States share a long history of trade, the latter has carried out a blockade policy against the former ever since its founding. In spite of the ceaseless frictions and conflicts in trade over the past more than 40 years since President Nixon's visit to China, the bilateral relationship between the two sides has kept progressing. Frictions and conflicts occur along with the development, and development is sustained along with frictions and conflicts. It is unknown whether it is friction and conflict that accelerate development or development that intensifies friction and conflict. In a nutshell, the process "from conflicts to development, to new conflicts and to further development" is a normal cycle, which we shall not address as a trade war but as the normality of trade conflicts. What is being manifested in trade, which stems from a specific political environment, a specific social climate, and at a specific time, is a kind of bargaining in trade as well as a new form of trade friction.

A famous proverb by Sima Qian, a great Chinese historian in the Western Han Dynasty, goes like this: "For some undesirable rules or social practices that have existed for long, the best method is to let nature take its course, and the second best method is to offer guidance for their improvement when there is a favorable condition; then comes the method of providing direct advice for a change, followed by the backup method of correcting them as required; and the most inadvisable method is to go against and resist them." In the eyes of the great historian, resistance is the most inadvisable policy whereas letting the rules or practices get improved in its natural course is the smartest measure, followed by less advisable methods of being kind and persuasive. According to such philosophical essence, confrontations over trade would be considered the most inadvisable policy as well as the most inferior means of trade competition. Harmony is a theme in Chinese traditional culture, as is shown by the example of the reinforced alliance of State Jin and State Qin in the Spring and Autumn Period (from 722 BC to 481 BC) (through the marriage between their key royal members). But the Thucydides Trap in Western culture is apparently a different example. It is clear that there is a distinct difference between Chinese and Western cultures: China advocates win-win cooperation and views confrontations as the worst means of competition. This is the philosophical perspective, based on which I comprehend the trade war.

Who Will Be the Winner of the Trade War?

Two basic conclusions must be drawn here before we continue: the United States will not be the winner, nor will China be the loser.

Why Can't the United States Be the Winner?

1. The United States is not strong and capable enough to win the trade war. The GDP of the United States and China account for 25 % and 15 % of the global GDP respectively. But China has now grown into the largest global trading country as its trade in goods has already surpassed that of the United States since 2013. According to the statistics of Chinese customs authorities in 2017, China's imports and exports valued about $4.1 trillion while those of the United States were about $3.89 trillion, accounting for 95 % of China's total. In addition, the statistics of Chinese customs authorities reveal a trade deficit of approximately $275.8 billion between China and the United States whereas those of the United States show a deficit of about $375.3 billion. Although the two countries have different statistical calibers for trade volumes, the U.S. trade deficit against China nearly accounted

for 40 % of its total trade deficit, to which China had contributed the largest share.

Only confined to the area of trade in goods for the time being, the current trade war has not yet influenced the trade in service and currency. In the trade war in which the largest trade-in-goods country contends against the second largest trade-in-goods country in the area of trade in goods, it would be hard and very unlikely for the less capable country to win the trade war. The power of trade is the product of the market emerging from its natural evolving process as well as the result of market competition. The United States is not as strong as it seems and less capable as we imagine in this regard. After playing the trump card of imposing additional tariffs on $400 billion worth of Chinese products, Donald Trump would have no other effective measures to count on. An analysis of the measures China can resort to reveals that despite the seemingly limited bargaining chips for the trade-in-goods war in the hands of China, it also has the means of bond and currency to make good use of thanks to its holding of the largest amount of U.S. government bonds. According to the Treasure International Capital released by the U.S. Department of the Treasury, the U.S. government bonds, bills, and treasury bills held by China had increased by $11 billion by March 2018, hitting the highest record in the past five months with a total of $1.19 trillion. If China, based on the risks of the trade war, reevaluates the risks of bond investment, carries out regulations against risks, and especially incorporates the risks of the trade-in-goods war into debt management, it will have more ways of defending itself. Since at the initial stage of the trade war, China doesn't have to adopt this countermeasure for the time being.

2. The United States is stuck with rigid strategies and old-fashioned thoughts. I admire Donald Trump for his smart brain as a businessman. He authors excellent books as well. In terms of trade negotiations, he sometimes gains the upper hand and sometimes fails, but manages to achieve his goals most of the time. When it comes to the exchanges and cooperation in trade between countries, however, the commercial approaches he prefers have limitations. The same game strategies, after being used twice, will be easily spotted by his opponents and their deterrent effects will weaken. What are rigid strategies? After imposing additional tariffs on $200 billion worth of products after the previous same policy against products of $50 billion, it cannot be considered innovative to plan increased tariffs against another butch of products worth $400 billion.

3. Kidnapped by the election, the United States does not have enough time for the trade war. Donald Trump is attempting to win re-election for his presidency, which will definitely influence his choices of trade strategies. Since trade develops in a continuous process, it is extremely difficult to end a trade war with a showdown in a short time. It is up to a country when to trigger a trade war, but it is out of its ability to decide when to cease fire for an agreement or to stop it, no cease-fire can be reached without the consent of both the initiator and the defender. In this sense, the United States does not have enough time for the trade war. Election kidnapping refers to the influence that partisan interests and the interests of interest groups exert on the choices of strategies regarding the trade war due to America's electoral system—the presidential tenure system—that is totally different from China's.
4. The United States is faced with internal disputes among its allies and the predicament of credit deficit. In response to America's additional tariff policy against the EU, the latter started to impose an additional 25 % tariff on €2.8 billion worth of products imported from the former starting from June 22, 2018; Canada started to levy extra tariffs on imported products worth $12.8 billion from the United States from July 1, 2018, as well. America's other allies, such as Türkiye, India and Russia, and some half-allying partners, had also begun to implement the additional tariff policy against it. Due to the disunity and internal disputes among its allies, the United States is affected in its trade confrontations with China and thus unable to end the trade war as fast as it initiated it. I disapprove of some people's opinion that Donald Trump is not trustworthy. As far as I'm concerned, he is very credible compared to all the Presidents of the United States before him. He is credible to American voters and has thoroughly fulfilled his campaign promises. But it is unnecessary for him to be credible to foreign countries because they are not rendered the right to vote for him—a cause for America's external credit deficit. The efforts of one or a couple of persons are far from enough to make up for the credit deficit as it is a demanding undertaking calling for the collective endeavor of a society for many years.
5. What the United States attempts to do is go against the trend of history and the development laws of trade. Trade is one of the greatest inventions of mankind. To what extent trade has developed embodies how advanced mankind is. Any actions standing in the way of the development of trade is to hinder the progress of human civilization as

well as the optimal allocation of transnational resources. Obstructing the development of trade is against the trend of history and the laws of economics. Therefore, the United States can't win the trade war given its actions and deeds deviating from the trend of history and the laws of economics.

Why Won't China Be the Loser?

1. China is growing stronger with superb capabilities. China has currently become the largest country in trade in goods worldwide. As trade frictions continue, what will occur in 2019? Trade diversion might be the answer: the trade volumes between the countries that are not allies of the United States and are in a trade war or conflicts with it may increase while the trade volumes between them and the United States may decrease. Then come the consequences that the United States may see the continuous decline of its position in international trade while emerging economies represented by China may enjoy a higher trade status. China has become the world's largest consumer market, a significant global economic change rarely seen in a hundred years.

China is a major manufacturing power. Surpassing the United States in industrial added value in 2010 for the first time, China has become the world's largest manufacturing power. Some scholars estimate that China's industrial added value, accounting for approximately 19 % of the global, has exceeded 26 % by 2016 whereas America's global proportion has slipped to less than 18 %. China owns the widest range of categories of manufactured goods listed by the United Nations. As a major emerging manufacturing power, China plays an irreplaceable role in the global supply chain system, a result coming along natural development. Will the largest trade-in-goods and manufacturing country lose the trade war? The answer is a positive "No".

2. China deals with the trade war with flexible strategies and a look-ahead mind. The Chinese government is typically of a superb administrative capacity and has established a unique administrative system of its own. It has demonstrated an impressive ability to deal with external changes since the founding of the People's Republic of China. With its effective combat against the severe SARS pandemic during the administration

of General Secretary Hu Jintao and Premier Wen Jiabao as an outstanding example, and with leaders equipped with forward thinking, China has a host of flexible and effective contingencies in the face of the threat of major calamities and disasters. The current leaders of China have a strategic vision because of their good knowledge of the world, strong competitiveness and forward thinking in the face of the trade war. The Chinese leadership is experienced with a strong ability to cope with challenges, and most of its team members have been trained and tested in long-term complicated grassroots work.

3. China has enough time to win the victory in the long run. Trade wars, especially those between major powers, are not fast campaigns that could be ended with feints but protracted battles, the truce of which is hard to decide. In addition to the endurance and determination that China has in the face of conflicts, the Communist Party of China is also experienced as a governing party. It was through a protracted war that China defeated the Japanese fascists and won national independence and liberation. Moreover, the strategic thinking of "independent warring tactics vs. the opponents' designed traps" is also prevailing in China.
4. China has the support of many partners and has the ability to turn an opponent into a friend. In the vicinity of China, some friendly countries, especially the developing countries to which Chairman Mao Zedong offered assistance when he was alive, cherish a natural sense of geniality toward and share natural trade ties with China. Because of such advantages, the support from China's partners is very stable. Chinese culture advocates the conception of "befriending the enemies", which advises people to turn their enemies into allies. This is also a strategy that China adopts in the course of trade competition.
5. China not only follows the trend of history but also makes use of it to its advantage. The development of trade conforms to the development trend of human history, so hindering the development of trade is tantamount to blocking the progress of human civilization. This is not only true to the Chinese and American people but also to the people of other countries, especially American farmers, workers and peasants who long for gains and mutual benefits through trade. The United States had been the world's most important advocate of free trade since the end of World War II and before Donald Trump's presidency. But now some changes have taken place with China's rise as the current major supporter of free trade worldwide, which not only follows the trend of history but also makes use of it to its advantage.

> Judging from historical experience, major countries with strong trade competitiveness are often in favor of free trade while declining countries, especially those major powers on the path of declining, usually discard the free trade that they once advocated.

According to what we have discussed previously, China will by no means be the loser, nor will the United States have a chance to win.

Will the Trade War Lead to Debt Crises and Financial Crises?

The period from 2008 to 2018 had only seen a debt crisis instead of another large-scale financial crisis. Trade wars usually lead to shrinking global trade, rising unemployment, and eventually the emergence of a global economic crisis, just like what happened in the Great Depression era. I published the *International Political Economy of Finance and Debt Crises* in 2015, in which the question of whether other major economic and financial crises will emerge from 2018 to 2020 is raised. The conclusion is that their happening is not inevitable despite a high possibility, and further observations of how the trade war will develop are needed for a better judgment.

Will Any Economic Crises Arise?

1. Trade crises. Trade wars may cause trade disputes and trade crises, while the latter will affect industries closely related to trade, like China's electromechanical manufacturing and chips industry, and may cause damage to agriculture and animal husbandry, especially soybeans, wheat and livestock products, of the United States. In fact, sporadic trade crises have already emerged. According to the data I acquired on June 21, after the United States imposed additional tariffs on steel and aluminum products of some countries, the steel prices in the United States have risen by 40 %. If such products are traded in the future market, the prices, as some people speculate, may have even increased by more than 50 %. The possible consequences may include inflation, waves of job losses, and even a possibility of debt crises. With a debt of more than $20 trillion (based on incomplete statistics), the United States is currently the most indebted country in the world, and the risk of holding U.S. government bonds is now rising. Since the tax cuts of the U.S. federal government have led to a reduction

in its revenue, it may borrow money from the bond market. After the breakout of the trade war, the U.S. government's fiscal revenue may continue to fall with increased borrowing costs. If a large sum of deficit occurs in fiscal revenue, the possibility of shutting down the U.S. federal government again cannot be ruled out.

2. Employment crises. Some scholars point out that although the levy of additional tariffs on steel and aluminum products will guarantee parts of employment opportunities in America, it may lead to the loss of more jobs in other related industries. Waves of job losses may arise if lost jobs outnumber the increased ones. Once the waves of job losses start to spread globally, employment crises will hit the whole world.
3. Other crises. Possible consequences also cover currency crises, reserve asset crises, financial crises, economic crises, social crises, and political crises. The reduction in trade between the United States and other countries may cause the global trade volume, which is priced in U.S. dollars, to drop. Consequently, the status of the U.S. dollar as the world's leading transaction currency may be replaced by the euro, the RMB and the currencies of other countries in some regions and some trading fields, thus leading to currency crises that will subsequently trigger reserve asset crises, financial crises and eventually economic crises; all of which may also spread to the social sectors to give rise to social crises and subsequently political crises.

The Contagion Effect of Trade Crises

The contagion effect of trade crises mainly covers the following eight aspects:

1. Global contagion. The trade war will spread across the whole world: I will certainly fight back and trigger a war between us if I'm challenged.
2. Market competition contagion. The trade war itself is a manifestation of market crises, which will spread globally.
3. Industry contagion. Economic crises will spread through industries. Since a global supply chain and a value chain have taken shape, a Domino Effect may occur if a certain link of the industrial chain system is broken.
4. Currency contagion. Trade crises will spread to the whole world through currency channels.

5. Financial contagion. Currency contagion is a manifestation of financial contagion, but the latter involves more fields and is more complicated.
6. Policy contagion. Trade crises are contagious globally through the mutual influence of each country' national policies.
7. Anticipation contagion. Anticipation will change, and people's changed attitudes toward the expected future will also trigger crises, especially leading to the global spread of financial panic.
8. Other contagions.

China's Strategic Responsibilities and Choices

China's Strategic Responsibilities

Since the 19th National Congress of the CPC, the leadership, represented by President Xi Jinping, of China has demonstrated an outstanding spirit of strategic responsibility in the following six aspects:

1. Safeguard and promote global free trade and global civilization by firmly upholding trade liberalization. This is the manifestation of China's belief in cosmopolitanism and universal goodwill as well as the "world as a family" concept advocated by Chinese traditional philosophy.
2. Advance the Belt and Road Initiative proposed by China. The Belt and Road Initiative is a strategic measure to prevent trade wars.
3. Continue strengthening and expanding China's manufacturing industry in parallel with the build-up of a new global industrial chain system, supply chain system and value chain system.
4. Promote the establishment of a new international currency system, China's reserve currency system and exchange rate will be examined and pondered over again.
5. Play a boosting role in the construction of an open world economy. There would be no open world economy to speak of without an open world.
6. Promote the construction of a community with a shared future for mankind. Proposed in the report of the 19th National Congress of the CPC, the construction of a community with a shared future for mankind aims to advance the shared destiny of mankind, especially the shared economic destiny of the people of all countries, embodying China's responsibility as a great power.

China's Strategic Choices

No one will benefit from a trade war in the long run, it is easy to initiate but extremely difficult to stop. Involved in the trade war, the Chinese government may decide its strategies from the following six perspectives:

1. A global vision: a foresighted strategy and tactical planning.

The contemporary China is different from what it used to be. As a global power, it must be equipped with a global vision as well as a foresighted strategy that looks deeper into the future. Having formed his unique strategic thinking before the founding of the People's Republic of China, Chairman Mao Zedong usually emphasized "despising our enemies strategically but never underestimating their specific plans tactically," which is influential to Chinese policymakers. In the trade war, such strategic thinking shall be manifested as making light of our opponents strategically while attaching great importance to their specific policies tactically. Strategic thinking and tactical planning are an organic whole. Chairman Mao's strategic thinking and ways of making decisions could shed light on the current ruling leadership and decision-makers as references.

2. Strategies for an enduring war: public governance and great rejuvenation.

China has undergone hardships and challenges with strong resilience and perseverance amid its five-thousand-year-long civilization. The whole process of China's counterattack against Japanese fascism in history is very similar to what Chairman Mao had expected in his masterpiece *On Protracted War*. Likewise, in the face of the changes in trade. It is impossible for Chinese leaders not to hold the thinking of "protracted-war", which will, in combination with public governance and the great rejuvenation of the Chinese nation, foster enduring determination against the fluctuations in trade.

3. The bottom-line principle: core interests and the art of the deal.

When it comes to the core trade interests of China, no Chinese decision-makers, governing officers, or elites shall make any concessions. Instead, they will certainly safeguard China's core interests and stick to the bottom-line principle. With a flexible mind and skilled at transactions, Chinese people are open to negotiations as long as their bottom line is safeguarded; mastering the arts of the deal, they are willing to make the deal if their core interests are guaranteed.

4. The people-oriented tenet: the world as a family and the mutual benefit and win-win pursuit.

In Chinese culture, the people are believed to be more important than the emperors. The CPC thinks highly of the people so the people-oriented tenet has been unswervingly stuck from the times of Chairman Mao to the administration of President Xi Jinping. Safeguarding the trade interests is tantamount to protecting the interests of the people. The "people" here not only refer to the Chinese people but also the people of the United States or even the world.

5. Due awards and punishments: opening up and cooperation vs. extra-extreme punishment.

Trade is mutually beneficial and win-win, but risks still exist and not everyone can earn a profit on an even basis. Since the development of trade is a process that keeps changing, the judgments concerning trade benefits during different periods differ. As General Secretary Xi mentioned at the Boao Forum for Asia, China will deepen its opening up to the outside, forge a new situation of all-around opening up and, especially, promote the opening up in the service sector. For countries that trigger a trade war, however, they are not allowed to enjoy such opening up across the board. Not only will China never open its market at an extensive scale to its opponents that launch a trade war on purpose, but it will also impose some punishment measures on them. Then how will China punish them? Since there are measures of maximum pressure and extreme blackmail, there are countermeasures of "extra-extreme trade punishment" (as I call it), which will never be ignored as an effective option by all the countries intending to defend their trade interests.

6. A united front: turn the enemies into friends and pursue great harmony.

As upheld by Chinese tradition, enemies should be turned into friends to achieve great harmony, so we shall win and unite all partners as much as possible.

(This article is compiled and edited based on Professor Bao Jianyun's lecture, part of the RDCY Master Series Lectures, on June 22, 2018)

7. *The United States' Engagement Policy toward China over the Past 40 Years*

Zhao Suisheng

Since the establishment of diplomatic relations between China and the United States, the United States has always attempted to shape China based on its engagement policy, to realize its strategic purposes and some other interests. While summing up the effect of its government's policies toward China in 2018, the U.S. political and academic circles voiced more and more reproaches and criticisms against its engagement policy, which is believed by some people to achieve none of the United States' strategic goals except for forging a competitor for itself. Then how should we decipher such reproaches and criticisms? Will the United States continue its engagement policy? In this article, the merits and demerits of the U.S. engagement policy will be discussed in detail through a systematic review of its evolution.

Change China—A "Misplaced Consensus" in the U.S. Engagement Policy Toward China

The origin and purposes of the U.S. engagement policy is the first issue we need to address in this article. The engagement policy refers to the policy proposed by the U.S. government after President Nixon's visit to China, with an aim to establish a normal state-to-state relationship between China and the United States. Such a policy was proposed for two purposes: firstly, geopolitical necessity. China and the United States were facing a common opponent—the Soviet Union, which constitutes a very important geostrategic background for the proposal of this policy; and secondly, America's strategic need to reshape China in the long run. The engagement policy was planned to help China realize modernization, sprout its middle class, and achieve the goals of political liberalization and democratization on the one hand, and help China to rise in the international order dominated by the United States and become one of its stakeholders on the other hand. In this way, China would pose no threat to the global leadership of the United States.

China was faced with the task of rebuilding the country from scratch at that time, so American technologies, investment, and the market played a positive role in its reform and opening up. In this sense, China and the United States had reached a consensus, but a "displaced" one. That is, the United States attempts to turn China into a Western-style democratic society like itself whereas China only wishes to enrich itself and strengthen its military force through modernization. Though "displaced", such a consensus paved the way for the successful contact between China and the United States from the late 1970s to the 1980s, making the latter believe that China was shifting toward the direction it desired.

After the end of the Cold War, the collapse of the Soviet Union, their common opponent, put China-US relations to the test. As the only major socialist country at that time, it was China's turn to be treated as a strategic competitor of the United States. Some people involved in the affairs of U.S. policies toward China started to question whether the engagement policy would accomplish its goals or not. During that period, China, under the guidance of Deng Xiaoping, kept a low profile lest it would become a political highlight, thus avoiding all confrontations and strengthening its cooperation with foreign countries. This convinced some Americans in support of the engagement policy to believe that China would certainly shift its original goals in line with the American engagement policy and its market-oriented economic reform would also definitely lead to political liberalization and democratization as long as they wait with patience.

The 2008 Financial Crisis: An Important Turning Point in the Development of China-US Relations

Nowadays, the United States denounces China for its changed attitudes toward it while China criticizes the United States for its suppression of its development. The United States has gradually come to realize that China won't accept some of its ideas, nor does the former have the ability to change the latter. After completely discarding the values of America, Donald Trump has become a challenger to liberalism and even the biggest challenger to the international order of liberalism, ideals of liberalism and American human rights values. The changes in the United States itself have greatly contributed to the loss of confidence in its engagement policy toward China. Consequently, it believes that its engagement policy toward China can no longer be sustained pursuant to its original strategic goals under such circumstances.

Meanwhile, China is full of confidence. China quickly shook off the impact of the financial crisis in 2008 in spite of its severe influence on the United States. At that time, many Chinese scholars believed that the United States relied more on China than China on the United States. During this process, Chinese political leaders and scholars have become more and more confident in their belief in China's development path. Meanwhile, China has grown more and more dissatisfied with the international order dominated by the United States because of its inherent unfairness and unreasonableness from the perspective of China. China was unable to challenge the leading position of the United States in the past, but it is exerting an increasing influence worldwide by speaking out about China's ideals, offering China's proposals, and contributing to China's wisdom. As a result, the United States has begun to worry whether China is planning to establish a new international order under its leadership to replace the one dominated by it.

In the context, where the United States is losing confidence and becoming less secure while China grows more and more confident, the misplaced consensus has evaporated. Therefore, there is a great challenge to the engagement policy. The following two popular viewpoints have started to emerge for the United States to reflect on: one of the viewpoints believes that the United States is so naive that it is fooled by China as the latter will never treat the former as an equal once it rises, while the other one holds that China has changed its mind after becoming stronger despite its original intention of heading toward the direction as the United States plans. Neither of them believes that the U.S. engagement policy can no longer be continued and should give way to tough policies, especially tough economic policies, against China.

The United States treats many economic issues from the perspective of politics. In terms of security, some scholars believe that there will be some problems like the "Thucydides trap" between China and the United States—mutual fear toward each other may give rise to conflicts and campaigns. After Donald Trump took office, he is still stuck in the same cycle during which the U.S. policies toward China keep changing. Implementing tough policies is a good choice for a new president to denounce his predecessor. Realizing the importance of the China-US relations in a later period, he has to soften with a kinder attitude. After some time, however, he will become tough again after new contradictions and problems emerge. Donald Trump has not gotten rid of such a cycle either. The two focuses of engagement policy he pays attention to are North Korea and trade issues. His concerns are quite concentrated, and the trade frictions he cares about are not exclusively aimed at China. So from this perspective, I don't think there is a fundamental change in Donald Trump's policies toward China.

Why Can't the United States Abandon Its Engagement Policy?

Why haven't fundamental changes taken place in Donald Trump's policies toward China? Why can't the United States give up its engagement policy toward China even if there are so many criticisms about it? In short, we can sum up the following reasons:

> Firstly, the engagement policy has not only benefited China but also the United States. China's economy has grown by 30 % after the financial crisis, a supporting factor for the U.S. economic growth. Even in the 1970s and 1980s when China and the United States had shortly established diplomatic relations and the latter was experiencing stagflation (coexistence of both inflation and economic stagnation) domestically, China's cheap products and labor played a great role in helping it to overcome stagflation. In recent years, China has contributed the most to the growth of foreign trade and employment in the United States. So apparently, to launch the trade war, the United States is launching a campaign at a huge cost even if it can bring greater damage to its opponent.
>
> Secondly, the United States has to cooperate with China if it plans to maintain its influence in the Asia-Pacific region. A decade ago, the trade volume between the bulk of East Asian countries and the United States exceeded 50 % of the total trade volume of all these countries but has now dropped to only about 20 %. More than 50 % of the total trade of these countries comes from their trade with China, indicating the United States' declining influence in the Asia-Pacific region. Under such circumstances, the United States cannot afford to cut off its ties with China if it still tries to guarantee its influence and maintain good relations with countries in the Asia-Pacific region.
>
> Thirdly, the engagement policy has prevented confrontations between China and the United States to a large extent, which is not only beneficial to China's development but also plays an important role in regional peace and stability.

And finally, instead of giving up the engagement policy, the United States has just made some adjustments. The engagement policy was conducted in an attempt to change China in the past, but now it is maintained to safeguard the interests of the United States rather than change China. In other words, the engagement policy in the past emphasized defining competition through cooperation while the current one stresses defining cooperation through competition.

(This article is compiled and edited based on Professor Zhao Suisheng's lecture, part of the RDCY Master Series Lectures, on June 19, 2018)

8. *How Can China Break through Amid Anti-dumping Encirclement Led by India and the United States?*

SONG LIFANG

Anti-dumping is a major form of trade friction in today's international trade. Among various forms of trade friction, anti-dumping has the greatest impact on China. To cope with the severe challenge of anti-dumping against China, innovation-driven strategies, manufacturing of high-value-added products, and realization of high-quality development are our fundamental solutions. Therefore, basic situations, industries of related products, characteristics, reasons and countermeasures of anti-dumping against China will be expounded in this article.

Since the establishment of the WTO in 1995, China has been positioned as the major target country of anti-dumping worldwide—precisely, the first target and object that many countries would aim at when it comes to anti-dumping affairs. It could be said that China has carried out its reform and opening up nearly in company with the anti-dumping of foreign countries. Shortly after the policy of reform and opening up was announced at the Third Plenary Session of the Eleventh Central Committee of the CPC in December 1978, anti-dumping measures of the European Community were raised against mechanical alarm clocks exported from China to the EU. The number of anti-dumping cases, anti-dumping investigations and anti-dumping measures against China accounted for approximately 25 %, 23 %, and 25 % of the global total respectively.

The impact of anti-dumping on China's foreign trade differs from that of other trade frictions because the latter only influences one or several companies or certain manufacturers in certain industries whereas the former usually affects the whole industry and the entire sector with catastrophic consequences. This is because once anti-dumping measures are put into practice, they will be implemented for the next five years, followed by further implementation of such measures for another five years if the anti-dumping country thinks it is necessary after a review when such measures are due in effect at the end of the first five years. Deprived of export opportunities for five or ten years, any country would see disastrous losses in its related industries. In addition, since anti-dumping measures usually involve and impair other similar manufacturers across the industry, the damages caused to the entire industry may amount to several billion or even tens of billions of yuan.

Anti-dumping: The Major Form of Trade Friction Faced by China

Anti-dumping constitutes the major form of trade friction faced by China. Due to the unfairness and unreasonableness of dumping in nature, anti-dumping, countervailing and safeguard measures have become the three trade remedies advocated within the WTO framework to maintain the order of fair competition and suppress unfair competition. It is considered an unfair and unreasonable means of competition if a country tends to suppress relevant industries of the importing countries by exporting products to them at low prices on purpose. Given such malicious actions of dumping, the WTO allows importing countries to take anti-dumping measures accordingly. Countervailing is treated similarly to anti-dumping as subsidizing is also unfair. Since subsidies render subsidized manufacturers an unfair competitive advantage, the WTO allows importing countries to take countervailing measures against subsidized imported products. Safeguard measures are mainly applied in a situation where the import of myriads of certain products in a short time will cause tremendous damage to the industries or sectors involved in the importing country.

In addition to the three major forms of trade friction mentioned above, there are also other forms such as green trade barriers and technical barriers that are associated with exchange rates, intellectual property rights, labor standards, etc.

All of them belong to non-tariff barriers in trade frictions. Nowadays, since tariffs in global trade have been reduced to a very low level since the establishment of WTO, countries across the world are prone to adopting non-tariff barriers like anti-dumping, countervailing, safeguard measures, green trade barriers, technical barriers, etc. Currently, the tariffs of developed countries and developing countries are maintained at the level of 4 % and 10 % on average respectively, which would only play an increasingly weakened role in curbing the import of foreign products and protecting domestic industries and markets.

As a result, more and more countries have turned to non-tariff protective measures, namely non-tariff barriers represented by anti-dumping, countervailing and safeguard measures, which are proper means approved of by the WTO for its member states to protect their domestic industries and markets. However, because relevant rules of anti-dumping, countervailing and safeguard measures are mainly qualitative in nature and manifested in forms of laws and regulations in practice, there are no distinct and strict operational procedures nor identification standards to follow, causing countries involved to take advantage of the loopholes in the rules as a protective means of their trade.

As shown in Table 8.1, there were 5,286 anti-dumping cases in total in contrast to only 445 countervailing cases and 323 safeguard measure cases from 1995 to 2016, revealing a much larger portion of the former than the latter two.

Speaking of the number of anti-dumping countries, a total of 62 countries or regions initiated anti-dumping investigations, among which India ranked first for 839 investigations, followed by the United States for 606 investigations, and then the EU, Brazil and Argentina.

During this period, China encountered 1,217 anti-dumping investigations, accounting for 23.02 % of the total worldwide, a typical datum clearly reflecting the severe situation faced by China in anti-dumping.

Basic Situations of Anti-dumping Faced by China since the Establishment of the WTO

Basic situations of anti-dumping faced by China since the establishment of the WTO in 1995 can be analyzed from the following three perspectives:

Firstly, what is the situation of anti-dumping against China overseas each year?

Anti-dumping cases against China not only accounted for the yearly largest share worldwide but also ranked first—1,217 cases in aggregate—over the 22 years from 1995 to 2016, with a total of 866 anti-dumping measures (see Table 8.2). The number of anti-dumping investigation cases, for instance, shows a general tendency of rise year by year, indicating that anti-dumping cases would increase rather than decrease in the short run as China's foreign trade continues to expand.

Although anti-dumping measures basically go hand in hand with anti-dumping investigations, the latter may not escalate into the former in the

Table 8.1. Number of cases of trade remedy measures worldwide and against China from 1995 to 2016

Trade remedy measures	Anti-dumping		Countervailing		Safeguard measure	
	Investigation	Implementation	Investigation	Implementation	Investigation	Implementation
Number of cases worldwide	5,286 cases (A total of 62 countries or regions initiated investigations, among which India filed 839 cases, the United States 606 cases, the EU 493 cases, Brazil 403 cases, and Argentina 348 cases)	3,405 cases (An implementation rate of 64.42 %)	445 cases (A total of 28 countries or regions initiated investigations, among which the United States filed 195 cases, the EU 77 cases, Canada 54 cases, Australia 28 cases, and South Africa 13 cases)	240 cases (An implementation rate of 53.93 %)	323 cases (India filed 42 cases, Indonesia 27 cases, Türkiye 23 cases, Chile 19 cases, and Jordan 18 cases)	155 cases (An implementation rate of 47.99 %)
Number of cases against China	1,217 cases	866 cases (An implementation rate of 71.16 %)	119 cases	74 cases (An implementation rate of 62.18 %)	—	—
Proportion of the cases against China to the global total	23.02 % (A total of 104 countries or regions subject to investigations)	25.43 %	26.74 % (A total of 49 countries or regions subject to investigations)	30.83 %	—	—

Table 8.2. Number of Chinese export products subject to anti-dumping investigations and measures from 1995 to 2016 unit: Case

Year	Number of Chinese export products subject to anti-dumping investigations	Number of Chinese export products subject to anti-dumping measures
1995	20	27
1996	43	16
1997	33	33
1998	27	24
1999	43	21
2000	43	31
2001	55	31
2002	50	36
2003	53	41
2004	49	44
2005	53	42
2006	73	37
2007	61	46
2008	78	54
2009	78	57
2010	44	57
2011	51	37
2012	60	35
2013	76	52
2014	63	40
2015	70	61
2016	94	44
合计	1 217	866

end. For cases filed with hollow grounds, China will certainly argue for its interests and proactively respond to the lawsuits, thus putting an end to them before subsequent measures can be implemented. Therefore, anti-dumping measures are usually outnumbered by anti-dumping investigations.

It should be noted that anti-dumping measures outnumbered anti-dumping investigations in some years, a result of statistical methods of anti-dumping cases that are based on the number of investigations and implemented measures registered in the year during which they are conducted or initiated. Therefore, a gap of one year to one and a half years usually exists before an investigation evolves into specific measures.

Secondly, what are the countries and regions that have raised the maximum amount of anti-dumping cases against China?

As shown in Table 8.3, the top five anti-dumping countries and regions against China are India, the United States, the EU, Argentina, and Brazil/Türkiye (Brazil ranks fifth in the number of anti-dumping investigations while Türkiye fifth in the number of anti-dumping measures), all of which are developing economies except the United States and the EU. Before the establishment of the WTO, it was the four developed economies—the United States, the European Community, Australia, and Canada—that played a leading role in anti-dumping affairs against China; after the establishment of the WTO, however, more and more developing countries have joined the ranks of anti-dumping countries against China.

In addition to the number of anti-dumping investigations and anti-dumping measures, we should also pay attention to the implementation rate (also called success rate) of anti-dumping against China of each country (region), namely the ratio of the number of anti-dumping measures to the number of anti-dumping investigations.

India, for instance, has filed a total of 199 anti-dumping investigations and implemented 152 anti-dumping measures against China over the past 22 years, achieving an implementation rate of 76.38 %. During the same period, there were 5,286 anti-dumping investigations and 3,405 anti-dumping measures in total worldwide, with an implementation rate of 64.42 %. Compared with the overall situation across the world, the number

Table 8.3. Chinese export products subject to anti-dumping policies of foreign countries from 1995 to 2016 top five anti-dumping countries (regions)

Countries (regions)	Number of anti-dumping investigations against China (case)	Proportion to total anti-dumping investigations against China in the corresponding period (%)	Number of anti-dumping measures against China (case)	Proportion to total anti-dumping measures against China in the corresponding period (%)	Implementation rate of anti-dumping against China of various countries (regions) (%)
India	199	16.35	152	17.55	76.38
The U.S.	141	11.59	111	12.82	78.72
The EU	129	10.60	91	10.51	70.54
Argentina	106	8.71	76	8.78	71.70
Brazil (Türkiye)	96 (80)	7.89 (6.57)	67 (71)	7.74 (8.20)	69.79 (88.75)

of anti-dumping investigations and anti-dumping measures against China initiated by India are relatively high.

And finally, what are the products or industries that are the commonest anti-dumping targets?

Judging from Chinese products or industries suffering from anti-dumping overseas, five major industries or sectors stand out as the commonest targets (see Table 8.4), among which base metals and the related products—copper, zinc, aluminum, lead and nickel with the largest proportion of steel—go top of the list. The Section 232 Investigations carried out by the United States on China, for example, targeted its steel and aluminum products. Then chemical products, mechanical and electronic products, plastic and rubber products, and textiles come as the commonest targets in order. The aforementioned five categories of products not only come from China's traditionally advantageous industries but also key competitive products for export. Textiles constituted

Table 8.4. Top five categories of chinese products subject to anti-dumping investigations and measures overseas from 1995 to 2016

Product	Number of anti-dumping investigations against China (case)	Proportion to total anti-dumping investigations against China in the corresponding period (%)	Number of anti-dumping measures against China (case)	Proportion to total anti-dumping measures against China in the corresponding period (%)	Implementation rate of anti-dumping against China overseas (%)
Base metal and related product (XV)	352	28.92	243	28.06	69.03
Chemical product (VI)	231	18.98	183	21.13	79.22
Mechanical and electronic product (XVI)	144	11.83	99	11.43	68.75
Plastic and rubber product (VII)	97	7.97	67	7.74	69.07
Textile (XI)	92	7.56	72	8.31	78.26

Note: A total of 17 categories of Chinese products (a total of 18 categories of products worldwide) have suffered from anti-dumping investigations and measures.

the largest portion of China's exports, especially before the middle of the 1990s, which then gave way to mechanical and electronic products in a later period. So it is natural that the five categories of products are positioned as the commonest targets of anti-dumping.

It's worth attention that among the five categories of products mentioned above, 352 anti-dumping investigations centered on base metals and related products (mainly steel), accounting for 28.92 % of the total anti-dumping investigations against China during the same period. In other words, nearly one-third of the products subject to anti-dumping investigations were base metal products represented by steel.

In addition, among the 18 major categories of products under the classification of the WTO, all other 17 categories of Chinese products have suffered from anti-dumping except for animal and vegetable fats and oils.

Characteristics of and Reasons for Anti-dumping against China since the Establishment of the WTO

The characteristics of anti-dumping against China can be summarized as follows:

Firstly, China is the primary target country of anti-dumping worldwide, with a comparatively high implementation rate. Secondly, most anti-dumping complaints against China come from India. Finally, in terms of products, base metal products represented by steel are the commonest target of anti-dumping investigations against China.

China: The Primary Target Country of Anti-dumping Worldwide

China is treated as the primary target country of anti-dumping worldwide mainly for the following reasons:

Firstly, China's position as the world's largest exporter. China's status as the largest exporter in the world has never changed ever since it surpassed Germany in 2009. Its colossal amount of exports naturally gives rise to controversies.

In addition to the large sum of exports, a huge trade surplus also plays a role. The increase in China's trade surplus means a larger trade deficit suffered by its trade partners. As we know, the trade deficit is usually a major reason for deficit countries to initiate anti-dumping investigations against surplus countries.

In terms of trade balance, China had been in deficit since the 1980s but started to see a generally increasing surplus each year from 1990 except for the year 1993. By 2016, China's trade surplus had reached $509 billion.

Both China's total trade volume and trade surplus have kept rising, naturally bringing about pressure on importing countries.

On the other hand, however, dumping indeed exists in some sectors in China to some extent. Without the concept of "dumping" in China before the 1990s, it wasn't until 1997 that the *Anti-dumping Regulations of the People's Republic of China* was enacted.

And secondly, the so-called "non-market economy status" of China. Countries labeled as non-market economy are often extremely disadvantaged in the face of anti-dumping issues. This is because if a country is regarded as a non-market economy, a surrogate country will be identified and appointed as the reference object, the normal market prices of which shall be considered as the basis for detecting its dumping activities.

In the face of accusations of anti-dumping, it is not China but the anti-dumping country that determines the surrogate country. However, the anti-dumping country usually chooses countries with higher prices and costs but lower productivity than China. Among all the countries, India is most frequently appointed as a surrogate country for China. There is no denying that India indeed resembles China in economic scale and structures of population, industry and economy, but the prices of Indian products are higher due to its lower labor productivity and higher costs compared with those in China. Therefore, China's non-market economy status is a great disadvantage in anti-dumping issues. As a result, it is very likely to be judged as a dumping country and thus suffer from subsequent anti-dumping actions.

At present, only 78 of the 164 WTO state members admit China's status as a market economy. The top anti-dumping countries or regions against China, including India, the United States, the EU, and Mexico, have not yet acknowledged its status as a market economy.

Therefore, China needs to make other countries, especially those top anti-dumping countries against China, admit its status as a market economy.

Thirdly, the low prices of Chinese export products. We have to admit that low-price transactions indeed exist in China, resulting in the export of products at lower prices than regular domestic prices and dumping as a result. Why are products sold at low prices? It comes along with the measurement of the means of competition. China enjoys a comparative advantage for its labor-intensive products and primary products, both of which embody low added value, low value, and low prices. Moreover, with price as the only focus of competition in China in the past, other non-price means of competition like product quality, after-sales service and advertising were ignored. Since China's export products mainly consist of primary products, labor-intensive products and low-value-added products, its trade would easily pose dumping.

Therefore, in response to anti-dumping complaints, China should stick to innovation and produce and export high-value-added products.

And finally, Chinese companies' inactive responses to lawsuits and allegations of anti-dumping overseas. The Chinese people and governmental departments knew little of dumping and anti-dumping at the initial stage of the reform and opening up, so they had no intention of dealing with lawsuits and allegations in this regard; moreover, their poor knowledge of the anti-dumping laws of other countries prevented them from taking corresponding actions. To get us prepared for the lawsuits and allegations, acquaintance with the laws of other countries is the premise for active responses.

India: A Leading Contributor of Anti-dumping against China

India contributes most of the anti-dumping complaints against China for the following reasons:

> Firstly, dramatically increased exports from China to India. China's exports to India amounted to $765 million in 1995 but $58.415 billion in 2016, an increase of 75.4 times over 22 years. With total imports and exports of $70.179 billion to India, China's exports stood at $11.764 billion in 2016, with a trade surplus of $46.651 billion. It is clear that both China's trade volume and surplus have grown significantly.
>
> Secondly, fierce competition between Chinese and Indian products due to great similarities in their economy.
>
> Thirdly, Chinese companies have scarce knowledge of the anti-dumping policies and practices of India.

Finally, China has taken very few anti-dumping actions against India, proof of China's failure to restrict or balance the anti-dumping actions of other countries. China had only filed 7 anti-dumping investigations against India from 1995 to 2016, in contrast to a total of 234 anti-dumping investigations it had initiated worldwide.

Steel Products: The Commonest Target of Anti-dumping Investigations against China

Chinese steel products are an easy target of anti-dumping investigations for the following reasons:

> China exports a large number of steel products at low prices. Of the approximately 1.6 billion tons of crude steel manufactured worldwide in 2017, China alone contributed more than 800 million tons, meaning half of the crude steel was produced in China. In addition to meeting its domestic demand, China also exports a great number of the steel it manufactures. The export destinations of China's steel products are relatively concentrated in Europe and the United States, which happen to be the leading anti-dumping countries and regions against China's steel products.

In addition, China's steel industry features low concentration. Although China has a high production capacity of steel, its steel industry is characterized by low concentration—the top three, top five and top ten steel companies only account for a relatively small share of China's total production output. HBIS Group, China Baowu Steel Group and Wuhan Iron and Steel Company, the three steel companies with the highest production capacity in China, account for only 16 % of China's total steel output. In contrast, however, the output of the top three steel companies in South Korea, Japan, Russia, India and the United States accounts for 90.66 %, 80.29 %, 68.86 %, 62.32 %, and 53.51 % of the total output of their countries respectively. Moreover, since the steel industry is under strict protection of each country given its status as a national pillar industry, Chinese steel products are prone to bear the brunt of anti-dumping.

China's Countermeasures Against Future Anti-dumping

China's countermeasures against accusations of anti-dumping in the future are listed below:

> Firstly, adjust the pattern of China's traditional export trade. Specific measures concerning the adjustment include: adjusting export goals and concepts; adjusting and optimizing the structure of export products, shifting from the original export that mainly relies on primary products and low value-added products to export of innovative and high value-added products and transforming China from a major exporting country to a great exporting power; adjust competition strategies for export products, shifting the focus from the competition of price to quality, after-sales service, and other non-price strategies; and adjust the

mode of export trade, shifting from the export of pure products to outward direct investment, through which direct investment can be made in the original export destinations to replace export of pure products.

Secondly, pay attention to and proactively respond to anti-dumping against China from developing countries represented by India. Above all else, we should deepen our understanding of and research developing countries' anti-dumping policies and regulations, and practices against China; secondly, China can take the initiative to establish free trade agreements or free trade zones with developing countries to avoid or reduce anti-dumping trade frictions, thus achieving mutual benefit and win-win relations; and finally, we can establish an anti-dumping warning mechanism aimed at major anti-dumping countries against developing countries, especially China, through which the governments or industrial associations can warn their member companies once there are signs of dumping.

Thirdly, strive to reduce the implementation rate of anti-dumping against China worldwide as well as the losses caused by anti-dumping. We should proactively respond to the anti-dumping lawsuits, safeguard our interests with solid grounds, and provide the anti-dumping countries with required materials in a cooperative manner; try our best to make countries (regions) across the world, especially India, the United States and the EU, admit China's status as a full market economy as early as possible; and resolve trade frictions through the WTO dispute settlement mechanism.

Fourthly, appropriately strengthen China's anti-dumping regulations against foreign countries. Without anti-dumping regulations, there would be no deterrence to speak of. Due to the qualitative nature of most anti-dumping regulations, it will be easy to contain the anti-dumping of other countries if China has a corresponding, complete anti-dumping law and regulation system.

And finally, take active measures against steel anti-dumping overseas to safeguard the safety of China's steel industry. For steel companies, China's current structural adjustments, mergers and reorganizations, and measures of expanding and strengthening the steel industry will all be of great help in addressing overseas anti-dumping actions against China's steel industry.

(This article is compiled and edited based on Professor Song Lifang's lecture, part of the RDCY Master Series Lectures, on June 12, 2018)

9. *China's Surrounding Security Environment and Strategies to Neighboring Countries*

FANG CHANGPING

Unlike most major powers in history, China rose in an undoubtedly complicated course: many major powers in history usually grew stronger within the framework of the nation-state system, the basically same social mechanism and a homogeneous civilization; China, however, is faced with the combined impact of the inherent pressure that a nation-state has to face, the special pressure that a socialist power has to bear, and the pressure of winning recognition of the West with an alien civilization. Considering the historical fact that the pressure and challenges coming along with the rise of a great power usually emerge first in its vicinity, we must maintain a harmonious and friendly relationship with our neighbors without doubt, which will pave the way for a sound peripheral environment for the great rejuvenation of the Chinese nation.

In terms of a neighborhood in the traditional sense, the security environment around China has continued to improve and can even be depicted as the best in recent years since 2018. What is the logic behind the changes in the environment around China? What are its relations with the overall external environment and China's strategic adjustments? What are the difficulties concerning security issues in China's neighborhood for the time being? And what should be taken into consideration when it comes to China's future strategic choices? Such issues will be discussed and communicated in this article.

China's Overall External Environment: Peace and Development Remains the Basic Theme of the Times

The report of the Nineteenth National Congress of the CPC depicted the international environment as follows: the world is in a period of dramatic development, transformation and adjustment with peace and development remaining the theme of the times. Due to the in-depth development of multi-polarization, economic globalization, social informatization, and cultural diversification across the world as well as accelerated progress in the transformation of global governance system and international order, interconnection and interdependence between countries have been reinforced over time, the pattern of international power has remained more balanced, and peaceful development has become an irreversible trend. In the meanwhile, however, the world is still faced with distinct instability and uncertainty, insufficient momentum for global economic growth, the increasingly widened gap between the rich and poor, emerging regional hot issues, and continuously pervasive non-traditional security threats such as terrorism, cybersecurity, major infectious diseases and climate changes, all of which are common challenges faced by mankind. It must be admitted that the Nineteenth National Congress of the CPC made a very accurate judgment of the international environment faced by China, based on which I summarized the following "new" characteristics of the overall international environment facing China:

> Firstly, a "new stage" for global politics. The prevailing international order of liberalism has been on the verge of collapse since World War II, especially since the end of the Cold War. It must be admitted that the international order of liberalism relies to a large extent on the multitude of public products provided by the hegemonic America for its stability. Due to the relative decline of its power, however, the United States is becoming less capable and unwilling to sustain the provision of public goods for the maintenance of such international order that causes it to "suffer a loss". In addition, the confluence of populism and nationalism has posed a severe challenge to the existing political order. Moreover, strongman politics has reemerged to some extent because of the failure of the existing system of liberalism to effectively address its internal problems and the pressure of nationalism and populism. And finally, the awakening of global politics as well as the return of identification politics. The awakening of global politics is driven by multiple factors, especially the possible participation of individuals and small groups in domestic and global political affairs thanks to the advancement of technological means; moreover, due to

the international flow of people as well as the imbalanced economic development, people's identification of and loyalty to a nation state in old days are being eroded by their identification of tribe, race, culture, religion, etc.

Secondly, "new changes" in the world economy. The first new change is the intensified economic and trade conflicts, evidenced by the currently escalating trade war initiated by the United States that does not exclusively involve China. Then comes the unbalanced economic development, which occurs not only between developed and developing countries but also between developing countries, such as, the widening gap between emerging economies including China and other developing countries. Imbalanced income distribution is another new change worth mentioning, which is not only normal between developed countries and the poorest developing countries, but also prominent within highly developed countries like the U.S. And finally, the imbalanced world economy and finance. After the financial crisis in 2008, the United States did not eradicate the problem through its governance of the financial sector, with uncertainties still remaining in it and international financial markets. In the context of interdependent world politics and economy, the new changes in the world economy will bring about an in-depth impact on the evolution of the international system as well as the changes in the international environment.

Thirdly, "new trends" in geopolitical competition. Above all else, geopolitical competition among systemic powers has intensified, such as the intensified competition and battle between China, America and Russia in recent years, evidenced by the incessant new records of military expenditures of major powers to some degree. In addition, "competition and conflicts" among proxies have started to emerge. Although not as severe and open as the "proxy war" during the Cold War, "proxy competition and even conflicts" have already loomed. And finally, the prominent Cold War mentality. Since the old Cold War is not completely over in the strict sense, it is by no means a good sign for us to talk about the new Cold War for the time being.

And finally, the appearance of "a new pattern" due to the rise and fall of great powers. With the rise of China, we have been fascinated by talks about its rise and the decline of other countries or regions. The first one is the decline of the United States. In terms of GDP alone, China is indeed narrowing its gap with America at a rapid speed, but it is only one of the indicators for estimating the rise and fall of a country as huge gaps in military strength, cultural and educational influence and the ability to influence the international system and shape international agendas still stand between the two countries. Then comes the concern of whether Russia has declined to such a point of no return to its former prime. Regardless of Russia's GDP which is just about one-tenth of China's and its hard times due to the continuous sanction by the West, Russia's strong military industry and scientific and technological strength are a well-known fact to everybody, not to mention its status as a major and powerful nuclear country; as a traditional empire in history, Russia has a variety of mature strategic tools that China does not possess; above all else, the mighty willpower and decisiveness that Russia has demonstrated while defending its core national interests at critical moments is indeed beyond doubt, which is evidenced by Russia's sudden dispatching of troops to Kosovo, Syria and Crimea years back that had shocked the entire international community. Our last concern is about the EU. At present, a popular view holds that even if the EU does not disintegrate, its future cohesion will weaken to such an extent that it will be unable to mount on the international stage as one of the powers of the world. Although the EU is currently faced with problems such as an integration crisis, debt crisis, refugee problem, and terrorism, we must understand that it is still a highly developed and mature organization because some of the problems are structural and some just temporarily exist in certain phases. Europe has always been a region full of creativity since modern times, giving birth to plenty of ideas and mechanisms that still exist in today's international society. In a nutshell, we should be as objective as possible while assessing the rise and fall of great powers, thus avoiding the misconception of China's rise and revival based on the pre-assumption of the decline of other countries.

To sum up, my opinions about the overall external environment faced by China are as follows: although peace and development remain the theme of the times, uncertainties concerning the security environment and development still exist and keep increasing; China-US relations will still function as a structural influence factor for China's overall external environment; and the environment around China will still affect its overall external environment as a key link.

Security Environment in China's Periphery

Understanding the Neighboring Environment of China

There are also some important non-neighboring countries, regional international organizations, and regional cooperation mechanisms in China's neighborhood, in addition to its 14 neighbors on land and 6 others on the sea which include: North Korea, Russia, Mongolia, Kazakhstan, Kyrgyzstan, Tajikistan, Afghanistan, Pakistan, India, Nepal, Bhutan, Myanmar, Laos and Vietnam (the 14 onshore neighbors), and South Korea, Japan, the Philippines, Malaysia, Brunei, and Indonesia (the 6 maritime neighbors). Non-neighboring countries that have a significant impact on the security environment around China include the United States, Australia, Singapore, Cambodia, Thailand, Uzbekistan, etc. Regional international organizations and regional cooperation mechanisms with important influence include the Shanghai Cooperation Organization, the Association of Southeast Asian Countries, the Asia-Pacific Economic Cooperation, the East Asia Summit, the "10+3" Summit, the "10+1" Summit, the -Japan-ROK Business Summit, the Conference on Interactions and Confidence-Building Measures in Asia, the Trans-Pacific Partnership Agreement, etc.

Believing that a greater neighborhood of China is beyond the scope confined by its neighboring countries geographically, some Chinese scholars uphold the conception of "6+2", namely the 6 traditional regions of Northeast Asia, Southeast Asia, South Asia, Central Asia, South Pacific, and West Asia plus other 2 regions of Western Pacific and North Indian Ocean, the latter two of which are important maritime pathways both in China's strategies and development. Some other scholars even propose that the greater neighborhood in geopolitics should also cover the United States for its key role in influencing, whether in history or contemporary days, the security environment around China.

Understanding the Peripheral Relations of China

To understand our peripheral relations, we shall focus on the following two kinds of relationship: firstly, three pairs of bilateral relationships. The first pair refers to the relationship between China and the United States (a structural relationship), the second pair the relationship between China and middle powers including Japan, India, Australia, etc., and the third pair the relationship between China and small countries; and secondly, the multilateral relationship, namely the relations between China and some regional organizations.

With the adjustment of China's diplomatic strategies since the end of the Cold War, the relations between China and its neighbors have improved and normalized. It was during this period that China shifted its diplomatic principles from the direction of master diplomacy to that of typological diplomacy—a brief classification of great-power diplomacy, neighborhood diplomacy, developing country diplomacy and multilateral diplomacy had taken shape. So the principles and tenets of neighborhood diplomacy derived from China's overall diplomatic system.

Understanding the Neighborhood Problems of China

The following aspects should be considered to grasp China's neighborhood problems:

> Firstly, the contrast of power in China's neighborhood and the strategic pressure China faces. With China's rise and shortened economic gap with the United States, the latter has reinforced strategic containment of the former to narrow its strategic space for worries of being squeezed out of its neighborhood in influence. Neighboring powers, such as India, Japan, and Australia, have strengthened strategic interactions with the United States to restrict China lest they lose their dominance in the sub-region they belong to. As for minor neighboring countries that are not confident in China's resistance to the temptation of hegemonic power—especially some that have territorial or territorial waters disputes with it, are not truly friendly to and even fearful of China despite their seemingly close relations with it. Therefore, China must deepen bilateral trust and disperse the clouds of doubt. Currently, the three types of countries have reached a quasi-consensus on their defense against China.
>
> Secondly, the constraints of economic and security dichotomy. As we know, China is currently the largest trading partner for most countries in its neighborhood, but such an influence in geoeconomics hasn't yet been transformed into a force in geopolitics. And it is even worse that China is frequently subject to the restriction of those trading partners in security issues. Economic and security dichotomy mainly originate from the consideration of such neighboring countries in hopes of maintaining their independence by not showing one-sided support because of their dependence on the United States for security while attachment to China in the economy.
>
> Thirdly, unbalanced security and economic mechanisms. At present, no security mechanism covering the entire neighborhood of China has ever been established. The US-Japan, US-Korea and US-Australia alliances are currently the major bilateral security mechanism and the SCO is a key multilateral mechanism, the former usually being the cause of regional tensions because of their exclusivity while the latter mainly focuses on issues of non-traditional security. Meanwhile, some

scholars also believe the surplus of economic mechanisms in East Asia is a problem. Because of the distinct forum characteristics of such economic mechanisms, they contribute little to substantially boosting the regional economy, not to mention the current competition among various economic mechanisms to a certain degree.

Fourthly, regional hot issues tend to become more and more complicated. These key issues in various regions around China include the North Korean nuclear issue, the China-Japan dispute over the East China Sea, the Diaoyu Islands dispute, the South China Sea dispute, the China-Indian border dispute, the India and Pakistan conflict, the reconstruction of Afghanistan, and "three -isms" (terrorism, separatism, extremism), which are typically enduring and complicated. These hot issues are hard and even impossible to resolve firstly because of their complexity. The forcible intervention of extraterritorial forces that has complicated the situation sits as another reason. And finally, since China's rise has led to a surge of nationalism in its neighborhood, emotional factors also make it harder to solve these problems.

And finally, the emergence of new situations in China's neighborhood. The relationship between China and the surrounding great powers is in progress, evidenced by the positive changes in China's relations with two major powers, Japan and India, based on the improved traditional relationship between China and Russia. The hotspot issues in the periphery of China are cooling down, with at least no further tensions in the North Korean nuclear issue in Northeast Asia, the South China Sea dispute in Southeast Asia, and the China-Indian border dispute in South Asia. However, uncertainties in the U.S. Asia-Pacific policy and China-US relations have also led to uncertainties in improving the environment around China. Whether it is the improvement of the relationships between China and major powers or the cooling-down of hot issues, it has a connection with in what direction and how vigorously the United States will adjust its future East Asian policy. Therefore, it is necessary for us to fully consider the vulnerability for the improvement of China's relations with its neighbors.

China's Neighborhood Strategic Choices

In a speech at the Neighborhood Work Symposium in October 2013, President Xi Jinping emphasized building a relationship between China and the neighboring countries that is more friendly in politics, more solid in economy, more in-depth in security cooperation and closer in cultural and people-to-people exchanges.

The neighborhood strategy of China since the Eighteenth National Congress of the CPC features as follows: strengthened diplomacy in economy with diplomacy in security to be improved; highlighted small-and-medium-country diplomacy with big-country diplomacy to be advanced; prominent multilateral diplomacy with bilateral diplomacy to be enhanced; and reinforced official diplomacy with people-to-people diplomacy to be promoted. The construction of a diplomatic mechanism in security is still relatively weak except for the release of some crisis response measures and statements of principle. In terms of big-power diplomacy, since China has focused more on small and medium countries since the Eighteenth National Congress of the CPC, its relations with big countries, especially with those neighboring ones, have not fundamentally improved. Speaking of bilateral diplomacy, due to China's common practice of developing bilateral relations within the multilateral framework, there is still room for the advancement of its bilateral diplomacy with the countries and regions in its neighborhood. In the field of people-to-people diplomacy, except for the comparatively robust tourism between China and the surrounding countries and regions, the exchanges in academic research, culture and education can be improved to a larger extent.

Based on the diplomatic experience accumulated since the Eighteenth National Congress of the CPC as well as the neighborhood principle of amity, sincerity, mutual benefit and inclusiveness, China's foreign strategies and schemes can be planned and conducted from the following six perspectives:

1. Gain objective knowledge of the United States' role in the peripheral relations of China and fully understand the independence of neighborhood diplomacy.

A long-standing opinion in the academic circle upholds that since the United States is the root cause of China's problems in neighborhood diplomacy, they can be resolved as long as the China-US relationship remains sound and harmonious. This viewpoint, to a large extent, believes in China's poor independence of neighborhood diplomacy and susceptibility to the influence of the United States, taking for granted an eased environment around China if the China-US relation is relaxed and a pressured one if it is under tension. We must admit that the United States not only has a strong ability to shape the situations in China's neighborhood for some reasons both in history and reality but also has the willingness to impose pressure on China by utilizing the hot-button issues in its neighborhood, which has become an increasingly overt tendency from the later period of the Obama administration to the

Trump administration. But such a conception is one-sided to some degree. Above all else, the United States is unlikely to play a dominantly decisive role in the diplomatic environment in China's vicinity, where there are not only small countries but also major powers like Russia, Japan and India. Moreover, there are also countries not allying and even intense relationships with the United States in this region in addition to its allies. To be precise, the United States is influential to its allies to a larger extent. Secondly, even its allies have their national interests to consider without easily binding them with their foreign policies. The United States' trust in and commitment to their allies have become extremely uncertain especially when the Trump administration's Asia-Pacific strategy has kept changing dramatically. In such a context, the United States' allies deal with their relationships with China from the perspective of their own interests rather than their alliance. For instance, the security environment around China hasn't deteriorated significantly regardless of the recent comparatively tense relationship between China and the United States. Instead, the China-Japan and China-India relations have presented positive momentum for improvement, with the relation between China and the ASEAN remaining generally stable as well as the comparatively alleviated tension in Northeast Asia. Finally, with China's increasing economic and regional influence, it is hard for small and medium countries around China to choose between China and the United States because the support for either side does not fit their interests. Therefore, we must admit that the China-US relationship indeed has a special meaning for China's overall diplomacy including neighborhood diplomacy; on the one hand, since the issues of neighborhood diplomacy have their own unique history and evolution logic, the faith in absolute dependence of China's neighborhood diplomacy on the China-US relation will give rise to the thought of conspiracy theory, insufficient understanding of independent neighborhood diplomacy, and reduced initiative in planning and implementing our neighborhood diplomacy.

2. Spare no efforts to reinforce diplomacy with small neighboring countries and improve the layout of neighborhood diplomacy.

China itself is a big power worldwide. China's rise at an accelerated pace has caused small countries around it to doubt and even fear it, which is understandable to some extent. The Chinese government has attached great importance to the work on neighborhood diplomacy after the new century. The diplomatic concept of amity, sincerity, mutual benefit and inclusiveness proposed in the Eighteenth National Congress of the CPC and the diplomatic principle of equality between large and small countries consistently emphasized by China particularly reflect how highly the Chinese government thinks of the neighborhood issues. But much meticulous and careful effort is needed to link such a concept and principle with the practices of handling China's relations with the small countries around it. For instance, we shall truly value how these small countries think, pay attention to details (the key of small-country diplomacy lies in details rather than scale) and forge China's image through details, and establish a correct view of justice and interests—as a big power, China should surrender part of its interests in its economic exchanges with small countries because mere focus on mutual benefit and win-win relationship is far from enough. Of course, the success of small-country diplomacy shall not be achieved at the sacrifice of our principles. Small countries cannot be willful, nor are they allowed to deliberately stir up trouble in cooperation with extraterritorial big powers. For things like this, we shall stick to the thought of the bottom line and the principle of differentiated thinking.

3. Properly handle China's relations with the regional middle powers and respect their regional influence.

As mentioned previously, along with the gradually narrowed gap between China and the United States because of China's rise, the gap between China and the regional middle powers in strength has kept widening, which will arouse a sense of uncertainty and even crisis among such regional middle powers while maintaining their traditional regional influence to a certain degree. Therefore, China should handle its relations with the middle powers as well as with the third parties under the influence of such middle powers in a balanced manner. Traditionally, China has never adopted any diplomatic concept of planning and designating a certain sphere of power, nor will it resort to the idea of expanding the so-called sphere of power at present. In terms of specific diplomatic practices, we shall be cautious not to concentrate our diplomatic resources on those large or small countries for a certain period of time, lest the large countries feel like being "undermined" or the small countries have a sense of being neglected for "unequal attention".

4. Take into consideration both the integrity and differences of neighborhood diplomacy to distinguish the priorities of issues in different sub-regions.

Considering the complicated environment around China and the differentiated issues in different regions, China should not propose a neighborhood diplomatic policy or strategy from a holistic perspective. On the other hand, it should develop strategies aimed at differentiated situations and security issues in different regions. For instance, the current hot issues in Northeast Asia are the North Korean nuclear dispute and the related problem of building a peace mechanism on the Korean Peninsula as well as the China-Japan, Japan-South Korea and Japan-Russia disputes over islands and territorial waters; the disputes between China and some ASEAN countries over the South China Sea constitute a major concern in Southeast Asia; in South Asia, it is mainly the border dispute between China and India and the possible geographical tension between the two sides in the course of China's rise; and the focuses in Central Asia mainly center on the combat against the "three -isms" and the cooperation under the Belt and Road Initiative framework. Other neighborhood issues also cover the possible impact on China from the Indo-Pacific strategy put forward by the United States. Due to differentiated issues of different areas around us, diplomatic problems in China's neighborhood are usually fragmented, leading to the failure of the formation of a holistic neighborhood diplomatic concept both structurally and systematically. To integrate neighborhood diplomacy in different directions into an organic and coordinated whole, we should, in addition to systematic thinking we demand, distinguish the priorities of issues in different sub-regions to reconstruct a neighborhood diplomatic system based on different themes of issues like sovereignty, security and development and guarantee the balance between different regions, between the land and the sea, and between different issues, thus ensuring the long-term stability and development in China's neighborhood.

5. Coordinate the two overall situations of maintaining stability and safeguarding rights and stress the integrated relationship between crisis management and control and development.

In a speech at the Eighth Collective Study Conference of the Political Bureau of the Eighteenth Central Committee of the CPC on July 30, 2013, President Xi Jinping pointed out that in order to solve this problem (territorial and territorial waters dispute), the general policy is to pursue progress while ensuring stability by coordinating the two overall situations of maintaining stability and safeguarding rights, insisting on the integration of the defense of national sovereignty, security and development interests, maintaining our maritime rights and interests and enhancing the overall national strength. This indicates that the Chinese government is calm and sober while considering hot-button issues, which can easily ferment nationalist sentiments in various countries, including China, and thus interfere with the rational decision-making process of these countries. Therefore, we should realize that although these neighborhood issues, especially those involving territorial and territorial waters disputes, are of extreme importance. However, China is facing an overall strategic environment and task that matters more and should be examined and dealt with under the framework of China's overall strategic situation. Territorial and territorial waters issues are key concerns in relations between neighboring countries. The outbreak of disputes is usually a manifestation, rather than the root cause, of the deteriorated relations between countries. In other words, territory and territorial waters do not determine the relations between countries, because it is the overall situation of such relations that determines how a country would address the territorial and territorial waters issues. Under such circumstances, what we need to pay attention to is crisis management and control rather than the pursuit of once-for-all solutions to hot-button issues; and what we need to do is to gradually erase the important role of these issues in bilateral relationships through bilateral ties that are positive, stable, and sound.

6. Identify the core issues of neighborhood strategy and maintain and improve China's stable relations with neighboring countries.

China needs to focus on the following core issues of neighborhood strategy at present and for some time in the future:

> Firstly, maintain and enhance China's core geostrategic position in Northeast Asia. First of all, we need to guarantee a stable security situation in this region, especially in the critical period for the development of the North Korean nuclear issue. We need to facilitate the simultaneous resolution of this problem as well as the peacebuilding on the Korean Peninsula by taking the initiative to step in and mediate and well-performing crisis management and control. Meanwhile, we also need to be cautious not to offer any excuses for the United States to hold China responsible for not making any progress or even worsening the North Korean nuclear issue. Secondly, strive for fundamental improvement and development of China's relations with South Korea and Japan to go beyond specific issues—such as the THAAD (Terminal High Altitude Area Defense) issue, island disputes and control of nationalist sentiment—as much as possible and strengthen the government-to-people exchanges and communication in the three countries respectively. Currently, the Trump administration's

Northeast Asia strategy is full of dramatic changes. In addition to the sharply volatile and puzzling interactions between the United States and North Korea, South Korea and Japan are also under pressure arising from the United States, readjustment of its alliance systems and alliance military expenses. Coupled with tariff sanctions, the aforementioned elements will offer space and opportunities for the development of China's relations with Japan and South Korea to a certain degree, as is shown by the frequent interactions between senior officials of China, Japan and South Korea. Finally, we need to improve our capacity to plan and set up diplomatic agendas for Northeast Asia, shifting the agenda of the North Korean nuclear issue, the focus of Northeast Asia for the time being, to that of economic cooperation. For China, it is particularly important to attract North Korea into the framework of regional and global multilateral economic cooperation when the latter is adjusting its domestic Songun Policy and focusing its national strategic priorities on economic development.

Secondly, greatly enhance China's power to shape Southeast Asia. We should first further strengthen China's economic radiation and influence in Southeast Asia. Although economic interdependence does not necessarily mean mutual understanding and support in politics and security, economic influence still cannot be ignored for small and medium countries in Southeast Asia in pursuit of economic development. Secondly, we should further advance our ability to consolidate multilateral initiatives and mechanisms—strengthening the existing multilateral mechanisms established with Southeast Asian countries has become more important, especially after the United States' withdrawal from the TPP. Thirdly, we should strengthen our efforts in communicating with the people, take into full account the psychological impact that China's rise may exert on the small and medium countries in Southeast Asia, advance their expectations of China's peaceful development strategy, and win their recognition through careful long-term effort. Finally, fully seize the opportunity to build the ASEAN community and forge a community of shared interests and destiny linking China and the ASEAN, thus hoisting the overall relationship between China and the ASEAN to a higher level.

Thirdly, well plan China's relations with India, Japan and other major powers in a proactive manner.

As a key neighbor to the west of China and a rising world power, India cannot be ignored for its resource conditions, development prospects and national aspirations. In comparison to India's significant strategic value, however, China's knowledge and understanding of this neighbor has been far from enough for long, not to mention the insufficient attention paid to its strategic intentions and influence. In this new period, we need to view the China-India relationship from a global perspective, wider than the traditional triangle relationship between China, India and Pakistan. We should put India in a higher position strategically and encourage it to maintain strategic independence, especially after the proposal of the Indo-Pacific strategy by the Trump administration. Meanwhile, we also need to transcend the specific issues concerning the China-India border dispute and develop the China-India relationship based on a wider range of issues. Strengthening extensive connections with Indian society and exchanges in education, tourism, and economy and trade is also necessary for us to consolidate the public opinion foundation for the China-India relationship. It is of particular importance if we pay attention to each other's core concerns and handle the disparities as regards the Belt and Road Initiative in a flexible manner. Moreover, sound planning for the China-Japan relationship is of equal significance as well and we should fully understand the independence of the China-Japan relation. In spite of the strong dependency of the Abe administration on US-Japan diplomacy as well as the essential function of the US-Japan relation in Japanese diplomacy, the China-Japan relation has its own development momentum and logic of evolution since Japan does not synchronically follow the United States for everything. There is no denying that Japan has demonstrated a more independent foreign strategy during the administration of Donald Trump. Meanwhile, we need to view the China-Japan relationship by getting rid of the shackles of specific issues, especially those territorial disputes and historical issues that would constrain the overall relationship between China and Japan. We still need to be cautious to prevent radical nationalism from hindering the development of the China-Japan relation—curb it in both Japan and China so as to consolidate the public opinion foundation for the China-Japan relation and improve and enhance the positive recognition of the people from both sides.

Currently, a critical period is coming for the improvement and development of the China-Indian and China-Japan relations. Top-level talks have been carried out between China and India as well as between China and Japan, bringing about new vitality into the two pairs of bilateral relations that have stayed stagnant for years. This is not only the outcome of China's active neighborhood diplomacy, but also a result under the influence of the proactive adjustment and consideration of India and Japan in the face of the Trump administration's uncertain domestic and foreign policies. Despite some vulnerable points in this round of adjustment of the China-Japan and China-India relations and uncertainties in the future, we still need to sustain the current positive momentum for top-level exchanges between China and India as well as between China and Japan as possible as we can, control the sensitive issues about the two pairs of bilateral relation, and enhance the awareness of independent bilateral relations, thus planning and maintaining sound relationships between China and India, Japan and other neighboring powers.

Finally, strive to maintain the stability of China-US relations strategically and minimize the negative impact of deteriorated China-US relations in China's neighborhood.

Whether we admit it or not, among all the structural factors influential to the environment around China, the United States plays a more important role than any other country. It could be said that a sound China-US relationship may not contribute to a favorable environment in the neighborhood of China, had the relationship between China and the United States kept worsening, however, it would be impossible to cool down the hot-button issues in China's neighborhood, and China would also face a bleak prospect to improve its relations with the neighboring countries. With the gradual rise of China, the United States' strategic blockade and containment against China tend to intensify over time. The United States is under significant strategic adjustment in an active manner, shifting from the Asia-Pacific rebalancing strategy during the Obama administration to the Indo-Pacific strategy. Since the Indo-Pacific strategy has not yet completely taken shape nor been implemented, we should not only maintain strategic focus on it to a certain degree but also pay great attention to its future changes, trends and aggressive influence. Under such circumstances, it is extremely necessary for China to take precautions by proactively planning and realizing sound relations with the great powers in its vicinity on the one hand and remain sufficiently rational and determined to maintain a strategically stable relationship with the United States from the perspective of the overall strategy on the other hand, thus avoiding the negative impact of the China-US relation on the improvement of its peripheral environment. Currently, preventing the escalation of economic and trade issues into security problems is our top priority.

Conclusion

Systematic thinking is required for observing the environment around China. Vertically, we should understand the current neighborhood problems of China that have emerged with an inherent logic of evolution in history; and laterally, the environment around China is subject to the structural constraints of foreign powers, especially those of the United States, and the strategic ambitions and interest tradeoff of the big powers and the small and medium nations in its vicinity, and the regional reorganization and strategic adjustments coming along with the changes of China's own strength. In the face of a complicated neighborhood environment, we should observe the shaping of it under the framework of the overall strategy for the great rejuvenation of the Chinese nation. To that end, we should fully understand the complexity and arduousness accompanying China's rise and remain fully determined and patient in strategic focus. Unlike most major powers in history, China rose in a naturally complicated course: many major powers in history usually grew stronger under the framework of the nation-state system, the basically same social mechanism and a homogeneous civilization; for China, however, it is faced with the combined impact of the inherent pressure that a nation-state has to face, the special pressure that a socialist power has to bear, and the pressure of winning recognition of the West with an alien civilization. Considering the historical fact that the pressure and challenges coming along with the rise of a great power usually emerge first in its vicinity, we have a reason to maintain a harmonious and friendly relationship with our neighbors, which will naturally pave the way for a sound peripheral environment for the great rejuvenation of the Chinese nation.

(This article is compiled and edited based on Professor Fang Changping's lecture, part of the RDCY Master Series Lectures, on October 26, 2018)

II. *Enriching the People*

10. China's Finance in the Past Four Decades: The Return of Common Sense and Logic of Finance

WU XIAOQIU

The thought behind China's great achievements over the past 40 years derived from the Third Plenary Session of the Eleventh Central Committee of the CPC. We must never forget the year 1978, a turning point in the history of modern China that marks the inauguration of the great undertaking of China's reform and opening up. It was at the Third Plenary Session of the Eleventh Central Committee of the CPC that the correct ideological guidelines of emancipating the mind, seeking truth from facts and making economic development as the central task were proposed. The Chinese nation has never been off the track in exploring the path to its rise as a prosperous and developed nation. From Sun Yat-sen to Mao Zedong and all the CPC members, exploring the right path for the rejuvenation of the Chinese nation is their eternal pursuit.

This article covers two major parts: an introduction to the history and achievements of China's financial reform over the past 40 years and a detailed explanation of the common sense and logic of finance, elaborated in the bulk of the article because people frequently go against them.

The Achievements of China's Financial Reform and Development over the Past 40 Years Have Laid a Solid Foundation for China's Future as a Financial Power

Great economic achievements have been registered during China's reform and opening up over the past 40 years. It is through the 40 years of reform and opening up that China has developed from a poor, backward, and isolated country to an open-minded nation that is advancing toward modernization and prosperity. The achievements that China has made in the past 40 years are remarkable in the history of mankind. Regardless of a large population and a vast territory, China was economically weak with a poor foundation and backward consciousness 40 years ago. It is indeed a miracle in human society that such an economically weak country can veer toward affluence and openness with ample vitality through 40 years of reform and opening up, as well as development. A short period of 40 years—time for just two generations—has made a change in the once-backward China. What's the reason behind it?

The Great Significance of Mind Emancipation

The thought behind China's great achievements over the past 40 years derives from the Third Plenary Session of the Eleventh Central Committee of the CPC. The year 1978, a turning point in the history of modern China, will never be forgotten because it marks the inauguration of the great undertaking of reform and opening up of China. The correct ideological guidelines of emancipating the mind, seeking truth from facts and making economic development the central task were proposed at the Third Plenary Session of the Eleventh Central Committee of the CPC. The Chinese nation has never been off the track in exploring the path to its rise of China as a prosperous and developed nation. From Sun Yat-sen to Mao Zedong and to all the CPC members, exploring the right path for the rejuvenation of the Chinese nation is their eternal pursuit.

We had groped in detours for long before 1978 because it was not until the Third Plenary Session of the Eleventh Central Committee of the CPC in that year that the right path of rejuvenating the Chinese nation, namely the path of socialism with Chinese characteristics as well as the path of reform and opening up, was found and established. Emancipating the mind and seeking truth from facts are the secrets of our success. China's success lies in the emancipation of the mind because it gives rise to the tremendous vitality and creativity of the Chinese nation. The Chinese nation is great, evidenced by a great number of Chinese thinkers who shed light on the direction for the development of human society in history. Few nations in the world have witnessed the emergence of a great number of thinkers as the Chinese nation has. The times of thinkers is certainly an era of prosperity. Emancipation of the mind is the source of a nation's vitality. Our decline in the past was the consequence of shackled thought—our mind was imprisoned. The imprisonment of people's thoughts stood out as the most typical feature of the decaying Qing Dynasty. Our minds remained imprisoned for many years after the founding of the People's Republic of China, explaining the dormant creativity of the Chinese people and China's backwardness as a result.

The concept of emancipating the mind proposed at the Third Plenary Session of the Eleventh Central Committee of the CPC in 1978 is of far-reaching significance for its liberation of people's creativity. The past 40 years have witnessed massive innovations as well as the emergence of a good many world-class fields in China, all benefits of the great campaign of emancipating the mind.

It is in such a context that China cultivated millions of talents in the late 1970s, 1980s, and even 1990s, who have grown into the mainstay of society. Emancipated in mind during that era, those people were fully aware of how important the creativity of the mind is. China's great achievements over the past 40 years are inseparable not only from the two generations who underwent the mind emancipation campaign but also from the spirit of the arduous struggle of the last generation. I always commemorate the Third Plenary Session of the Eleventh Central Committee of the CPC in a very grateful manner for the new vitality it has rendered us. Without it, many people might have been laboring in midst of their farming chores in their dwelling places. China hadn't completely opened its doors for reform and opening up in 1977. To solve the problem that kept gnawing numerous talented people, Deng Xiaoping proposed to restore the national college and university entrance examination. As for some suggestions of putting candidates in the examination under political review for superior leaders' approval, Deng Xiaoping rejected them resolutely. The tremendous courage, great wisdom, and unparalleled spirit of responsibility that he displayed in that era are worthy of our admiration. No matter what we do, we should have a sense of responsibility for the future of our country. In fact, all youth should be guaranteed access to equal and free education. It is impossible for China to develop without the fostering and growth of talent generation after generation.

How should we define talented people? Above all, they must be equipped with a sense of responsibility. Dodging everything with excuses doesn't make a talent. Without a sense of responsibility, China can't develop at such a fast pace because considerable things are in need of innovation and exploration. China adopted a closed planned economic system 40 years ago (1978), with obsolete concepts and the common practice of labeling people with various political accusations. Without a great number of people with a sense of responsibility and ideals, how could China gain such achievements today? There was a popular slogan—Revitalize China—in the 1980s, an inner voice embodying the spiritual pursuit of that era. The great idea of "Revitalizing

China" was heard echoing at the playground when the Chinese women's volleyball team won the world championship. The youths of that era indeed possessed such an ideal, giving less priority to their personal interests. We hope that people with ideals, a sense of responsibility and aspirations for accomplishments will serve China generation after generation.

Promotion of an All-round Marketization Reform

Many people have no idea how influential the planned economy in that era was and how rigid its concepts were. The planned economy and the market economy are completely different economic systems, with the latter giving full play to everyone's competence while the former only encourages the enthusiasm of a single person. In the context of the market economy, the initiatives of millions of enterprises and hundreds of millions of people have been brought into play—this is the power of the market. The market economy renders people huge free space, space for creation, imagination and realization of ideals. The planned economy, however, has bound people completely. Under such a system, people are always like immovable screws, and even geniuses have to stay where they are supposed to be. Therefore, promoting market-oriented reforms across the board is of extreme significance.

For some time, I was worried about some strange comments made by people. Many people seem to have forgotten our experience and lessons from the past after the 40 years of reform and opening up, so they are subject to decaying thoughts again. How could this work? The market-oriented reform and the path of the socialist market economy are irreversible. As President Xi Jinping has particularly emphasized on various occasions, the reform and opening up is the only way to rejuvenate the Chinese nation.

Therefore, we must adhere to the direction of the market-oriented reform. The core of the reform is to motivate everyone's initiative. The market plays a decisive role in allocating resources—the experience and theory summarized at the Third Plenary Session of the Eleventh Central Committee of the CPC showed its in-depth comprehension of the role and value of the market. From a key role in resource allocation to a fundamental force and finally, to a decisive role in resource allocation, our theoretical understanding of the market has been under continuous progress.

The Significance of Opening Up

Opening up has bestowed the Chinese nation with tremendous confidence, which is rational and attained through competition. China should never shut up its doors. Instead, it must keep them open forever with more and more fields to be opened. The downfall era of China was when it shut up its doors in seclusion. Whichever country shuts itself up will decline because of its lack of confidence, short-sighted views, and self-conceit. We must become confident during competition. In the 40 years of reform and opening up, especially after China entered the WTO, China has indeed seen a take-off of its economy. But it was only after China joined the WTO that its economy started to take off in the true sense. There is no denying that we were already well-prepared institutionally by promoting the reform of the market economy system before China acceded to the WTO. But we started to know what a modern market economy is only after our entry, so opening up is very important. Without it, the reform will be conducted without any criteria or directions to follow, nor will there be any link-up rules and regulations to consult. As we have learned from the reform and opening up, all the rules and regulations must link up with those of the modern market economy—link up ours with the WTO protocol as well as globalization in other words. We have achieved great progress after joining the WTO, such as the reinforced protection of intellectual property rights. It was from then that Chinese society started to advance towards the rule of law and modernity in the true sense.

China advocates opening up, through which we gain our knowledge of the world. As a set of rules formed after World War II, the WTO is labeled with the mark of that era. Generally speaking, this set of rules is fair and reasonable enough to reflect the disparities in development among various countries. However, China's rise has brought about significant changes in the global economic structure as well as in economic business forms, with wider penetration of science and technology into the economy and an increasingly pronounced tendency of globalization. At this moment, we must study a new set of globalization rules to push forward the development of the global economy. Systematic thinking is needed to determine this new set of rules. In the old rules, some tariff and non-tariff barriers are useful in global trade. But they hinder the effective flow of goods and capital although their existence is allowed within the scope of the rules. In other words, the rules of the old days are reasonable as they embody the characteristics of the past era. With the advance of the times, however, we need to find new rules which are applicable in this new era of globalization.

Then what new rules of globalization are needed for a new type of globalization? What are the differences between the new trade rules, investment rules, and other rules and those formed after World War II? The General Agreement on Tariffs and Trade, the predecessor of WTO, is an important system of global trade rules established after the end of World War II, which played a key role in global trade. International organizations such as the International Monetary Fund (hereinafter referred to as IMF), the World Bank, and the United Nations are all systems of political, economic, and financial rules established after the World War II.

Today, after 40 years of reform and opening up, parts of all these rule systems are in need of improvement. Therefore, we must treat these changes in a rational and dynamical manner to observe the role of the IMF and the World Bank as well as the structure of the international monetary system from a new perspective. As a great emerging country, China has the responsibility to study new rules according to fresh changes.

The Significant Role of Finance

Economy and finance are inseparable. China's GDP hit ¥360 billion in 1978 and may exceed ¥90 trillion in 2018. Its per capita GDP was only over $100 about 40 years ago but had reached nearly $10,000 by 2018. Finance has played a particularly important role in such a dramatic achievement. Over the past 40 years, financial indicators have kept growing at a much higher rate than economic indicators.

For instance, the savings deposits of urban and rural residents nationwide, recorded as ¥21 billion in 1978, have currently exceeded ¥70 trillion. The total national financial assets were no more than ¥300 billion in 1978 but have reached ¥360 trillion at present. With M2 surpassing ¥170 trillion, the current financial assets have registered ¥360 trillion according to larger statistical caliber (covering tax revenue, non-tax revenue, tax rebate revenue, and transfer payment revenue from superior units) and ¥220 trillion calculated by smaller statistical caliber (covering tax revenue and non-tax revenue) in addition to a securitized financial asset of ¥110 trillion. The current foreign exchange reserve has been stably maintained above $3 trillion, compared to that of $167 million in 1978 which was earned through China's huge sale of oil to other countries.

A comparison of these data reveals that various financial assets have kept growing at a much higher rate than the economy, indicating that the economic financialization ratio is accelerating from 0.318 in 1978 to the current 2.1. This figure stands for the monetization ratio of the economy, namely the ratio of M2 to GDP. Judging from this indicator, some people argue that huge bubbles exist in financial assets, so precautions against financial risks are necessary. Because of such a rapid growth of financial assets, many people believe that there is a possibility of financial crises in China—the growth of financial assets is so rapid that it sharply increases the degree of a financial asset bubble and subsequently the probability of crises. But some people also believe that this is the deepening of financialization in China's economy, a manifestation of deeper penetration of finance into the economy. This reveals how dramatically finance motivates China's economy. The point is how we should interpret it.

As far as I'm concerned, there are bubbles in financial assets to a certain degree in the current situation, but the influence of finance on China's economy has greatly increased, along with the significantly reinforced financialization of China's economy. Therefore, it is more appropriate for us to regard such a financial phenomenon as the deepening of indicators. Why hasn't any hyperinflation occurred in China during the fast growth of its currency or financial assets? Why hasn't it suffered from any financial crisis in the true sense? These are questions worth our research. Some people point out that RMB is seriously over-issued in China, for which the central bank should be held responsible. But I do not agree with such an opinion.

In fact, China has created and maintained a unique and wise leverage relationship between the real economy and finance during the 40 years of economic development. The central bank has made good use of financial leverage as well as unique financial resources to promote economic growth. From this perspective, the relationship between the economy and finance of China is forged with unique Chinese experience. Considering no occurrence of hyperinflation nor severe financial crises in the past 40 years, China has generally guaranteed a sound and healthy economy and finance, improved its economic competitiveness in all respects, and hoisted the competitiveness and soundness of its finance to a level better than any other period in the past—its competitiveness is under continuous progress compared to all periods in the past, let alone the years of 1978 and 1980. Academic research cannot be conducted with a superficial vision.

That China's central bank is excellent is the undertone of my words. I always think highly of the People's Bank of China for its good knowledge of the status quo of China' economy and good usage of financial leverage in promoting China's economic growth. When the economy is in different cyclical stages, the central bank is able to regulate China's economic problems by making good use of the counter-cyclical principle. Moreover, the central bank has also performed a series of financial innovations including those in tools. While innovating a set of monetary tools, it blazed new trails of liquidity tools in combination with flexible adjustment of market liquidity, instead of being confined to the traditional three major monetary regulation tools. We have a lot of space and subjects to research, for example, China's economic development model, China's foreign exchange settlement and sales model, China's currency issuance model and characteristics, and, above all else, the relationships between such models. The series of monetary policy tools created by the central bank has played a positive regulatory role in strengthening market liquidity.

Meanwhile, we must also admit that some of our policies may not be as reasonable as we think. Apparently, the primary function of fiscal policy is to regulate the macroeconomy and boost, in line with the principle of counter-cyclical regulation, the economy out of the recession cycle by cutting down taxes and fees and increasing expenditures when there is an economic downturn. This is the basic common sense of macroeconomic policy. In fact, the primary goal of fiscal policy is not to ensure the growth of fiscal revenue and tax revenue at a rate higher than that of economic growth. Besides, no proactive fiscal policy pursues higher growth of tax revenue than that of GDP. Indeed, China has never expressed that it would adopt some sort of expansionary monetary policy and has always stuck to a prudent and neutral one, but it has actually abided by an expansionary monetary policy for a long time. Since the concept of the conversion period does not exist in fiscal policy, monetary policy is the only tool to rely on for macroeconomic regulation, a difficult situation to deal with since the double tools are reduced to a single one. Considering the significant role that finance has played in the past 40 years, we should appropriately treat financial indicators.

Over the past 40 years of reform and opening up, China has gone further in constant marketization of its financial structure, prominently evidenced by the increased proportion of its securitized financial assets which have currently reached approximately ¥110 trillion with stocks accounting for over ¥40 trillion and bonds for over ¥60 trillion. At the same time, China has also achieved diversified forms of financial business. The impact of high technology on China's finances has become more apparent than in any other period before due to the in-depth penetration of technology into finance in an all-around manner. China's finance is actually driven by the following two forces:

Firstly, the force of market disintermediation is based on income growth and changes in social demand. Because of the growth of income, social demand for financial functions has accelerated financial disintermediation. The so-called disintermediation refers to financing through the market instead of through financing intermediations. With financing activities gradually realized through the market, disintermediation is carried out at a faster speed both in investment and financing. The market has helped to accelerate disintermediation recently, in contrast to its resisted disintermediation effect in China's financial reform for some time in the past. Banks are under increasing pressure as a result, but it is a sign of financial progress in China if commercial banks have to bear more and more pressure. If commercial banks could operate without pressure, it means they can easily harvest huge profits as well as the disadvantageous state of China's finances. The key goal of financial reform is to shatter monopoly and to put commercial banks under pressure because pressure forces commercial banks to transform, thus causing their clients to flow out downward. We often talk about the financing difficulties of small and medium-sized enterprises. This is because if banks could finance large corporations like PetroChina and Sinopec, they would not loan to small and medium-sized enterprises; if such large state-owned enterprises could go to the market to raise funds through bonds or stocks and need no more the loans of the banks, the banks' clients would flow out downward. When the needs of such clients flowing out downward from the banks cannot be fully met, it is time to kick off the structural reform of commercial banks, which would lead to changes in financial functions as well as the transformation of financial systems. Because of the dominant position of commercial banks in China's financial system, it will be difficult for China to progress in finance without a transformation of its commercial banks. Therefore, the force of disintermediation will promote disintermediation in the field of traditional financial financing.

And secondly, the force of technology. Technology will push forward the changes in the form of financial business, in which technology will facilitate the disintermediation in the means of payment and the market of the disintermediation in financing. Disintermediated through technology, the means of payment will be divided into digital payment and third-party payment, of which the latter will play a significant role. Currently, the central bank is preparing to incorporate the payment and clearing system as well as the reserve funds into its jurisdiction, for which I'm engaging in a study of related rules. Some people point out that even under the framework of the new payment system, either WeChat or Alipay will still have stock funds that will give rise to disputes over the ownership of the incomes generated by them. I wonder whether this problem will be solved if the stock funds are designated as an issue of the central bank. Apparently, it will exist as previously. Some people will also argue that digital payment is not secure. Then why is it insecure? Is there any evidence? All of them are issues in need of research.

Technology has certainly improved the efficiency of the means of financial payment in China, freeing finance from the constraints of time and space in terms of the function of payment and providing everybody with convenient and efficient means of payment realized through technological progress.

From the perspective of financial structure, degree of marketization, and internationalization ratio, China's finance has begun to manifest characteristics of a major financial power and form fundamental architecture for the establishment of a modern financial system. In consideration of the current situation, it was proposed to build a modern financial system in the report of the Nineteenth National Congress of the CPC.

The different data of the past 40 years of reform and opening up reveal that China has possessed basic conditions for establishing an international financial center and becoming a major financial power. This is the reality for the time being as well as the starting point for the future. To name the great achievements over the 40 years of China's financial reform and opening up, the efforts to lay a solid financial foundation for China to build a globally competitive and influential financial system as a major financial power should not be ignored.

Return to the Common Sense and Logic of Finance

We usually forget some common sense when we have made some marvelous achievements, which seems to be some kind of behavioral inertia. In times of a comparatively better economic environment, some people would grow restless after forgetting the benefits the market has brought us and begin to believe mankind's superb abilities over the laws of nature and the dominance of subjective will over objectiveness. In fact, people's subjective will is weak in the face of the market, so we must respect the laws of the latter. It is only in times of adverse economic conditions that we will think of the market and resort to it to get through the predicament. All of them are misunderstood by common sense.

Common sense and the logic of finance will be the key topics in the following sections.

Some changes have taken place in the common sense of finance over the past 40 years of reform and opening up. First of all, what is common sense? And what is the common sense of finance? I once tutored a postdoctoral researcher of finance with a Ph.D. in Law, who has worked as a judge in the Supreme Court for many years and knows well about the law. I once asked him what the common sense of law is. He found it difficult to answer after pondering for a long time. This indicates that common sense is elusive to capture. As I understand, the common sense of law is: the spirit of law must be founded on the starting point of goodness and it must praise the virtuous while punishing the evil because only goodness can develop into fairness and justice. The law must safeguard the following fundamental values: the law must protect basic human rights and must be a mechanism in praise of justice and in support of social fairness and justice. This is the essence of the law as far as I'm concerned. To put it more concisely, the law must embody kindness and conscience and would veer towards evil for lack of such common sense. It should reflect the equal status of every person as equality is the basic value in law and build a normative system that embodies the advancement of both society and goodness. If I were a jurist, I would be certainly full of this kind of emotion.

What Is Finance?

Why must we talk about the common sense of "what finance is"? It is because we go against the common sense of finance and break the regular laws of finance so frequently in practice that the understanding of common sense is very important for us. Society will keep moving ahead as long as we respect common sense—in other words, respect for common sense is the driving force of social progress.

What is the essence of finance? Some people may give this answer—fund financing, which cannot be considered a wrong answer because the concept of "fund financing" is believed to have covered the basic key points of traditional finance. Given its development by now, finance may be bestowed with new meanings as well as new functions because how funds are financed must also be considered in addition to the function of fund financing since the forces affecting finance have changed.

Although fund financing is important, intertemporal allocation of risks may also of great significance—an understanding under the framework of modern finance. The essence of finance is risk as any financial activity is accompanied by endogenous risks. This is actually an implicit warning that financial risks cannot be eliminated from their inherent relationship with finance. Striving to eradicate the risk and control and suppress it at the budding stage completely violates the common sense of finance. An in-depth understanding of this piece of common sense will help us to formulate policies and legal norms in line with the laws of modern finance. Risks, essentially deriving from finance, can be allocated but not be wiped out.

How Should Financial Risks and Financial Crises Be Comprehend?

Some people are afraid of talking about financial risks and even fear more when it comes to financial crises. As an inherent element of finance, risks undergo a complicated and long derivation process before evolving into crises. Sometimes, they may be just the seeds of crises and may not necessarily develop into the latter. Therefore, how to view financial risks is of great significance. At least the following stages are covered before a risk evolves into a crisis: individual risk, partial risk, systemic risk, and overall financial crisis. In theoretical research, the nodes of the risk derivation process must be identified to figure out in which nodes risk multiplier will be amplified.

I co-authored the *Stock Market Crisis* with my colleagues a couple of years ago, which exclusively focuses on the stock market crisis in 2015 and sorts out the processes of financial crises in various countries across the world. The researched crises include the Black Monday in 1987—the first financial crisis in the history of modern finance, the crisis caused by the bubble economy in Japan around 1990, the Asian and Russian financial crises in 1998, the Nasdaq market crisis in 2000, the global financial crisis triggered by the U.S. subprime crisis and the Chinese stock market crisis in 2015, all of which are typical in the history of global financial crisis. It is very interesting to study these crisis cases as each of them had a unique derivation process in logic due to the diversified economic development models of all the countries involved and varying degrees of their dependence on external capital.

A thorough study of these cases would provide experience for reference if China were in similar situations. Logically, we should clearly sort out and classify them for research. However, what China can learn from the processes and experience of the financial crises in Southeast Asian countries may be limited because of their economy, which is highly dependent on foreign countries for their small size and overdependency of their economic development model on foreign capital due to a high proportion of foreign capital.

We need to study the situations in Japan and more necessarily those in the United States, both of which could offer meaningful significance for China to borrow. In addition to cultural similarities between China and Japan, they also have nearly the same fervent bubbles in the real estate market. It's just that China has tried to maintain generally secure finance amid such severe bubbles in the real estate market thanks to the business separation model it has adopted. Some people think highly of the bank-enterprise cooperation model in Japan, through which businesses of the two sides are mutually embedded in the form of cross-shareholding. I always object to this model because, to isolate the risks of the real economy from the financial system, we need to separate them into property rights as well as controlling rights to avoid the influence of real economy crises on the financial system. Problems in the real economy are not devastating because the force of the market can make up for the losses of a certain industry or enterprise; had any crisis happened to the financial system, however, the consequences would have been catastrophically far-reaching.

China should build a risk barrier for its finance, the most correct thing China has accomplished in the field of finance over the past years. For some time, we had blindly worshiped the bank-enterprise model of Japan, which is actually not suitable for China. China's finance is secure despite huge bubbles in its real estate market, and its financial system is safe as well regardless of such an influential stock market crisis—a benefit from China's business separation supervision and business separation development model, the latter of which was and is still an appropriate measure for China. We must study the American financial system and its structure. There is no denying that the United States is a great financial power, so we need to carefully research its financial system and structure, which will offer us a lot to learn.

Objectively, the financial model of the United States is very scientific for its extremely flexible structure that is highly efficient in dealing with risks with a strong ability of resilience. The impact of the financial crisis in 2008 on the United States had only lasted as shortly as a couple of years, which was solved only through several times of quantitative easing. As a result, the U.S. financial system regained its most powerful competitiveness worldwide in 2018. For a financial system able to regain such a powerful competitiveness only ten years after the strike of a severe financial crisis, we must find out about its secrets. China needs to forge a future financial system that is structurally resilient and sticks to the path of marketization and opening up. It is certain that closed financial systems are fragile. Given an environment of underdeveloped marketization in which all financing and financial activities must be realized via traditional commercial banks, the construction of a modern financial system in China will be out of the question.

A study of these cases has led to a series of conclusions that shed light on our comprehension of which links need to be controlled. Figure 10.1 presents a logical diagram of the formation of a stock market crisis.

The real estate bubble turns out to be the trigger of the financial crisis as is shown by the situations in Japan and the United States. A crisis will soon come if the real estate bubble continues to expand in the financial system. Then what does the so-called Minsky Moment mean? It means that a crisis will come soon when the return on assets is lower than the cost of debt. The crisis in Japan started to emerge exactly when the earnings of real estate collateral were significantly lower than the debt yield. The stock market crisis in 2015 also proved this. A long process is involved before a financial risk evolves into to a financial crisis, and the same for a potential risk to develop into a real risk in reality. But many risks will naturally die out in the financial system, so we don't need to be afraid of them. Nevertheless, it is necessary for us to gain an in-depth understanding of every node in the process from a risk to a crisis.

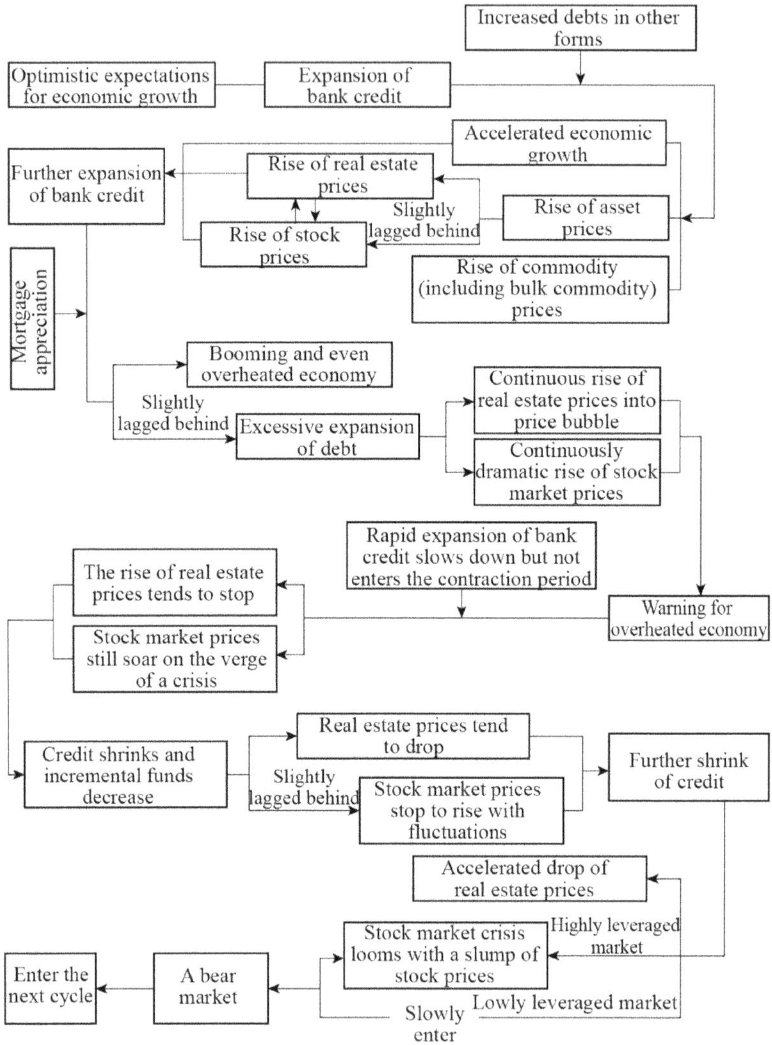

Figure 10.1. Logic diagram of the formation of a stock market crisis

In What Direction Will the Financial Structure Be Shaped?

The progress of a country's finances lies in the transformation of its financial structure rather than the expansion of the total amount. As mentioned previously, China's financial assets have increased from no more than ¥300 billion 40 years ago to ¥360 trillion at present. In comparison to the changed total amount, it is more important that structural changes have taken place.

The proportion of securitized financial assets is rising on an expanding scale. Structural changes will cause transformed functions of a country's financial system, shaping it more resiliently. The resilience comes as a result of the reform and adjustment of the financial structure. China's financial structure is being shaped toward the direction of marketization, along the process of which the proportion of securitized financial assets will continue to rise in an inevitable trend. Then why is this considered a piece of common sense or logic of finance? This is because people's intense apprehension about possible financial risks is frequently reported when they see declined savings deposits of residents in commercial banks, revealing their unawareness of the right direction for the development of finance. If residents' savings deposits grow at a rate faster than their increased incomes, it would mean that residents' increased incomes flowing to the capital market would become less and less, causing the country's financial system to become more traditional and under-developed, and less resilient. Only with this common sense can we view the changes in the distribution of resident assets in a rational manner. When more and more resident assets are invested in the sector of non-savings deposits, it means that the country's financial system has started to veer toward marketization with a more resilient structure and in the right direction. Fortunately, some people do not have such conception and theoretical judgment.

Diversification of the form of financial business is a basic trend. The form of financial business in China should not be confined to a single type, nor should the financial industry go back to the days of traditional commercial banks. For a certain period, I held different opinions on the financial supervision that seemed to compulsorily designate all kinds of financial activities a responsibility of commercial banks again. This cannot work and would definitely drag finance back into an inferior situation! In fact, residents have more financial demands after their incomes increase, which can only be met by diversified financial services provided through diversified forms of financial business as any single form of financial business can no longer satisfy their needs. Even low- and middle-income people have wealth management demands, but minimum requirements still exist to some extent though the access threshold to the financial market has been lowered. Only when the wealth management service for a sum of ¥1 is provided can it be crowned as the best, but its realization calls for a corresponding form of financial business. I hold high expectations for the new form of financial business as it has realized numerous things beyond the abilities of traditional finance. But it's a pity that some people always wish to eliminate it. They have no idea what an "epoch-making" feat digital payment and digital financial management have achieved by allowing the middle-income community to earn a monthly incremental income from a remaining sum of ¥1000 after all consumption costs are deducted. Whoever could provide value-added services for a sum of ¥1,000 provides the best financial services. It is inappropriate for the Chinese financial community to always target rich people like Wang Jianlin and Jack Ma as the focus of service. Instead, it should improve the inclusiveness of its services by serving low- and middle-income people. Since most people belong to the low- and middle-income community, services corresponding to the level of their incomes should be provided—this is the so-called inclusive finance.

The essence of inclusive finance is to guarantee everyone's access to financial services, including payment, wealth management, financing, etc. Low income is not an excuse for being deprived of financial services. That's why new forms of financial business must be created. If you request a major bank to offer wealth management services for a sum of only ¥500, no major banks will agree because the management cost is too high; but some new forms of financial business are willing to serve you even for a sum of ¥1. So why shouldn't we support it? If numerous people invest ¥1,000 or ¥2,000 for wealth management, the total sum would amount to tens of billions or even hundreds of billions yuan. In fact, we still fall behind in inclusive finance in spite of our high-profile publicity in this regard. When such financial services are about to be implemented—such as the development of third-party payment, some people would propose to curb the innovation in the form of financial business with high-sounding excuses like the safeguard of national financial security. Will the provision of financial services for the low- and middle-income community affect financial security? I don't think so. In fact, allowing new forms of financial business to serve the low- and middle-income community will help the regulatory authorities to supervise their transparency. A variety of exaggerated and labeled excuses are commonly used to discourage people. But is there any evidence for the threat of digital payment to national financial insecurity? Making a breakthrough in China's financial system is by no means an easy job, so it is valuable that new forms of financial business are freed from traditional thinking and traditional technological barriers.

Finance must be inclusive, which means that financial services cannot be confined to large corporations or the community of wealth. The rich people can enjoy customized services, of course. For example, they can go to Milan for a pair of customized shoes which cost at ¥50,000. But the shoe manufacturer can by no means stop making shoes for other clients just for a pair of shoes sold at ¥50,000. Most people need shoes priced at ¥100 or ¥200, after all. Apparently, financial innovation is needed to extend financial services to low- and middle-income communities. Since financial innovation is the only way to realize the mission of inclusiveness of finance, we must view the form of financial business correctly. There would be no diversified and abundant financial services without diversified forms of financial business. Like "diversified prosperity of different schools" in the academic circle, the same diversification cannot be achieved with just a few banks offering services. The diversification of the form of financial business is the prerequisite for the provision of diversified financial services as well as the fundamental path leading to inclusive finance.

On Shifting Finance from the Fictitious Economy to the Real Economy

Scholars like to decipher the logic behind problems. The "shift from the fictitious economy to the real economy" is frequently mentioned, which originally means that finance should serve the real economy and would exist meaninglessly otherwise. It is a piece of common sense that the vitality of finance derives from the real economy, so does the prosperity of finance from the prosperity of the real economy. Scholars also ponder over why funds are in favor of asset management, PE, VC, and insurance while why some real economies are short of money. Theoretically, if a country has a highly developed market economy and a market with the power to achieve a balanced allocation of resources, then it will not probably experience the so-called "shift from the fictitious economy to the real economy". Because of the profit-seeking nature of capital in market economy, a relative balance between various sectors can be achieved through the force of market.

Companies are able to attract funds if they have the potential to grow. No funds will go to companies without the potential to grow because such companies themselves are the target of the supply-side reform. No funds will flow into companies troubled with environmental pollution and overcapacity. Does Huawei fall short of funds? Are Unicorn companies in want of money? Of course not. Both VC and PE chase after them, so does the bank loans. This is because venture capital knows well the growth potential of this kind of company. Funds are profit-seeking and the rate of return and the degree of risk must be calculated for the flow of funds or capital—this is the law of capital flow. Be it commercial banks or market funds, they will judge the risks involved in this manner. Subjective beliefs, such as financial institutions or the market will certainly loan money to companies in lack of funds, are not erroneous. Who will be held responsible if the companies are insolvent for the loans? We shall never be overconfident in the subjective role of a certain department or institution, nor shall we believe they have a good vision just because they enjoy a higher position on the ladder of the market that helps them look further. In a word, we still must believe in the power of the market. The soul of a market economy lies in its ability to achieve a balance between gains and risks.

Erroneous conceptions lead to distorted policies. Such a reform will only give rise to numerous problems in the future. For instance, had some problems happened to P2P (peer-to-peer leading), some people would blame it on the shift from the fictitious economy to the real economy. In the field of P2P, there are indeed dishonest people who cheat and swindle on the pretext of online finance and P2P and they must be severely punished by the law. But it is also true that some lawful P2P institutions have closed down due to the draining of liquidity under strict supervision. Why did crises break out one after another during a certain period of time? Polices played a role to some extent. Therefore, an understanding of financial logic is of great significance for the formulation of financial regulatory policies. We must abide by the laws of financial development and formulate policies helpful to stabilize financial expectations.

On Deleveraging

The word "deleveraging" kept worrying me for a long time whenever it came to my mind. It means to reduce the leverage ratio as well as the debt ratio so as to guarantee a relatively safe economy, which is a correct idea. But the meaning of a word would be ambiguous if it is mentioned too frequently. Although finance cannot be deleveraged, some people indeed call for deleveraging. This kind of deleveraging is to halt the originally normal financial innovations under strict supervision. What do those financial innovations aim at? Many of them aim to provide services for the real economy, especially for micro, small and medium-sized enterprises. Because it is difficult for these enterprises to borrow on-balance sheet loans from the bank, and they have to finance through off-balance sheet lending and shadow banking. In spite of the higher cost of financing, they are granted access to funds. In fact, few private companies have access to off-balance sheet loans, so most of them resort to on-balance sheet lending and shadow banking, which are what deleveraging mainly deals with, however. The essence of deleveraging is to cut down the debt ratio. Then whose debt ratio should be lowered? Since it's difficult to drop the debt ratio of state-owned enterprises, it is better to cut down that of private companies. These companies, whose operations might be normal, may run into difficulties after liquidity shrinks.

Financial innovation involves two areas: firstly, commercial banks mainly innovate in off-balance sheet lending because innovations in on-balance sheet lending are hard to achieve for capital constraints; and secondly, technological innovation. These two kinds of financial innovations lead to tool innovations as well as asset diversification, innovation in financing tools, transformation of asset structure, and innovation in the form of financial business, all of which are key contents of financial innovation. Such innovations have a significant connection with offering services to low- and middle-income communities and private enterprises. The services for the rich and the financing services for large state-owned enterprises are the focuses of the traditional financial system. Why is finance in need of innovation? This is because traditional financial services for low- and middle-income communities and small and micro enterprises are badly scarce or insufficient. It is only through financial innovation that such a community and enterprises can gain access to corresponding financial services. Although they may acquire the funds at a higher cost than through on-balance sheet lending, they are offered a relatively stable channel of financing at any rate. The higher cost is understandable because returns correspond to risks and the risks of this kind of financing channel are relatively high. If such a channel is cut off, then private companies and small and micro enterprises will run into great trouble.

In a nutshell, I believe that "structural adjustment of leverage" is a better measure than "deleveraging".

What Is Financial Supervision and Regulation?

Financial supervision and regulation refers to regulating people's behaviors as well as restricting and constricting risks through the formulation of a series of codes. No risks would break out if such codes of conduct are followed; even if they do break out, they would be constricted with a significantly reduced probability of financial crises. Can financial supervision and regulation eliminate risks? Of course not. Some people believe that reinforced financial supervision and regulation can eradicate risks, which is a ridiculous viewpoint from the perspective of a layman. Risks can never be wiped out. They will be there as long as finance exists. This is the case whether it is in the sector of market-oriented finance or intermediary finance. It is an issue involving the core concept of financial supervision and regulation. Codes and standards for financial behavior are formulated to diminish financial risks rather than eliminate them. Through corresponding institutional design and technical indicators, financial supervision and regulation can facilitate the risk of recession or constriction and subsequently lower the probability of financial crises. Why should we study the characteristics and formation of the risks of modern finance carefully? Because it is of great significance for the formulation of corresponding supervisory and regulatory standards. Why do problems occur in new forms of financial business and online finance from time to time? It is because we haven't yet formulated a set of financial supervisory and regulatory standards fitting online finance nor established a corresponding mechanism for risk recession.

Why do Chinese commercial banks have a relatively better performance in general? It is because they have learned from the experience and lessons accumulated over the past years and, in particular, based on the *Basel Agreement III*, established China's own version in line with its actual conditions, which China strictly follows to supervise and regulate its commercial banks. There are indeed some problems with China's finances, but its commercial banks are sound in general, indicating how important rules must be clearly positioned. Turbulence is unavoidable in the capital market due to poor knowledge of the essence of rules. Since online finance belongs to the third form of financial business while the capital market is the second form, there are differences as regards the formulation of standards and comprehension of the risks of the two forms to a certain extent. In fact, transparency is the most important element in the capital market. Since supervision and regulation of transparency is the cornerstone of the supervision and regulation of the capital market, it must be placed in a very important position.

Why various laws, including the *Securities Law of the People's Republic of China*, in the capital market are called the "blue-sky laws"? It is because the core of these laws is to ensure the transparency of the market. It is important to understand that the focus of the responsibilities of the China Securities Regulatory Commission (hereinafter referred to as CSRC) is to guarantee the transparency of the market. As for the pricing of stocks, it has nothing to do with the CSRC. Whether listed companies disclose information in accordance with the rules is regarded as a focus the CSRC needs to supervise and regulate. The U.S. Federal Reserve occasionally intervenes in the market during special periods for the sake of stabilizing the entire financial system, which the U.S. Securities and Exchange Commission does not fully approve of. Chinese securities supervisory and regulatory authorities perform their responsibilities in a dilemma: they feel uneasy when the stock market slumps or soars dramatically. The securities supervisory and regulatory authorities indeed feel their work difficult. In fact, securities supervision and regulation should go back to the old track of supervision and regulation over transparency and remain unchanged regardless of the changes in the market cycle because transparency is always the only standard for it to follow. It would be inappropriate if supervisory and regulatory measures became a key mechanism affecting the trend of the market. Since the changes in the market occur in line with their own laws, the laws of the market must be regarded with due respect. If the changes in the market really affect the security of the entire financial system, the central bank—the last mechanism to maintain the stability and security of the financial system—will not hesitate to take action. What the market supervision and regulation authorities need to do is to supervise and regulate market transparency.

We must gain an in-depth understanding of the core mission of financial supervision and regulation, thus avoiding strengthened or weakened supervision and regulation subject to the changes in the market. In this sense, I do prefer the expressions of legal or standardized supervision and regulation to something like reinforced or strict supervision and regulation. There are no periodic variations when it comes to supervision and regulation.

Why Should Financial Innovation Be Carried Out?

Why financial innovation should be carried out is also an issue in need of research for its connection with the relationship between financial innovation and financial supervision and regulation. For China, financial innovation plays a key role in advancing China's finances and is also a fundamental driving force behind the continuous progress of China's finances. China's finances are still relatively behind, however. The criterion for judging whether financial innovation is appropriate is: that financial innovation must derive from the needs of the real economy, which refers to the needs of both the industries and the people. Since people are calling for new types of financial services, we must create such financial services accordingly instead of ignoring the calls for financial innovation from the real economy or the people. Some people wonder if there are any financial institutions that can not only provide insurance financial services and perform asset allocation but also guarantee necessary liquidity. Such kind of financial institution does not exist in China because of the limitation of its financial system. How to meet the needs of customers and the real economy is the only judging criterion for financial innovations. We must support any financial services that can efficiently and conveniently meet the needs of customers to the greatest extent at a low cost.

Financial innovation involves two aspects: institutional innovation and technological innovation. Institutional innovation covers a series of innovations in tools, structures, services, and mechanisms. Tool innovation, including innovation in financing tools and types of assets, is of great significance. The central bank has creatively provided a large number of convenient financing tools, offering excellent portfolio choices for the monetary liquidity of financial institutions, especially commercial banks. The current problem lies in insufficient innovation in tools and mechanisms in the face of financing demands from the real economy. For instance, it is difficult for ordinary people to loan from banks. The fact that extra fees must be paid before people can pay off their housing mortgage in advance is another example. All this happens because each rule is formulated to the interests of financial institutions, but financial innovation essentially means a challenge to this kind of monopoly. Since society, residents, and companies are in need of convenient financial services, financial services with various barriers cannot protected.

In short, innovation in mechanisms, tools and markets is required. Stocks mean a lot for asset allocation, for instance. Stocks of heavy and chemical industrial enterprises established in the industrial age, which lack the potential to grow, account for a great share of China's stock market. Therefore, we need to reform the stock issuance mechanism in China and comprehend the functions of the capital market in the true sense.

What Are the Functions of the Capital Market?

Some people believe that the capital market is the place for financing, a conception not completely correct. We indeed thought of it this way at first, treating it the extension of traditional financial financing. It is because of such an understanding that we give priorities to the services for financiers and listed companies but attach less importance to the interests of investors when we formulate a great number of rules. In fact, wealth management is the most important in the capital market because it is not a function of the traditional financial system or commercial banks but a function of the capital market. The fact that the capital market has the function of wealth management means that the listed companies in the capital market must have the potential to grow. This is the logic of the capital market. Basic assets in the capital market must have the potential to grow, so do the listed companies. But where does such potential come from? Apparently not from mature companies. There is no denying that mature companies have a glorious history, but they have lost the potential to grow. Since they have been clearly priced with a glorious past, they may decline in a gradual process.

Companies with a glorious history would sometimes mean a burden to the capital market. On the contrary, companies in their youth or even adolescence are often the best in spite of some weaknesses, deficiencies and losses for the time being. It's exactly because of that that they will have a promising future. When we select listed companies or formulate the listing criteria, we usually don't consider too much about the future of companies. The capital market is simply positioned as a market for financing, onto which the principles of bank credit are grafted. This is a totally incorrect conception. In the capital market, the soul of listed companies actually lies in their growth potential rather than maturity because the over-maturity of a company means no possibility of growth. This is the reason why China's fast economic growth hasn't been reflected in the capital market. China's GDP hit ¥1 trillion in 1990 and ¥83 trillion in 2017, but the market hadn't revealed such a growth potential for China's economy. This is because listed companies from the sector of the real economy used to pay more attention to their historical performance and status quo than their growth potential in the future. As a result, companies like Tencent, Alibaba, and Xiaomi went public overseas while the domestic stock market was filled with traditional companies of steel, coal, and cement. How can a market like this get developed? Are these traditional industrial companies important? Of course, they are. How can China achieve modernization without modern steel companies? How can the real estate market develop in the absence of cement companies? But they are companies without the potential to grow.

When the capital market is positioned as a market of wealth management, the listing criteria will be adjusted accordingly based on the future growth potential of companies, thus avoiding a preference for historical performance, status quo, and profits. This is the logic of the capital market.

What Is the Connotation of the M2-GDP Ratio?

The M2-GDP ratio embodies the special relationship between the economy and finance of China to a larger extent, reflecting a trend of financial deepening. China has endowed the indicator with a unique meaning. We have skillfully taken advantage of financial leverage to promote economic development, ensuring no major economic problems in China over the past 40 years since the reform and opening up.

How to Build China into an International Financial Center

Building a new international financial center is a financial strategic goal of China. This is both common sense and logic. We drew a research conclusion ten years ago that Shanghai and Shenzhen would definitely grow into new global financial hubs by 2020. Judging from the current situation, we might be a bit optimistic. While planning the 2020 goals for the CSRC in 2010, I came to realize that RMB would definitely become fully convertible and China's capital market the world's second-largest financial center ranked only second to the New York market by 2020. As of 2018 when this article was authored, it seems a bit difficult to achieve the goal as there are only two years to go. Nevertheless, I'm still confident in its realization because major countries are all international financial centers judging from the development of their finance in the past. As a major country, China is heading in that direction as well. President Xi Jinping mentioned the need for further opening up, especially in the financial sector, in his keynote speech at the 2018 Boao Forum for Asia. So I believe that China will speed up its opening up in the field of finance in the upcoming years. The internationalization of RMB is unavoidable—we are advancing the process in an extremely careful manner. Although RMB is not particularly influential in the global market by ranking fourth and fifth in the global reserve currency market and the trade settlement market respectively, it ranks third in the field of special drawing rights with a share of 10.92 %.

In my opinion, the goal of establishing China as an international financial center will certainly come true between 2020 and 2030. For China, forging a new financial center worldwide is more important than its entry into the WTO because it will fundamentally promote the modernization of Chinese society, facilitate its integration into the international community, and hoist its level of the rule of law. As the assets in the Chinese market are globally allocated, the international community will raise higher requirements for the level of the rule of law as well as the spirit of contract in China after it develops into an international financial center. In this sense, similar to the dramatically improved awareness of the Chinese people about the importance of intellectual property rights protection after China acceded to the WTO, the level of the rule of law in China will also be sharply promoted after it becomes an international financial center, thus exerting unimaginable motivation effect on China's modernization. Therefore, building the Chinese capital market into an international financial center is of strategic significance for both the modernization of Chinese society as well as the sustained growth of the Chinese economy.

(This article is compiled and edited based on Professor Wu Xiaoqiu's lecture, part of the RDCY Master Series Lectures, on December 4, 2018)

11. Re-interpretation of "China's Political Reform Falls behind Its Economic Reform"

YANG GUANGBIN

When it comes to state power, it also means political power because it usually stands for the former. Of course, state power is a broader concept covering four kinds of power: economic power, ideological power, military power and political power, among which political power emerges as the result of the game of the other three types of power. For instance, how did the CPC gain its power when the People's Republic of China was founded in 1949? It is natural that the military, economic and ideological power must be grasped before one can take control of political power from being powerless. In addition to the CPC affairs, Chairman Mao was also in charge of ideological affairs when he was in Yan'an—he was responsible for both military and administrative affairs.

Speaking of the relationship between politics and economy in China, many people would unhesitatingly come to the conclusion that China is good at economic reform but falls behind in political reform. A considerable number of people are in favor of this opinion, which will be the focus of the discussion in the following part.

The Failure of the Soviet Union and the Success of China and the United States

The Soviet Union, the United States and China were all stuck in great crises from 1965 to 1980.

The Soviet Union witnessed rapid economic growth from 1927 to 1974 but a slowdown afterward. Moreover, the death of several key leaders in succession after the 1980s complicated the situation. The economic crisis, social stagnation, rigid politics and leadership transition were beyond the Soviet Union's abilities to bear.

The United States experienced two campaigns in the mid-1960s: the civil rights campaign and the anti-Vietnam War campaign. Back then, black riots happened in all inhabited towns from east to west and from south to north in the United States. Showing off military force as much as possible while curbing its use of it was a policy adopted by the Nixon administration at that time. It was not until the 1970s that the black issue basically subsided, but the anti-Vietnam War campaign remained a hot issue. It was a common scene that hundreds of thousands or even millions of people would gather on the Washington Monument Square for protest from 1965 to the mid-1970s.

After 2008, when the American crises are mentioned, it is believed the first one happened in the 1960s, especially in 1970 when economic inflation arose from the oil crisis. From the perspective of social science, the thought of "why can't we sustain anymore" was popular in the community of Western social science from the late 1970s to the early 1980s, evidenced by the *Dilemmas of Pluralist Democracy: Autonomy and Control*, the most famous work of the renowned democracy theorist Robert Dahl, and something alike.

China was also in a crisis, namely the Cultural Revolution spanning from 1966 to 1976, which needs no further elaboration here.

In the end, the Soviet Union disintegrated while China and the United States were currently under favorable conditions.

I prefer the word "favorable" because I have come to the following conclusion: while making a comparison between countries, we should compare their difficulties and abilities to pull through the difficulties rather than their favorable conditions. Transcending individuals and groups, social science targets the result as a whole. Therefore, from the perspective of the country, China and the United States are currently under favorable conditions.

Then why did China and the United States make it while the Soviet Union failed?

Mikhail Gorbachev failed to carry on the reform any further after taking office in 1984, so he authored the *Reform and New Thought*, in which he proposed openness, transparency and democratization. The reform of the Soviet Union failed because of the fetters of the colossal interest group of the Communist Party of the Soviet Union (hereinafter referred to as CPSU)—a fundamental hindrance to its success. Mikhail Gorbachev initiated the political reform in 1987, bringing himself an opponent, Boris Yeltsin who successfully undermined the CPSU just in a couple of years. The Soviet Union was a party-state regime from the Western perspective. There would be no state to speak of if the party collapsed.

As for the United States, it resolved the crisis through neo-liberal economic reform after Ronald Wilson Reagan came into power in 1981. The process was cruel as it aimed for liberalization and marketization. At that time, the United States was in the midst of extreme opposition. For instance, believing his inhumanity as a president and disqualification as a father, Reagan's second daughter even severed her relationship with him. However, the U.S. economy started to improve after 1983.

In China, the Third Plenary Session of the Eleventh Central Committee of the CPC kicked off the prelude to a reform both ideologically and theoretically. The economy was the real field to be reformed, commenced with the establishment of the household contract responsibility system with remuneration linked to output and the urban enterprise contract system.

Why did the Soviet Union fail while China and the United States make it? What is the significance theoretically? From my perspective, we might need to rethink the variety of opinions we have gotten accustomed to.

Interpretation of the Theory of State

After taking office in 2012, President Xi Jinping delivered a speech lasting for nearly two hours in his inspection tour along the route, which witnessed the famous Talk in the South of Deng Xiaoping. I was so impressed when President Xi Jinping stressed, "I cannot agree with such an oversimplified viewpoint that China's reform falls behind in a certain field." In other words, he does not agree with the popular opinion that China's political reform falls behind its economic reform. Economists have the greatest faith in this opinion because some of them are departmentally-centered.

When it comes to state power, it also means political power because it usually stands for the former. Of course, state power is a broader concept covering four kinds of power: economic power, ideological power, military power and political power, among which political power emerges as the result of the game of the other three types of power. For instance, how did the CPC gain its power when the People's Republic of China was founded in 1949? It is natural that the military, economic and ideological power must be grasped before one can take control of political power from being powerless. In addition to the CPC affairs, Chairman Mao was also in charge of ideological affairs when he was in Yan'an—he was responsible for both military and administrative affairs.

Judging from history both at home and abroad, political power is the result. But when people run into problems like corruption in life, they may consider them as system problems, which are fundamentally related to political power. What kind of system is free from corruption? Some people may think of the "free and democratic" countries like the United States and the United Kingdom, but a large number of cases show that in developing countries that have copied the U.S. system, such as India and the Philippines, corruption is more common than that in China.

When Chinese girls bring their boyfriends home to see their parents for the first time, the elders will usually admonish the young men to abide by their leaders' instructions and work hard. This is what the older generation expects of the younger generation. In India, however, whether a man's position in work could grant him a chance for corruption and personal gains has become the criteria for people to pick up a would-be son-in-law. In the Philippines, a "jerry-built project" is called the "shadow project", which doesn't exist at all and only serves as an excuse for related interest groups to persuade a certain regional constructor into jointly fabricating a plan after the budget of such a project is set up. After the deliberation and approval of the Congress and government departments, the granted budget will be split among all the parties involved.

We've heard about too many complaints in our life: once there is a problem, it is usually considered a problem of the system; and the United States will always serve as the most ideal reference when it comes to such a problem. But the fact is that many countries following the U.S. system are troubled with corruption. A country will not be fundamentally influenced whether its economy grows by 6.5 % or 7 % as political power is the result in the true sense; when politics is in disorder, however, the structure that all people of that country rely on for survival will disappear in an instant. Both the Hundreds Days Reform in 1898 in the late Qing Dynasty and the reform of the Soviet Union attributed all the problems to the national system, so they aimed at it and quickly ruined the state power.

During the over 200 years since the founding of the United States of America, it has gone through from agricultural capitalism (Slavery in fact) to the industrial revolution and then to industrial capitalism and lastly financial capitalism after the middle of the 20th century. In spite of revolutionary changes in the economic system, the U.S. Constitution remains unchanged even if someone wishes to amend it—as stipulated by the Founding Fathers of the United States, consent by two-thirds of the House and Senate representatives must be obtained for the amendment of the Constitution. This is really difficult.

Hasn't the U.S. political system been reformed at all despite the dramatic changes in its economic system? Of course not, because it cannot be reformed at all. Since there is no chance to reform it, gun abuse comes as a result. Since things like the use of guns are stipulated in the Constitution, it cannot be curbed without an amendment. Some opinion polls reveal that 80 % to 95 % of Americans have a strong demand for banning and controlling guns. Nevertheless, public opinions are still extremely weak and powerless in front of the law. Terrorism across the world only causes a yearly mortality of no more than 10,000 persons, but approximately 30,000 people are killed or injured in gunshot accidents annually.

The situation in the United States shows that the relationship between politics and economy is not as simple as we thought. Andrew Nathan, an expert on Chinese issues at Columbia University in the United States, proposed in 2003 that more than 70 countries have fallen since the third wave of democratization in 1974, so the collapse of China is just a matter of time. However, instead of falling apart, China has become increasingly stronger. Therefore, he further put forward the concept of Authoritarian Resilience to explain the large amount of flexibility of China's authoritarian system.

From history to reality, the so-called conclusion of political reform falling behind economic reform may need to be re-comprehended.

Why Has China Achieved a Sound Development over the Past 40 Years of the Reform and Opening Up

What's the logic behind China's sound development since its reform and opening up? It could be summarized as follows: "Stick to the right direction and give priority to integration."

How should we stick to the right direction? It is mentioned in the *Selected Works of Deng Xiaoping* that the discussion of principles and ideological guidelines would soon be carried out after the Third Plenary Session of the Eleventh Central Committee of the CPC in December 1978. The discussion conference would last from January to March 1979 and be further continued. However, the Publicity Department of the Communist Party of China thought it was inappropriate for the conference to be convened without a deadline and it should have ended with someone making a summary speech. Since no one was willing to give the speech, the department could only turn to Deng Xiaoping.

Deng Xiaoping agreed readily. He mentioned the Four Basic Principles and set up the basic tenet—the reform. But how should the socialist reform be carried out? Having no idea what to do, we must safeguard the leadership of the CPC. Once we lose it, everything will be gone with it. Therefore, the starting point of the reform is of great significance.

There are many successful revolutions worldwide, but only a few successful reforms. Revolutions are relatively easy to achieve because the enemies and goals are so clear that all that needs to be done is to organize and motivate people to fight, but the reform aims at one's own problems. China succeeded in its reform because Deng Xiaoping grasped the right direction.

When Mikhail Gorbachev reformed, he first aimed at the basic foundation and successfully undermined the CPSU within two years. From 1987 to 1991, intellectuals and the working class launched stormy protests against the CPSU. Hundreds of thousands of Soviet miners went on strikes at every turn, while Soviet intellectuals played as the vanguards of the reform and counterattack. Consequently, the CPSU was downed. These Soviet intellectuals would ask for several cups of Erguotou (a Chinese liquor) if they could visit the Renmin University of China because they couldn't afford alcohol anymore in the Soviet Union. This is how the intellectuals suffered, let alone the Soviet workers.

Therefore, it is inappropriate to believe in economists' nice words about the disconnection between denationalization and ordinary people because what happened to the Soviet Union is a very typical example. This is why Deng Xiaoping was wiser than Mikhail Gorbachev. An apparent gap exists between them in wisdom.

Deng Xiaoping is considered a great man. Therefore, everybody worships him as a model for comparison. For instance, Narendra Damodardas Modi is regarded as the "Deng Xiaoping of India". As regards the national system of India, how could that be possible? There are thousands of public welfare organizations in India. When Modi wanted to establish factories or level mountains, a variety of public welfare organizations made his plans unfeasible. Consequently, Modi was so upset that he closed the accounts of more than 9,000 nongovernmental organizations to break off their operations, otherwise, the reform would never be carried on. Even in such a context, after Japan won the right to construct high-speed railways in India in its bidding competition with China, the land expropriated for that purpose didn't amount to two kilometers in two years. Therefore, how could Modi be the "Deng Xiaoping of India"?

"Spontaneous Order" and "People-oriented Order"

Nowadays, different from many countries which stick to the "spontaneous order", China is committed to the "people-oriented order".

The first step of "spontaneous order" is to have a market economy.

Without the market economy, there would be no competition to speak of, let alone more innovation and wealth. No matter how much some people dislike the market economy and labor employment system, they have come into being, rendering no chance for the return of the days before the market economy. If a country wishes to own wealth, it will have no access to it without the market economy.

Deng Xiaoping visited Singapore before the Third Plenary Session of the Eleventh Central Committee of the CPC was convened. Lee Kuan Yew told Deng Xiaoping that China was the only country that was short of development in the Chinese world, which should be the very one to have been under development because it has profound connections with the Chinese people worldwide and all its educated citizens choose to stay in the mainland while those who came to dwell in Malaysia and Singapore are all fishermen. Why can't the Chinese mainland become affluent? There must be something wrong with the path of development. Hearing this, Deng Xiaoping started to smoke cigarettes one after another in silence. He took a different path after returning to China and subsequently commenced the market economy.

The market economy will inevitably lead to social differentiation and the gap between the rich and the poor.

The market economy is the world of the capable, but people have different abilities. For instance, Beijing people like to talk about politics for their attachment to the homeland while Shanghai people prefer financial securities. Social differentiation will eventually give rise to people like Jack Ma and Ma Huateng. As for most of us, we have to count on education and subsequently live a routine life of striving to be a civil servant or figuring out what to do tomorrow and how to make a fortune after every day's work but slipping back into our offices again the next morning. The party of poor people is the "party of the poor" while the party of rich people is the "party of the rich". This is an uncontrollable "spontaneous order". In the 19th century, the parties were all class parties, classified in accordance with their wealth. Multiparty politics belong to representative democracy, which is elected to perform legislation and decision-making rights; but oligarchy comes as the result of representative democracy, leading to minority power control.

I've engaged in the research of democracy theory for over a decade and have reflected a lot, but Western scholars have conducted much more and more in-depth reflections on their own liberal democratic system.

In 2014, two professors from Princeton University and Northwestern University studied 1,881 American policy cases during the 30 years from 1981 to 2011 to figure out how many of them have evolved into laws and how many haven't. The study showed that the appeals of the rich community had basically evolved into laws and policies, while those of the poor and other disadvantaged communities that have been set as laws accounted for less than one-third of the former. The conclusion of the study is that the United States is not a democratic country but an oligarchic one, or it is an oligarchic democratic country at best.

Some people may question the conclusion as follows: even if there is a problem with the American system, the situation in the United States is excellent and its people are extremely wealthy. Westerners like to attribute things like this to a sound institution as well as a sound system. This is the result. But where does their wealth come from? "Two advancements and one retreat" is my summary for the reason.

One of the "two advancements" was realized through direct plunder in wars. After the signing of the *Treaty of Shimonoseki* in 1895, China paid Japan 230 million taels of silver as compensation. With the money, Japan successfully launched the Russo-Japanese War in Northeast China in 1905. Plundering through wars is a very common strategy in Western countries.

The other of the "two advancements" was achieved through the global purchase of Western industrial products. The total value of the industrial products of the East and the West was nearly the same in 1840; by 1980, however, the industrial products of Western countries had accounted for 90 % of the global total, and the whole world had to rely on Western products for consumption. This generated a tremendous amount of wealth for them. As a result, the Western countries have the money for welfare politics and have established themselves as welfare countries.

"One retreat" refers to the elimination of peasants through industrialization and the rise of new classes. How was the so-called "one retreat" realized? The departure of the people. Statistics show that the population of Edinburgh gradually fell to below 20 % from 1800 to 2000 because almost all the Scots had moved to the United States, New Zealand, and Australia. There was only a total of 50 million people in Italy from 1900 to 1930 after 6 million had migrated elsewhere. But the internal conflicts did not subside for the drain of people and eventually gave rise to fascism. When the Mussolini regime was created, the U.S. Department of State sent a telegram to Mussolini: "Congratulations to you on avoiding the emergence of a socialist democratic regime."

Therefore, the first step of "spontaneous order" is to implement the market economy; the second step will eventually lead to social differentiation like the gap between the rich and the poor, regional problems, urban-rural problems, etc; and in the third step, the rich people will attempt to organize parties.

A comparison between the two paths of "spontaneous order" and "people-oriented order" will lead to two sets of data: "1:9" and "1:150".

"150" refers to approximately 150 emerging countries after the World War II. This figure was calculated based on the current 200 member states in contrast to the 54 original ones when the United Nations was founded. For each country, the figure of 150 is the big data that tells us that no country has become developed for their practice of freedom and democracy, namely following the path of the United States.

"1:9" refers to the 10 developing countries with a population of over 100 million, of which 6 are Asian countries (China, India, Bangladesh, Pakistan, Indonesia, and the Philippines), 2 are African countries (Ethiopia and Nigeria), and 2 are American countries (Brazil and Mexico). Among the 10 countries, only China adopts democratic centralism while the nine others abide by the "spontaneous order". China is relatively comparable with India in terms of national governance, with insignificant comparability with the others. Therefore, we usually make comparisons between China and India.

The ambassador of the Ministry of Foreign Affairs to India once shared an interesting experience: when the Chinese delegation visited Mumbai, whose status in India is like that of Shanghai in China, the Indians raised a question for the delegates. "How many years do you think Shanghai is behind Mumbai?" Though stunned at this question, the Chinese delegates answered, "Many years, so we are expecting your guidance." Six months later, when the Indian delegation paid a return visit to Shanghai, the head of the delegation pinched his thigh and shouted, "Wake up! This is not New York. This is Shanghai!"

There is also another interesting story. When one of the Chinese leaders visited India, he saw colorful banners written with words all the way from the airport to the state guesthouse. The translator told him what the words read: "Let's speed up our development, or China will catch up with us."

In fact, China and India cannot be compared in some areas. For instance, since the transformation of the slums in Mumbai and Delhi involves social issues like infringement of property rights, it needs about 1,500 years based on its current speed.

The Philosophy of China's National Governance

Judging from history, the past 100 years were filled with various extreme ideologies that ebbed and flowed in turn. Several major ideologies came into being starting in 1900: the laissez-faire liberalism prevailing from 1900 to 1930, the Keynesianism emerging and collapsing in the 1930s, the Soviet-style Stalinism popular from the 1930s to the 1970s, and the neo-liberalism promoted by Reagan and Thatcher from the 1970s to the 1980s.

Even the best ideology will eventually collapse if it goes to extremes. This is because it does not meet the demands of mankind. People have different interests, which can be divided into superior or inferior categories. This is an objective reality. Vertically, different classes have different demands; and people's concepts are left, neutral or right horizontally. Any single ideology can only meet the demands of a certain number of people. Therefore, a country (probably) has different values, some mainstream values and some other lesser ones.

A survey reveals that the value of the Chinese people is a governance-oriented ideology. When Chinese people talk about democracy, they actually point at the demands of people's livelihood. Governance-oriented ideology aims at a situation in which people's demands are similar, the ideologies are not extreme nor onefold, and the public policies are inclusive.

How can inclusiveness be achieved? The politics in China is stratified with the system of government as the core. China's constitution stipulates that the system of the People's Congress is the fundamental political system of China and adopts democratic centralism. So democratic centralism is China's system of government. This is how it was defined in Yan'an years back.

It is hard for foreigners to understand democratic centralism because they think in a binary-opposing manner. The basic clues of social development since the Middle Ages are as follows: firstly comes the opposition between religious power and imperial power, then the opposition between imperial and state power and the power of merchants and society after religious power weakened. Society has always been characterized by binary opposition, thus giving rise to the same thinking mode. Since binary opposition has clear boundaries, duality is irreconcilable. This kind of thinking is determined by the history of the West.

In Yan'an, a Western reporter once asked Chairman Mao how it was possible to integrate democracy and centralism. Foreigners cannot understand it, but it is very natural in the eyes of the Chinese. Democracy goes before centralization; there would be no desirable centralization for lack of a sound democratic basis.

China's fundamental political system lies in the following aspects:

> Firstly, the relationship between the central and local governments is both democratic and centralized.

Centralization means that the relationship between the central and local governments is politically unitary, with the local power being granted by the central government and local legislation in line with national laws.

Economically, "economic federalism" has been put in place over the past 40 years of reform and opening up. Decentralization actually means the sharing of power between the central and local governments. For example, taxation collected nationally and locally can be shared by the central and local governments. Knowing nothing of the Chinese fiscal system, some people, merely based on financial statements, believe that the cities of Beijing and Shanghai and the provinces of Guangdong, Shandong, Jiangsu and Zhejiang enjoy a fiscal surplus while all the other provinces (municipalities and autonomous regions) suffer from a deficit. In fact, China adopted a tax-distributing fiscal system, through which 60 % of the tax revenue is turned over to the central government for subsequent transfer payment. Though various provinces seem to be in deficit, the gap will be made up after the transfer payment.

Secondly, the relationship between the government and the market.

On the one hand, the state leads economic development. For example, the various government departments led by the National Development and Reform Commission play a key role in promoting economic development.

Some so-called market economists uphold that since all governmental planning has failed, it should not be led by the government. Such an opinion neither fits reality nor is in line with the history of the West. In Western countries, many scientific and technological projects are now led through national planning. Some private enterprises also succeeded in this regard when they were allowed to do so. But the capitalist countries have engaged in this area for hundreds of years, how can our private enterprises compete with theirs without national power?

On the other hand, with the right to make decisions during the decision-making process, companies can influence the process to some degree.

And finally, the government-people relationship between the state and society.

One needs concentration while the other calls for democracy. Concentration is manifested through strict regulation of four types of associations, including those in the legal, political, ethnic, and religious sectors; economic and cultural organizations need to get registered—there are currently at least 1.5 million such organizations registered in the national civil affairs system.

As for the decision-making process, I address it as a democracy based on negotiation and consensus.

Politics is hierarchical, so it is impossible to explain all of its levels with a single concept.

1. Public policy. For instance, since the *Property Law of the People's Republic of China* involves the interests of everybody, tens of millions of people participated in the discussion concerning its formulation. This process involves the negotiation for institutional laws.
2. Departmental decision-making is also called market pressure-driven negotiation. For example, people think that car-hailing apps are very convenient at present, but they also give rise to safety problems. This kind of car-hailing service cannot be legalized in many countries or regions (such as Hong Kong, China) because it poses a challenge to existing interest groups and trade unions.

It can be said that middle and high-level government officials have all grown up in the market economy because they have formed the awareness of seeking solutions from the market whenever there is a problem. In my opinion, marketization of economic relations is necessary; but if both social relations and political relations are shifted toward marketization, the country will face a terrible situation. If social issues such as birth, senility, illness and death are all market-oriented, many people can't afford them. For the pro-market mindset of some government departments, it is time to make a reflection.

3. Local decision-making is considered a struggle or dialogue-driven negotiation. If local officials make decisions against the interests of the people, the people will stand out and protest; then the two sides will negotiate until both of them accept and be satisfied with the final result.

For instance, three plans were proposed before the construction of the Guangdong-Hong Kong Expressway: firstly, the construction of an expressway passing through the flat ground; secondly, the construction of a sunken expressway; and thirdly, the construction of a fully enclosed expressway. The government and the people finally settled on a plan through negotiations, which cost the government more than ¥1.3 billion and a construction period of nearly two years longer. At last, the people call the park on the side of the highway the "harmonious park". Cases like this are particularly common in affairs of local decision-making.

4. Grassroots governance is a way of democratic communication, with informal talks provided. However, if people are really granted democratic rights, they may not necessarily exercise them. For example, the elevators in the community where I live are used without considering their exclusive use for freight or passengers and are in urgent need of replacement for problems of serious aging and equipment depreciation. But all these problems remained unsolved after a two-year absence of the owners' committee, without the approval of which no large sum of money is allowed to be spent. Democracy and freedom are required in theory. Though the community is a place where democratic rights can be really exerted, residents are still unable to exercise their democratic rights in the true sense. This is really upsetting.

Conclusion

Politics should be re-interpreted, and the re-interpretation is summed up as follows:

> The constitutional system is unchangeable while all other sectors, such as the relationships between the central and local governments, between the government and the market, and between the state and society, are subject to and have experienced structural and revolutionary changes. Such changes in the non-political sectors—changes in people's livelihood and social relations—have strengthened the political constitutional system. These political reforms, which seem to be unpolitical, have currently led to sound achievements—when you think in this way, it means you have accepted the current constitutional system.

What is politics? In form, the relationships between the party and government as well as between the central and local governments and the system of government are all related to politics; in essence, however, politics is about the ability to govern. I especially admire Samuel P. Huntington for the first line he wrote in the *Political Order in Changing Societies* in 1968: "The difference between countries is not the political system, but the degree of governance." The difference between countries lies in the governments' abilities to govern rather than in the form. This kind of ability to govern refers to the livelihood of the people, which is the politics of the highest significance.

Then what is "good politics"? It is the dynamic balance between democracy, authority and the rule of law. A fundamental symbol of modernity is the sovereignty of the people, but such power only occurs in an authoritative order. Without order, the power of the masses may eventually evolve into populism or fascism. Democracy can also turn into something terrible. Tocqueville once said, "Democracy is the tyranny of the majority"; his students added that democracy would become class legislation, through which the class of the majority would legislate to their own interests at the cost of the minority's interests. Democracy will go stray, so will authority. That's why the rule of law is needed.

Whether it is democracy or authority, the rule of law is used to distribute and restrict power. Francis Fukuyama proposed that the United States is a veto-driven regime because of its multi-party system, interest groups and the "doctrine of the rule of law" put forward by Huntington.

The feudal system is highly stable, but the United States is a country established by a group of modern British people, who had run into the New World by mistake. Therefore, Huntington expressed that the United States is a modern society that welcomed its modernity in advance before any revolutions could happen, but its government is a Tudor-like feudal regime. The rule of law, namely making the law the principle for everything, is a very important feature of the Tudor regime.

In modern society, the government needs to push society forward; but the rule of law is a constraint of the government, so we advocate the rule of law. But, to what extent should it be upheld? With a dynamic balance between democracy, authority and the rule of law, a society would not be terrible. Without democracy, the people will not be satisfied no matter how good the governance is; without the rule of law or authority, democracy will be excessive and result in chaos. Things like these were summed up after the third transition of democratization.

Capitalist democracy and socialist democracy are what we frequently hear about. Is there something like feudal democracy? In fact, the Tudor regime is a feudal system. Why is it difficult to control guns? It is because since this land belongs to mine, outsiders are not allowed to intrude—this kind of thought is called feudalism. The French Trade Union is also feudal. When such a feudal system of trade union was continued to 2018 when Emmanuel Macron proposed to increase a fraction of petrol fees, the Yellow Vest Movement emerged. There are still numerous countries, such as the Philippines, India, Bangladesh, Pakistan and other developing countries, which feature feudal social structure. With the social structure unchanged, it is more difficult for them to develop when they have access to democracy.

(This article is compiled and edited based on Professor Yang Guangbin's lecture, part of the RDCY Series Lectures, on December 11, 2018)

12. *Review of the Chinese Banking Industry over the Past 40 Years and Its Status Quo and Prospect*

DONG XIMIAO

Some people argue that banks will disappear in the 21st century. As far as I'm concerned, however, banks will be everywhere, instead of disappearing, in the midst of financial technology. There is a concept of an "Open Bank". With the help of an application programming interface or software development kit, the banks can open up data and standards on the premise of ensured data security and protection of customer privacy. In this way, they can establish in-depth connections with various partners and third parties to innovate products and services, thus enabling customers to enjoy banking services without direct businesses with the banks.

> Three major focuses will be shared in this article: Firstly, the development of the Chinese banking industry over the past 40 years will be reviewed; secondly, the status quo of its development will be discussed; and finally, its development in the future can be expected.

The Starting Point of the Reform and Opening Up of the Chinese Banking Industry

It was in the year of 1978 that China initiated its reform and opening up in banking.

While reviewing the starting point of the reform and opening up of the Chinese banking industry, we shall not ignore some of Deng Xiaoping's speeches. 2018 marks the 40th anniversary of China's reform and opening up. As the chief designer of China's reform and opening up, Deng Xiaoping's report of *Emancipating the Mind, Seeking Truth from Facts, and Looking*

Forward with United Efforts, delivered before the Third Plenary Session of the Eleventh Central Committee of the CPC, has attracted many people's attention. In addition to this extremely important report, his report of the *Several Opinions on Economic Work* published on October 4, 1979, is also of key significance and has served as a guideline for many years. In his speeches, Deng Xiaoping clearly pointed out that economic work is the most significant politics at present, and economic issues should precede all political issues.

Although there was not much about banks in Deng Xiaoping's speeches, they still seem to be instructive even at present. "The banks must be run in the way that real banks are operated." But we still haven't achieved this goal by now. Deng Xiaoping also emphasized that any units must pay interest if they want to obtain resources or borrow money from the banks. This opinion is very ordinary and commonplace in today's world because it has become the common sense everyone agrees with; but at the time when it was proposed, it had a particular purpose. It was after this important speech of Deng Xiaoping that China commenced its reform and opening up in banking in the true sense. Therefore, Deng Xiaoping's speech marks the starting point.

The reform and opening up in banking involves two aspects: the deepening of the reform domestically and the expansion of opening up internationally. The deepening of the reform domestically consists of two parts: the reform and improvement of the operating system and mechanism and the reform of the supervisory system, which constitute a key part of the reform in banking. As for the opening up in the banking industry, it can be divided into four stages and will be discussed in detail later.

Generally speaking, China has made great efforts in deepening reform with remarkable progress since 1978. Currently, the Chinese banking industry has ranked first worldwide for both its total assets and profitability, indicating a gradual growth from a large force to a strong power. Although the expansion of opening up has also led to some achievements, there is still a lot of room for improvement. Over the past 40 years of reform and opening up, "reform" has become the keyword of the banking industry; in the future, however, the keyword may shift to "opening up" to a larger extent—facilitate the reform through opening up.

Review of the History of the Reform in Banking

Over the past 40 years of national reform and opening up, the reform of the bank operating mechanism and the improvement of the banking system have undergone the following four stages in general:

The first stage: professional transformation from 1978 to 1992.

The second stage: commercialization transformation from 1993 to 2003.

The third stage: marketization transformation from 2004 to 2016.

The fourth stage: high-quality development and transformation of the Chinese banking industry since 2017.

The First Stage: Professional Transformation

After 1978, in order to adapt to the reform of the economic system, the "uniform" institutional pattern dominated by the People's Bank of China was shattered for the exploration of corporate development of professional banks. Nowadays, the People's Bank of China has earned the nickname of "Central Bank Mother" because it was entrusted with everything in all respects at that time; as the only bank back then, it had to assume all responsibilities just like "parents" in a family. The existing several large banks were successively established or separated from their original parent institutions starting in 1978: the Agricultural Bank of China (hereinafter referred to as ABC) was re-established, the Bank of China (hereinafter referred to as BC) was separated from the People's Bank of China, and the China Construction Bank (hereinafter referred to as CCB) was broken up from the Ministry of Finance. CCB used to be an internal institution of the Ministry of Finance and was in charge of fund appropriation. It was through CCB that the Ministry of Finance allocated funds to various key projects. But such funds were not loans, but fiscal capital. There was a popular saying at that time. "The State Planning Commission 'orders dishes' while CCB pays the bills." Separated from the People's Bank of China in 1984, the Industrial and Commercial Bank of China (hereinafter referred to as ICBC) has developed into the largest commercial bank. Nowadays, it is widely called the "Universe Bank", but it is in fact the youngest one among the four key state commercial banks. Both BC and the Bank of Communications have a history of more than 100 years.

The first stage, namely the stage of professional transformation, was carried out to adapt the Chinese banking industry to the needs arising from the transition from a "planned economy" to a "planned commodity economy". During this stage, the Chinese banking industry started to explore diversified development.

In the meanwhile, some joint-stock commercial banks were established one after another, such as the establishment of the China Merchants Bank and the China CITIC Bank in 1987. At present, there are 12 national joint-stock commercial banks in total, constituting the most dynamic and innovative cluster of banks in the Chinese banking system. Some time ago, under the leadership of the China Banking Association, I participated in the compilation of the *Thirty Years of National Joint-stock Commercial Banks* in memory of the 30 years of the development of the joint-stock commercial banks.

In this stage, although banking institutions indeed had autonomy in management and operation to a certain degree, their rights were much limited; and they mainly offered single financial products like deposits and loans.

The Second Stage: Commercialization Transformation

After the Fourteenth National Congress of the CPC in 1992, the Chinese economic system ushered in a new stage of transition toward the socialist market economic system. In 1993, the commercialization reform in banking began. After 1978, professional banks were gradually transformed into commercial ones. For instance, the four major banks[1] were originally state-owned professional banks, but now they have all developed into state-owned commercial banks. What did we do during this process? Policy-based finance and commercial finance were separated to form a financial organization system in which state-owned commercial banks play as the main body and various financial institutions coexist. In 1993, three policy banks were established one after another, to which the policy-based businesses are designated. Currently, the State Council has clearly positioned the China Development Bank as a development-oriented financial institution. In 1999, four major asset management companies (hereinafter referred to as AMC) were set up, of which ¥1.4 trillion of non-performing loans were divested. 20 years later, we not only have the four major banks but also a large number of local AMCs.

A slang expression vividly depicts the transformation process of the Chinese state-owned professional banks into state-owned commercial banks, which says, "ICBC shall extend its businesses into the countryside while ABC shall shift its focus back to the city; BC shall pay attention to domestic services again while CCB shall shift from its major business of offering loans to construction companies." In this process, the proportion of commercial institutions in the banking industry has risen, with the set-up of joint-stock banks in succession.

The Third Stage: Marketization Transformation

The banking industry has entered the stage of marketization transformation since 2004, marked by the commencement of the shareholding transformation of state-owned commercial banks by the State Council to promote the establishment of a modern financial corporate system in 2014. The reform is very important and can even be considered as the most successful achievement in the entire reform of China's financial industry. Since 2004, several sets of plans have been proposed to explore how restructuring should be conducted. Dai Xianglong put forward one of them when he served as the governor of the central bank—the four major state-owned commercial banks should continue their former services, namely divesting their non-performing loans to the four AMCs by making use of the fiscal funds injected to them. Zhou Xiaochuan has taken in charge of the central bank since 2003. He then led the shareholding transformation of state-owned commercial banks and adopted the capital injection model through foreign exchange reserve. As a result, the Central Huijin Investment Ltd. was established at the end of 2003 and injected $22.5 billion to CCB and BC respectively, initiating the shareholding restructuring of the four major banks.

Why is the restructuring of the four major banks believed to be the most successful reform in the Chinese financial industry? As mentioned previously, ¥1.4 trillion worth of non-performing loans of the four major banks were divested to the four major AMCs in 1999. Then, what was their non-performing loan ratio by 2002? It was 21.2 % according to the statistical caliber based on "overdue, idle and bad loans", and 26.1 % at the end of 2002 if measured in line with the five-tier classification of loans; except for a non-performing loan ratio of about 15 % of CCB, the non-performing loan ratio of the other three major banks was all over 20 %; ABC even hit 36.6 % in this regard, indicating that more than one-third of its loans were non-performing. Back then, many foreigners believed that the Chinese banking industry had already gone "bankrupt technically". At present, however, the Chinese banking industry ranks first worldwide both in industrial scale and profitability. The four major banks of China ranked in the top four among the ten global institutions listed by *The Banker*, a British magazine, in 2018. Such an achievement is indeed difficult to accomplish.

Therefore, this reform is both important and successful. During the reform, financial burdens from the past were eliminated by national funds injection and financial reorganization; the shareholding transformation of state-owned banks was conducted along with the introduction of qualified foreign institutional investors in accordance with the *Company Law of the People's Republic of China* and the *Law of the People's Republic of China on Commercial Banks*, a measure to introduce both "intelligence" as well as "mechanisms" to improve both corporate governance and internal control and management and facilitate Chinese banks to go public in domestic and foreign public markets under market supervision. For instance, CCB took the lead in going public in Hong Kong in October 2005, kicking off the prelude for the four major banks to become listed; BC was listed in Hong Kong in June 2006; and ICBC went public on the Shanghai Stock Exchange and the Hong Kong Stock Exchange simultaneously in October 2006, the largest IPO in history worldwide at that time. Some people argue that the introduction of foreign strategic investment is tantamount to selling state-owned assets at low prices. I cannot agree with such a viewpoint, of course.

The shareholding reform of the four major banks is a major achievement. China was in the gradual process of establishing a diversified and market-oriented banking system and had accomplished the shareholding transformation of policy-based banks such as the China Development Bank. The 12 joint-stock banks were under reform and innovation, and some of them had begun to set up branch institutions overseas and gone public in capital markets both at home and abroad. A good number of city commercial banks had been listed on the market, with many of them running businesses across regions. With the restructuring of the rural credit cooperatives underway, provincial rural credit cooperatives were set up while prefectural and municipal rural credit cooperatives were transformed into rural cooperative banks and rural commercial banks with their status as independent legal persons remains. ICBC is said to be the "universe bank". But the people of the rural credit cooperative don't think so because the rural credit cooperative is the real "universe bank" in their eyes. Adding up the number and assets of all the rural credit cooperatives nationwide, they will indeed exceed those of ICBC; but it's a pity that there is not yet a nationally uniform management agency of the rural credit cooperative at present.

During this stage, China relaxed restrictions on the entry of private capital into the banking industry. Pilot private banks, such as WeBank, started to emerge in 2014 and have amounted to 17 in number by 2018. The 17 private banks are not the only achievement of the relaxed access for private capital into the banking industry, of course. Prior to this, many private companies in the eastern coastal regions had already invested significantly in banks. For instance, private capital accounts for more than 75 % of the shares of small and medium banks in Zhejiang.

The Fourth Stage: High-quality Development

China has entered the stage of high-quality development since 2017. With the implementation of strict and reinforced supervision policies starting from March 2017, such as the release of a series of documents addressing "three violations, three interest arbitrage conducts, four inappropriate behaviors and ten major problems", the entire banking industry has encountered a dramatic change. It must be admitted that such a change is both painful and profound. The change mainly involves the following aspects: "deleveraging" on the liability side, including tightening of liquidity, reduction of inter-bank reliance on financial management and certificate of deposit services, and the increasing difficulty of off-balance sheet financing; "de-channeling" on the asset side, including constraint of idle circulation of funds between banks, strict control of inter-bank investment, standard regulation of shadow banking, prevention of substantial risks, and promotion of the return of off-balance-sheet funds to on-balance-sheet credit; "de-pooling" of business models, including the shattering of rigid redemption, standardization of capital pools, restriction of multi-level nesting, implementation of penetration supervision, and prevention of regulatory arbitrage; and the enhancement of the build-up of supervisory capacity, including the prevention of supervisory gaps or overlapped supervision by improving weak links, the strengthening of the unification of regulatory standards and data sharing by advancing regulatory coordination, and the reinforcement of regulatory accountability.

Of course, the pace of strict and reinforced supervision has slowed down in general because of the changes in the external environment and increasing uncertainties. Nevertheless, the overall direction will remain unchanged.

The Reform of the Banking Regulatory System

The four stages of the reform of the Chinese banking industry were reviewed previously and the reform of the banking regulatory system will be discussed here. As a key link in the internal reform of the banking industry, the reform of the regulatory system has gone through the following stages:

The first stage: resumption of the central bank's supervisory responsibility from 1978 to 1994.

The second stage: formation of the separate supervision from 1995 to 2002.

The third stage: full establishment of the supervisory system from 2003 to 2007.

The fourth stage: continuous adjustment of the supervisory system after the U.S. financial crisis from 2008 to 2016.

The fifth stage: the era of reinforced supervision since 2017.

The First Stage: Resumption of the Central Bank's Supervisory Responsibility

The central bank has become independent of the Ministry of Finance since 1978 to take charge of banking-related issues. Though established in 1948, it only performed its functions as a nominal supervisory authority before 1978, especially during the Cultural Revolution. After being separated from the Ministry of Finance in 1978, it has not only assumed the responsibilities as the central bank but also performed businesses as a commercial bank; therefore, in addition to its status as a macro-policy formulation agency as well as a financial supervisory department, it also ran businesses directly. It was not until 1984 that the central bank transferred operational businesses to ICBC.

In 1983, the State Council issued a document to especially announce the establishment of the central bank. The *Interim Regulations of the People's Republic of China on the Management of Banks* was released in 1986 to legally clarify the responsibilities of the People's Bank of China as the central bank and financial supervisory authority. The *Law of the People's Republic of China on the People's Bank of China* was passed in 1995 to formally establish the status of the People's Bank of China as the central bank through national legislation.

The Second Stage: Formation of the Separate Supervision

China has adopted a separate supervision system since 1995, marked by the passage of the *Law of the People's Republic of China on Commercial Banks.* Since then, the reform and development of the banking industry have been legally secured.

As a milestone event, the First National Financial Work Conference in November 1997 is of great significance for plenty of decisions it made, such as the implementation of the commercial bank reform and the establishment of the four major AMCs. In terms of the supervisory system, the decision to implement the separate supervision was made: the China Banking Insurance Regulatory Commission was established on the one hand and the reform of the China Securities Regulatory Commission (hereinafter referred to as the CSRC) was initiated on the other hand. In fact, the CSRC was established in 1992, but there was still the State Council Securities Committee (hereinafter referred to as the SCSC) at that time. As the executive department of the SCSC, the CSRC was relatively limited in power. It was only after 1997 that the CSRC became the real regulator of the securities market. In this way, securities and insurance were separated from the central bank, leading to the establishment of a separate supervision system.

It was at the Second National Financial Work Conference that the separate supervision system was further consolidated. It was decided at the conference that the People's Bank of China would no longer be responsible for the supervision of financial institutions and shall be dedicated to monetary policy formulation, safeguarding of financial stability, and macro regulation. The *Law of the People's Republic of China on the People's Bank of China*, passed in 1995, officially established the status of the People's Bank of China as the central bank through national legislation. At that time, however, the People's Bank of China was also in charge of financial supervision. It was designated as the department of macro regulation in 2002 when the decision was made to set up the China Banking Regulatory Commission (hereinafter referred to as the CBRC).

The Third Stage: Full Establishment of the Supervisory System

The CBRC was formally established in 2003 to supervise banks and manage financial assets, to which the responsibility of supervising the trust industry was transferred from the central bank. It was after 2003 that the separate supervision system consisting of "one bank and three commissions" finally took shape. A proverb proved by history goes like this: "A long-lasting split is always followed by a reunion, and vice versa." Formally coming into being in 2003, the system consisting of "one bank and three commissions" was altered to a new one consisting of "one bank and two commissions" 15 years later, which is another story.

The CBRC was officially established after 2003. If the central bank can be nicknamed the "Central Bank Mother", then we have a formal institution to play the role of "father". With the release of the *Law of the People's Republic of China on Regulation of and Supervision over the Banking Industry* at the end of the same year, a supervisory framework of the banking industry has gradually taken shape—a compliance supervisory framework with capital adequacy rate at the core was established in addition to the restructuring of the banking industry. The year 2004 ushered in the stage of marketization transformation. With the establishment of the China Banking Association, China has sped up its pace of opening up to the outside world.

The Fourth Stage: Continuous Adjustment of the Supervisory System

The supervisory system has undergone some adjustments after 2008. The 2008 financial crisis indeed influenced the Chinese economy to some degree. Considering both the new development trends of international finance and the reality of China's economic and financial development, China has carried out a series of reforms and adjustments to the banking supervisory system to address the weaknesses and deficiencies exposed in the crisis. A reflection on the 2008 financial crisis reveals that it is of great significance to strengthen and improve the macro-prudential policy to better prevent and eliminate financial risks and avoid systemic financial risks. Issues of finance were mentioned at the Nineteenth National Congress of the CPC, such as the novel expression of "a two-pillar regulatory framework realized through sound monetary policy and macro-prudential policy". The State Council Financial Stability and Development Commission was set up at the Fifth National Financial Work Conference, indicating the advent of the era of the supervisory system consisting of "one commission, one bank and two conferences". Moreover, there is also another link in the Chinese financial supervisory system—the local governments. As for their roles and functions in financial supervision, they're worth being further studied.

The Fifth Stage: The Era of Reinforced Supervision

The reinforced and strict supervision in recent years is indeed faced with the problem of excessively fast pace. One of the key areas targeted by the reinforced and strict supervision is "shadow banking". I prefer to call it the "shadow of banks", however. "Shadow banking" has dramatically shrunk at a rapid speed under the influence of reinforced and strict supervision. Why are the difficulties and high costs of private companies in financing a problem so prominent in 2018? It is because many private companies do not finance through formal institutions or formal channels, but through "shadow banking". Fast-paced supervision will cause the businesses of "shadow banking" to shrink sharply, from which private companies will suffer the most. Sometimes we say that the strengthening of financial supervision is like "removing landmines". There are indeed "landmines" in the banking industry, which we need to remove instead of detonating them directly. No landmines will exist anymore whether they are removed or detonated, but the impacts are completely different: there will be a relatively mild consequence with no risks if they are removed, but it'll bring about a destructive result if they are detonated. Therefore, both the pace and intensity of financial supervision have been eased, which I think is a very necessary adjustment.

Expansion of the Opening Up

Financial opening up is the future trend. Many studies have shown that the economy of the countries opening up in finance grows faster than those that are financially closed. But financial opening up will certainly bring about risks, and the opening up of capital projects at a rapid speed may lead to huge impacts. The Asian financial crises in 1997 and 1998 are typically negative examples. It should be noted that China has indeed made great achievements in its financial opening up, but there are still areas in need of improvement. Following the pace of the national opening up in all respects, the Chinese banking industry has steadily opened up to the outside world step by step with remarkable progress. The whole process covers the following four stages:

The first stage: before the entry into the WTO.

The second stage: from the accession to the WTO to the 2008 financial crisis.

The third stage: from the 2008 financial crisis to 2016.

The fourth stage: from 2017 to the present.

The First Stage: Before the Entry to the WTO

China opened up its banking industry mainly in coordination with the process of its national reform and opening up. A better investment environment was created by introducing foreign-funded banks and foreign exchange funds and improving financial services for foreign-funded enterprises. In order to improve the level of opening up, the opening up in the Chinese banking industry was further expanded. The businesses of foreign-funded banks kept growing at a fast pace thanks to the rapid growth of foreign-funded enterprises in China and the development of international businesses of Chinese-funded enterprises. During this stage, foreign-funded banks established representative offices or branches in China in succession, mainly engaging in some of the banking businesses in association with foreign currencies.

The Second Stage: After the Accession to the WTO to the 2008 Financial Crisis

The opening up of the Chinese banking industry during this period centered on the fulfillment of the promises that China had made for its membership of the WTO, for which a series of independent opening-up measures had been adopted. With the expanded business scope of foreign-funded banks in a gradual process, foreign-funded financial institutions had begun to invest in Chinese-funded banks as strategic partners. The customers of foreign-funded banks' RMB services gradually went beyond foreign-funded corporations and foreigners to cover Chinese enterprises and Chinese residents; constraints of foreign-funded banks' operations in China were relaxed step by step, and the restriction that foreign-funded banks' RMB liabilities shall not exceed 50 % of their foreign exchange liabilities was abolished. In the meanwhile, foreign-funded banks would be gradually rendered national treatment in addition to promised conditions.

The landmark event during this stage was the Hong Kong and Shanghai Banking Corporation's investment in the Bank of Communications in 2004, through which the former acquired 19.9 % of the shares of the latter. Subsequently, a number of foreign-funded banks began to invest in Chinese-funded banks as strategic investors and especially took the initiative to participate in the shareholding transformation of large commercial banks. Some foreign-funded banks even invested in joint-stock banks and city commercial banks, such as Citibank's investment in the China Guangfa Bank, Hang Seng Bank's investment in Industrial Bank Co, Ltd., and BNP Paribas' investment in the Bank of Nanjing.

The Third Stage: From the 2008 Financial Crisis to 2016

After the global financial crisis in 2008, China strengthened risk prevention in banking as well as international supervision and coordination to curb cross-border financial risks. Consequently, the pace of opening up in the Chinese banking industry had slowed down to a certain degree.

With the diminishing impact of the financial crisis, the international financial market tended to regain its balance and the global economy started to recover. Therefore, China sped up the pace of opening up banking to the outside world again. It released a series of management measures for foreign-funded banks, such as legal personalization in 2007, which were carried on with continuous efforts during this stage. The legal personalization of foreign-funded banks played a favorable role in preventing cross-border risks associated with foreign-funded banks. The State Council announced the *Decision of the State Council on Amending the Regulations of the People's Republic of China on the Administration of Foreign-funded Banks* in December 2014 to properly relax the access standards for foreign-funded banks to enter China and the requirements for their operation of RMB-related businesses, thus creating a more relaxed and independent institutional environment for the set-up and operation of foreign-funded banks.

The Fourth Stage: From 2017 to the Present

Zhu Guangyao, the then Vice Minister of the Ministry of Finance, announced a new round of opening-up policies for the Chinese financial industry on

November 10, 2017. In terms of the banking industry, China had lifted the restriction that the single shareholding ratio and total shareholding ratio that foreign funds account for in a Chinese bank shall not exceed 20 % and 25 % respectively, and had adopted a banking equity investment ratio that was consistent both internally and externally. With such measures, the pace, scope, and depth of the opening up of the Chinese bank industry continued to improve. The former CBRC issued the *Decision of the CBRC on Amending the Implementation Measures for the CBRC Administrative Licensing of Foreign-funded Banks* in February 2018, intending to further open up the Chinese banking market and expand the service scope of foreign-funded banks in China. After that, the China Banking and Insurance Regulatory Commission announced the revised *Detailed Rules for the Implementation of the Regulation of the People's Republic of China on the Administration of Foreign-funded Banks* on November 28 of the same year. Recently, a good number of market access programs in the banking industry have been examined and approved.

Generally speaking, remarkable achievements have been registered in the opening up of the banking industry. The assets of foreign-funded banks in China hit ¥3.2 trillion in 2017, with the number of legal persons institutions and operating institutions reaching 39 and 1,013 respectively. In other words, two breakthroughs were accomplished in 2017—the assets of foreign-funded banks in the Chinese Mainland had exceeded ¥3 trillion and foreign-funded operating institutions had totaled more than 1,000. However, there were also outstanding weaknesses in the Chinese banking industry, evidenced by the relatively slow development of the businesses of foreign-funded banks in China and the comparatively low proportion of each of their businesses. The market share of foreign-funded banks started to shrink in a gradual process, especially after 2011. The assets of foreign-funded banks in the Chinese Mainland accounted for 1.93 % of the total of the banking industry in 2011, followed by a drop year by year. Although the assets of foreign-funded banks in China had surpassed ¥3 trillion by 2017, the proportion had fallen to 1.28 %. Therefore, there is still much room for further opening up of the Chinese banking industry in the long run. Cutting off ourselves from the outside world will hinder our development, and only competition with excellent rivals can improve ourselves. The logic of China's opening up of its banking industry is as follows: firstly, introduce high-quality competitors to enhance the overall competitiveness of the Chinese banking industry and improve our banks' service efficiency; and secondly, introduce more institutions to increase the main body of supply in the market and promote the diversity and variety of products and services, thus facilitating China's economic development.

The Status Quo of the Development of the Chinese Banking Industry

The deepening of the internal reform and the expansion of the opening up of the Chinese banking industry during the 40 years of China's reform and opening up were briefly reviewed previously. Then the focus will be shifted to the current situation of the Chinese banking industry, which mainly covers six aspects.

Firstly, rebounded profitability and optimized revenue structure. Take listed banks as an example. In the first half of 2018, 41 listed banks earned a total operating income of ¥2.31 trillion, a year-on-year growth of 7.28 %, and realized a net profit of ¥910.755 billion, a year-on-year increase of 6.72 %. In terms of income structure, the proportion of non-interest income of listed banks had increased significantly: at the end of the first half of 2018, the proportion of non-interest income of listed banks averaged 28.4 %, 7.38 % higher than the same period last year. Among the reasons behind the better performance of listed banks, the stabilization of the net interest margin of large and medium-sized banks played a key role in the recovery of their profits. This benefited firstly from the monetary policy the central bank had adopted in the first half of 2018 to maintain a reasonable and adequate liquidity that successfully reduced the cost of bank liabilities; and secondly, from the increased average loan interest rate of financial institutions in the first half of 2018, which helped boost the yield rate of interest-bearing assets.

Secondly, the growth of the scale of listed banks has slowed down with the proportion of deposits and loans increased. In the first half of 2018, the growth of the scale of listed banks slowed down, but the asset-liability structure has been further optimized with an increased proportion of deposits and loans. In the first half of 2018, the total assets of listed banks reached ¥173.27 trillion, a year-on-year increase of 6.15 %; and the total liabilities hit ¥160.51 trillion, a year-on-year growth of 5.71 %. In terms of structure, the loans of listed banks accounted for 52.32 % of the total assets, a year-on-year increase of 2.0 %; and the deposits accounted for 74.0 % of the total liabilities, 0.6 % higher than the same period last year.

Thirdly, the transformation of the retail business has registered initial achievements. The China Merchants Bank is the best for its retail business among all the banks. Established in 1987, it has specialized in the retail banking business for more than 30 years, possessing the highest valuation in the entire banking industry at present. Looking back to the 40 years of the Chinese banking reform, the China Merchants Bank should be named if a real commercial bank must be recommended. Its corporate governance is worth our study because it has only three presidents in total by now, including the incumbent one, and has implemented stable strategies ever since its establishment. No other banks can do things like these. All listed banks have regarded extensive retail business as one of their strategic development priorities.

In terms of the transformation of retail business, joint-stock banks achieved the most outstanding performance among all types of banks in the first half of 2018, with the retail business revenue of 7 listed joint-stock commercial banks (excluding the Hua Xia Bank and the China Zheshang Bank) totaling ¥222.07 billion, a year-on-year increase of 17.2 %. Of course, Ping An Bank is enterprising in attempts to catch up with China Merchants Bank in retail business, but whether its ambition can be sustained remains to be seen. In the Chinese banking industry, the transformation of retail business is a phenomenon worthy of attention. But it is inappropriate that some banks are too rash in pursuit of fast success.

Fourthly, asset quality tends to stabilize. A profound connotation is implied in the tendency to stabilize. To be honest, I'm worried about the asset quality of the Chinese banking industry. The balance of non-performing loans of listed banks reached ¥1.37 trillion in the first half of 2018, indicating an overall trend of increase. Of all the aforesaid loans, special mention loans accounted for 2.86 % on average, a decrease compared with the same period last year. In terms of non-performing loan ratio, the overall non-performing loan ratio of listed banks was stabilized; and the average non-performing loan ratio of 43 listed banks was registered at 1.50 % in the first half of 2018, nearly the same as that in the same period of 2017. In terms of provision coverage, listed banks have improved dramatically in this regard with promotion of prudent operation capabilities. In the first half of 2018, the provision coverage of listed banks averaged 229.04 %, a year-on-year increase of 15.54 % over the last year.

Fifth, increased capital adequacy ratio. The tier-1 capital adequacy ratio of 42 listed banks (excluding Bank of Jiujiang) averaged 10.49 % at the end of the first half of 2018, a year-on-year increase of 0.37 % over the last year. In 2018, the tier-1 core capital adequacy ratio of listed banks was basically the same as that during the same period last year. In addition, the tier-1 core capital adequacy ratio of 42 listed banks reached 9.75 % on average at the end of the first half of 2018. In general, the tier-1 core capital adequacy ratio still limits the expansion of banks in scale, and the capital adequacy ratio of small and medium-sized banks is especially in need of improvement. In the future, the off-balance-sheet assets of banks will continue to "flow back as on-balance-sheet assets", credit assets with high risks and weights will consume more capital, and the pressure on small and medium-sized banks in supplementing core capital shall not be ignored. Many people outside the financial circle believe that the banks should loan more money because the Central Bank Mother has granted them more funds by carrying out a targeted reduction of the bank-required reserve ratio four times in 2018 and another targeted medium-term lending facility. In fact, banks may not be able to lend even if they are provided with enough money. In addition to liquidity, they are also subject to capital constraints. Why is capital replenishment necessary? Because banks still cannot lend if the capital adequacy ratio is insufficient. Lending of banks is not that simple. Therefore, we are still faced with huge pressure as regards capital replenishment at present. Why do so many banks go public? Capital replenishment is what they need fundamentally.

Finally, the subsidiary system is advancing steadily. A new asset management regulation was implemented in the first half of 2018, requiring qualified commercial banks to set up subsidiaries for wealth management business. Under the guidance of this policy, small and medium banks among the listed banks have begun to take the initiative to explore the establishment of subsidiaries. As of 2018, 27 banks have announced to set up wealth management subsidiaries. It is expected that the supervisory authorities will soon approve of the banks' applications of setting up wealth management subsidiaries. In November 2017, the supervisory authorities approved of the establishment of the subsidiary of the Ai Bank, the first direct bank in China. Financial technological subsidiaries of banks are also underway, with seven or eight of them already established at present.

Prospect of the Chinese Banking Industry

The future development of the Chinese banking industry may lie in the following aspects:

> Firstly, accelerated opening up and intensified market competition. Although a variety of uncertainties may exist in the future, the opening up of the banking industry will certainly accelerate with intensified competition. Although reform has played a key driving force in the development of the Chinese banking industry over the past 40 years, the keyword has shifted to opening up at present. Through the deepening of reform and the expansion of opening up, China has reconstructed the pattern of the banking industry along two guidelines: incremental reform and stock transformation. Opening up involves the following three aspects: the lowering of access standards,

the simplification of approval procedures, and the expansion of business scope, through which more foreign-funded banks will be attracted to China.

In the future, competition in the banking market will intensify for sure. As of the end of 2017, there were 4,249 banking legal person institutions in China, of which about 3,900 are real banks (including rural credit cooperatives) if trust companies, finance companies, auto finance companies, and consumer finance companies are excluded. With so many banks in the market at present, the competition is becoming more and more fierce. The growth of both deposits and loans of listed banks in the first half of 2018 slowed down compared with that in the same period last year. Also in the first half of 2018, the loan balance of listed banks reached ¥90.66 trillion, with the deposit balance hitting ¥118.79 trillion. In terms of growth rate, the loans of listed bank grew at 16.47 % on average in the first half of 2018, a year-on-year decrease of 2.15 % compared with last year; and the deposits grew at 8.78 % on average, 3.69 % lower than the same period of 2017. In the context of strict supervision, interbank, financial management and off-balance-sheet businesses have become the key targets of supervision; moreover, as deposits remain the most important source of liabilities, they have become more and more important. Since the limited low-cost deposits in the market are the "anchor" of the banks' profitability, they have become the major target the banks compete for.

Secondly, return to the original focus on enhancing service capabilities. As mentioned above, both the proportion of bank deposits in total liabilities and loans in total assets is rebounding, a manifestation of the return to the original focus of the banks. Implementing national strategies and serving the real economy are the responsibilities of banks in nature, and also the fundamental source for the sustainable development of finance. Banks must strive to follow up major national decision-making deployments and key programs, such as promoting coordinated regional development, reinforcing financial support for the Belt and Road Initiative, facilitating Chinese-funded enterprises to go global, advancing the internationalization of RMB, etc.; additionally, they should work hard to cultivate new momentum, support innovation-driven development and the construction of pilot free trade zones, and improve consumer financial services. At present, they also need to further improve the services for the private sector and small and micro enterprises.

The two principles of marketization and legalization must be abided by in the process of serving the national strategy and the weak links of finance, otherwise, the mistake of the so-called Four-trillion-yuan Economic Policy[2], from which we have drawn an impressive lesson, may happen again. Now many voices are calling for an increase in credit supply, expecting the bank's net profit to grow at a faster rate in 2019. Many banks requested enterprises to loan from them ten years ago, and now a similar situation seems to be happening again.

> Thirdly, shift of businesses and accelerated integrated operations. To cope with the marketization of interest rates and meet the customers' needs for diversified financial services, various banks have deployed integrated operations to give full play to multiple operational licenses and strengthen the linkage and coordination between multiple operational threads; they have shifted from provision of traditional credit to resource integration so as to implement the "customer-oriented" conception and strengthen integrated financial services in a pragmatic manner. Generally speaking, the integrated operations of the banking industry are not only conducive to the realization of the synergy between banks and non-banking financial services but will also play a positive role in improving the social financing structure at the macro level and reinforce the banking industry's ability to withstand the impact of economic cyclical fluctuations at the micro level.

We also need to heed that with the optimization of the business structure of the banks and the transformation of business models, the staff structure will change accordingly. In the future, although the total staff of some banks may decrease, part of the banks will still increase their investment in talent, especially in the cultivation of professional talent in financial technology, Internet technology, products and marketing. In a nutshell, there is no such problem as large-scale layoffs in the Chinese banking industry, nor branches or outlets of banks will be removed or merged in large quantities.

> Fourthly, take a leading role in innovation and in-depth integration with scientific technology. With the deepening of innovation, financial technology has indeed become a significant driving force for the transformation and innovation of the banking industry. As a result, finance and scientific technology will be further integrated, from simply "being grafted" to in-depth "integration". The banking industry has always been the pioneer and role model in the application of

advanced technology. For instance, the first large computer in the world was first used by Bank of America. With the continuous deepening of the special rectification of Internet financial risks, faster and better development will be achieved in the financial technology of formal financial institutions represented by banks. When it comes to specific financial technologies, either "ABCD" or "ABCDT" should be mentioned. "ABCD" refers to artificial intelligence, blockchain, cloud computing and big data, while "ABCDT" means Internet of Things plus "ABCD". All these technologies will be profoundly applied in the banking industry, and are helping to reconstruct the operational and business models of banks in customer service, product design, operation model, risk control, etc. At a time when the banking industry is facing the risk of pattern reshaping, scientific technology will become the core competitiveness that determines the strength of banks in the future.

The Chinese banking industry will leave its footprint everywhere in the future. Some people argue that banks will disappear in the 21st century; as far as I'm concerned, however, banks will be everywhere, instead of disappearing, in the midst of financial technology. There is a concept of an "Open Bank". With the help of an application programming interface or software development kit, the banks can open up data and standards on the premise of ensured data security and protection of customer privacy. In this way, they can establish in-depth connections with various partners and third parties to innovate products and services, thus enabling customers to enjoy banking services without direct businesses with the banks. Therefore, banks will become more and more open. In the future, people may forget about the services of the bank when their banking businesses are processed. The focus is being shifted from the banking outlet service in the past to the scenario-based service and may to the scenario-free service in the future. This is the power of financial technology.

In short, financial technology will promote the transformation of the banking industry in three directions: digital transformation, light-weight transformation, and platform-based transformation.

Finally, guarantee operations in compliance with regulations and further improve risk control capabilities. There will be three key areas in need of extreme attention in the future. Firstly, the prevention and elimination of major risks. In this regard, the priority is to prevent and resolve financial risks, the focus of which lies in the prevention and elimination of banking risks. Since banks are the main body of the Chinese financial system, they assume a great responsibility in this regard. "Preventing and eliminating existing risks, curbing incremental risks, and facilitating the return of finance to its original function of serving the real economy" is the current leading guideline for the supervision of the banking industry. Therefore, the prevention and control of financial risks in the banking industry has become a key task at present.

Specifically, three major risks—credit risk, liquidity risk, and operational risk—need to be prevented and controlled. To prevent and control credit risk, we must resolutely implement the pressure relief policy for high-risk customers, high-pollution and high-energy-consumption resourced-based industries and overcapacity industries, and "zombie companies", manage and control the risks of "high leverage" customers, optimize the disposal portfolio of bad assets, and accelerate the process of risk disposal. The pressure on the asset quality of the banking industry is relatively huge at present and in the future, so the disposal of existing non-performing loans will generate the greatest pressure for the banking industry in the upcoming years. In terms of the prevention and control of liquidity risk, it is necessary to enhance the expansion of self-operated deposits, arrange credit progress in a rational manner, optimize the asset-liability structure, expand diversified financing channels, carry out the active liability management, issue financial bonds at appropriate moments, and strengthen the business asset-liability maturity-matching management, such as the set-up of separate liquidity risk limits for bills, wealth management and other businesses. In preventing and controlling operational risk, we shall conduct inspections of key risk indicators, improve outsourcing risk management mechanisms, strengthen credit investigation compliance risk management, enhance information technology risk management, and carry out full-coverage monitoring of the availability of key systems.

(This article is compiled and edited based on Professor Dong Ximiao's lecture, part of the RDCY Series Lectures, December 20, 2018)

Notes

1 The four major state-owned commercial banks of China: the Agricultural Bank of China, the Bank of China, the China Construction Bank, and the Industrial and Commercial Bank of China.

2 An economic policy proposed by the Chinese government in November 2018 to address the 2008 international economic crisis and stabilize economy, with a total investment of ¥4 trillion.

13. *How Will the Chinese Economy Develop under an Economic Downturn?*

Chen Yanbin

As is shown by macroeconomic practices, macropolicy is of great significance because of the importance of short-term economic and financial stability. Short-term financial instability will lead to financial crises and subsequently economic collapse. The Great Depression of the United States from 1929 to 1933 occurred because people understood the importance of short-term economic stability poorly while focusing too much on market clearing—it was believed that the companies and banks able to pull through the crisis would be of high quality and efficient and could facilitate better economic development. However, economists at that time did not expect that it would be unwise to directly apply the principles of marketing and market clearing in macroeconomics. From a modern point of view, this will cause debt deflation as well as the trap of a vicious circle. Consequently, short-term problems will worsen in the long run and eventually cause economic collapse.

The current development of China's economy calls for reinforced macro policy as well as more profound policy coordination. This article mainly focuses on the basic situations of China's economy and what macro policy we should adopt in response to the current economic development. It consists of the following four parts: firstly, an introduction to the current economy; secondly, a brief analysis of the current finance; thirdly, an evaluation of the current macro policy; and finally, some recommendations about the policy.

The Current Economy

China's economic growth has slowed down in 2018, faced with increased downward pressure. With a GDP growth expected at 6.6 % in 2018, it remains high globally despite a percentage point 0.3 lower than that in 2017. Although it met the target of growth of "approximately 6.5 %" set at the beginning of the year, the macro policy in 2018 hasn't achieved its goal of economic stability satisfactorily. To realize economic stability, it'll be infeasible if China pins all its hopes on macro policy; further structural reforms and even cooperation with other economic policies are needed as well. The economic downward pressure can be spotted in the following aspects:

1. A trend, "a low rate in the wake of a high one, of the annual GDP growth highlights the failure of the macro policy in effectively addressing the economic downward pressure."

China's GDP grew at 6.8 % and 6.7 % in the first and second quarters of 2018 respectively. But its economy has witnessed "a change in the midst of steady growth" in the second half of 2018, evidenced by the drop in GDP growth rate to 6.5 % in the third quarter, a quarterly record low since the first quarter of 2009; and a GDP growth rate of only 6.4 % hasn't shown any improvement in the fourth quarter. Therefore, signs of slowing economic growth are obvious. In terms of employment, the unemployment rate was maintained at a relatively ideal level of around 5 %, but it began to change in the second half of the year. As for labor demands, the purchasing managers index (PMI) of both manufacturing and non-manufacturing sectors has dropped dramatically to below the critical value of 50 % since the second half of 2018, remaining at a low level in recent years. When it comes to residents' actual feelings, the survey data of the central bank show that the employment experience index in the third quarter of 2018 (44.2 %) fell by 1.6 and 0.8 percentage points respectively compared with that in the first and second quarters respectively; and the employment expectation index (51.6 %) was 2.5 and 0.7 percentage points lower than that in the first and second quarter respectively. Since a time lag exists between the implementation of the macro policy and the manifestation of its effect, the economic downward pressure in the second half of the year may reflect the insufficient effect of the macro policy on stabilizing the economy in 2018.

2. China's GDP growth rate, calculated through the production method, mainly embodies the changes in total supply; in terms of aggregate demand, however, the downward pressure on the Chinese economy in 2018 is more obvious.

Ways to account GDP cover production method, income method and expenditure method. In recent years, it has been found that a comparatively huge gap would exist between the GDP calculated with the production method and the expenditure method. The gap has seemed to be significantly widened since 2015, and the GDP growth rate calculated with the production method was substantially higher than that based on the expenditure method in 2016 and 2017 (see Figure 13.1).

A detailed analysis will be conducted from the perspective of aggregate demand structure—the trio of economic growth (consumption, investment and export)—in the following part.

First of all, in terms of consumer demand, the growth of residents' consumption expenditure on both commodities and services has sharply declined. The consumer demand of Chinese urban residents has remained weak since the beginning of 2018. Judging from the overall consumption expenditure of urban residents, although the nominal growth of per capita consumption expenditure of urban residents in the first three quarters of 2018 registered 6.5 %, a year-on-year increase of 0.3 % over 2017, it was mainly due to the accelerated growth of residents' spending on residence, daily necessities, services and other passive consumption expenditures. Since it is difficult for consumers to control expenditures on rigid demands like these as freely as they wish, the faster growth actually indicates the rising living cost of the residents, instead of their stronger willingness to spend money. After excluding

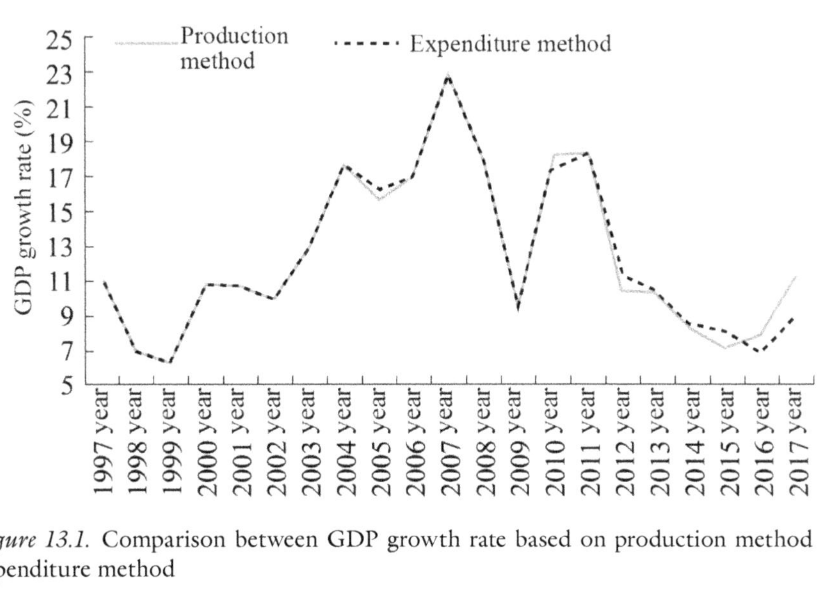

Figure 13.1. Comparison between GDP growth rate based on production method and expenditure method

passive consumption expenditures, it can be found that the growth rate of per capita consumption expenditure of urban residents in the first three quarters of 2018 only reached 5.2 %, 0.3 percentage points lower than the same period in 2017 and a record low since the implementation of the new statistical caliber of household consumption expenditure by the National Bureau of Statistics in 2013.

The growth of the consumption of both commodities and services, the two major sectors of consumption, is slowing down. In commodity consumption, the changes in its growth rate can be more precisely reflected by the growth rate of total retail sales of consumer goods without considering catering revenue. The total retail sales of consumer goods (excluding catering revenue) from January to October 2018 grew only at 9.2 %, a year-on-year decrease of 1 percentage point from 2017 and the lowest one in the same period since 2000. When it comes to service consumption, it mainly refers to experiential consumption of education, medical care, culture, entertainment, etc. Currently, due to the lack of adequate statistics on the scale of service consumption, China usually forecasts and calculates the results based on the sub-item data of household consumption expenditure released by the National Bureau of Statistics each quarter. In 2018, the rapid growth momentum over the past few years hasn't been sustained in the service consumption of urban residents, with the growth rate in the first three quarters only maintained at 7 %, a year-on-year drop of 0.7 and 4.1 percentage points compared with 2017 and the average growth rate of service consumption from 2012 to 2016 respectively.

Secondly, from the perspective of investment demand, the actual growth rate of fixed asset investment is close to zero. Although the growth rate of private fixed asset investment has rebounded, the momentum is not yet stable.

The fixed asset investment grew at a rate of 24 % in 2011, a continuous decline for several years. It only reached 5.7 % from January to October 2018, a year-on-year drop of 1.6 percentage points over 2017. With the price factor further excluded, it only grew at 0.1 % in the January-October period of 2018, basically in a state of zero growth. Though the land purchase fees grew at a rate as high as 63.4 % from January to October 2018, the nominal growth rate of fixed asset investment during the same period would drop to 3.6 % if the impact of land purchase fees is excluded, significantly lower than the current level of 5.7 %.

As for the accelerated growth of private investment in manufacturing since the beginning of 2018, an over-optimistic prospect should not be held. Private investment in the manufacturing industry increased by 9.7 % from January to October 2018, a year-on-year increase of 5.7 percentage points over 2017. But with such a faster growth the period mainly benefited from the sharp increase of investment in the fields of steel, construction materials and non-ferrous metals, and other traditional energy-intensive industries. Without considering the impact of energy-intensive industries, the growth rate of private investment in manufacturing would drop from 9.7 % to 6.9 %. After the impact of price factors is further excluded, there would be actually no dramatic change in the growth rate of private investment in the manufacturing industry compared with 2017. No practical improvement has been achieved in issues like market access restrictions, heavy tax burdens, the difficulty in financing and expensive financing costs that have long constrained private investment; moreover, some of the problems have become more prominent in 2018. The financing cost of private enterprises, for example, has clearly risen in 2018, evidenced by the rapid growth of interest expenditures of industrial private enterprises.

We can use the incremental capital-output ratio to measure the efficiency of investment. In 1978, only an amount of ¥3.3 was needed to push up the GDP by ¥1; the figure gradually rose to ¥6.6 for the same rise in GDP in 2016, indicating that higher investment was needed to drive the same amount of GDP. This means that the efficiency of converting investment into GDP had declined (see Table 13.1). This is a phenomenon in need of our attention.

Finally, the growth of exports has slowed down in terms of export demand, with the contribution rate of net exports to economic growth turning from positive to negative. Exports had exceeded expectations in some months before November 2018, but such an increase was mainly due to the depreciation of the RMB exchange rate, export tax rebate policies and the phenomenon of "export rival", all of which are unsustainable factors. Statistics show that under the influence of trade frictions and other factors, the growth of exports in 2018 has dropped significantly compared with last year. The most direct manifestation is the new export orders reflected from the manufacturing PMI indicators, which only reached 47.0 in November 2018, far below the critical line of 50 and lower than the level of 51.9 in December of the previous year, indicating that the situation of export is not too optimistic.

3. In terms of benefits, the growth of residents' income has dropped dramatically, so have the profits of private enterprises.

In 2018, the national per capita disposable income—only at 6.6 % in the first three quarters—has not "outperformed" GDP in terms of actual growth rate, 0.1 percentage point lower than that of GDP and a drop of

Table 13.1. Capital-output ratio between 1978 and 2016

Year	GDP (%)	Capital formation ratio (%)	Incremental capital-output ratio (ICOR)
1978	11.7	38.9	3.3
1979	7.6	37.3	4.9
1980	7.8	35.5	4.6
1990	3.9	34.4	8.8
2000	8.5	34.3	4.0
2001	8.3	36.3	4.4
2002	9.1	36.9	4.1
2003	10.0	40.4	4.0
2004	10.1	42.7	4.2
2005	11.4	41.0	3.6
2006	12.7	40.6	3.2
2007	14.2	41.2	2.9
2008	9.7	43.2	4.5
2009	9.4	46.3	4.9
2010	10.6	47.9	4.5
2011	9.5	48.0	5.1
2012	7.9	47.2	6.0
2013	7.8	47.3	6.1
2014	7.3	46.8	6.4
2015	6.9	44.7	6.5
2016	6.7	44.1	6.6

0.9 percentage points from the same period of 2017; and the growth rate of per capita disposable income of urban residents only reached 5.7 %. In addition, the growth rate of per capita wage income of urban residents (the nominal growth rate was 7.7 %—hereinafter the same indicator) was not only lower than that of per capita disposable income (7.9 %), but also substantially lower than that of per capita property income (9.2 %), revealing that the income growth of low- and middle-income groups who mainly rely on wage income was lower than that of high-income groups who primarily depend on property income. This means that along with the decline of the overall income growth, the income distribution pattern of residents has also worsened.

As for corporate profits, there is a huge gap between the estimated and published growth rates. Take private enterprises as an example. The growth rate of private enterprise released by the Nation Bureau of Statistics was 9.3 %, but the year-on-year growth rate calculated on the basis of total profits

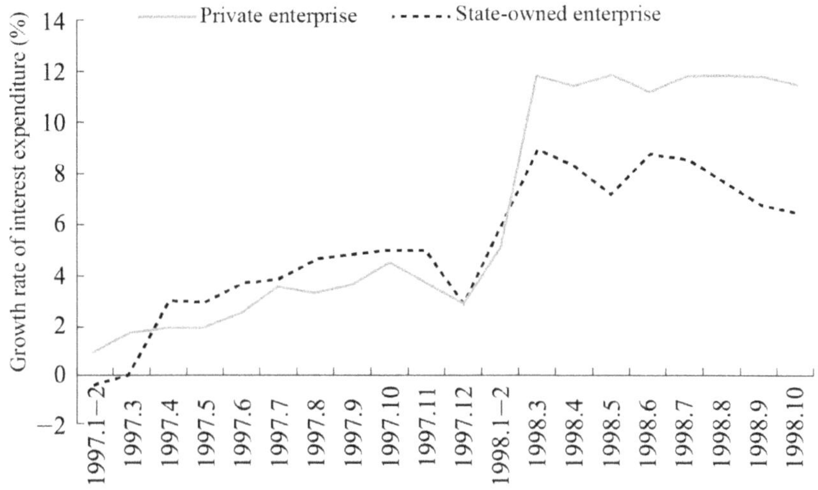

Figure 13.2. Comparison between the growth rate of interest expenditure of private enterprises and state-owned enterprises above state-designated scale

was -30 %, revealing a gap of nearly 40 percentage points. This shows that private enterprises are facing severe problems of survival and profitability. The increased production and operation pressure on private enterprises mainly comes from increased tax burdens and rising financing costs. For example, the gap between state-owned enterprises and private enterprises in the growth rate of interest expenditures has gradually widened since the beginning of 2018—state-owned enterprises is relatively low in this regard while private enterprises maintain a relatively high rate (see Figure 13.2). Therefore, helping enterprises, especially small and medium-sized private enterprises, tide over their difficulties shall be the next direction to be considered in policy making.

The Financial Situation

To assess whether an economy will suffer from high financial instability or not, six financial risks—foreign exchange risk, the risk of substantial asset price fluctuations, high debt risk, credit risk, liquidity risk, and the risk of improper financial innovation—should be taken into consideration.

Improvement has been witnessed as regards some financial risks, mainly in liquidity risk and the risk of improper financial innovation. In terms of liquidity risk, the proportion of short-term liabilities of financial institutions has declined, thus easing the problem of maturity mismatch between assets and liabilities. In the meanwhile, the money market rate has fallen, offering greater market liquidity. As for the risk of improper financial innovation, with the continuous enhancement of financial supervision, chaotic financial phenomena in the past few years have been cured to a certain extent, the disorderly expansion of financial institutions has slowed down significantly, and the proportion of the output value of "shadow banking" in GDP has substantially dropped.

But some financial risks have worsened. Firstly, the foreign exchange risk. Though the pressure of RMB depreciation has increased in 2018, it is controllable in general. Secondly, the risk of substantial asset price fluctuations. In 2018, housing prices in third- and fourth-tier cities have kept rising rapidly, further increasing the risk of the potential sharp decline in prices. Meanwhile, the continued drop in stock prices has not only disrupted market expectations but has also substantially increased the risk of large-scale defaults in the pledge of stock rights. Thirdly, high debt risk. Enterprises and local governments are still facing heavy debt pressure, and the debt risk of the residential sector has increased sharply. And finally, the credit risk. The non-performing loan rate of commercial banks has risen further, with the risk of default in the bond market increased.

Generally speaking, the "gray rhino" risk, such as the risks of real estate, high debt and credit default, still poses a comparatively huge threat to financial stability, with a sign of worsening in 2018. Therefore, the overall stability of the financial system is still in need of improvement.

Evaluation of the Macro Policy

The Monetary Policy

Several rounds of cuts to the required reserve ratio, operated promptly with comparatively strong intensity, have provided the market with sufficient liquidity. As of the end of November 2018, the central bank has carried out targeted cuts to the required reserve ratio four times, reducing the deposit reserve ratios of large financial institutions and small and medium-sized financial institutions by 2.5 percentage points. The four rounds of cuts to the required reserve ratio have not only released funds enough for the repayment of the matured medium-term lending facility (MLF) but also an extra ¥ 2.3 trillion in liquidity. In 2018, the central bank provided ample liquidity for the monetary market by lowering the required reserve ratio. As a result, the interest rate centers of various monetary markets have gone down in general, further revealing the relatively abundant liquidity in the interbank market. Firstly, the weighted average interest rate of interbank offers and that of pledge-style repos have both dropped. By the end of October 2018, the weighted average interest rate of interbank offers and that of pledge-style repos had been kept at 2.42 % and 2.39 % respectively, a decrease of 0.49 and 0.72 percentage points from the end of 2017 and a drop of 0.4 and 0.52 percentage points over the same period of 2017 respectively. And secondly, the continuous decline of the Shibor interest rate. In 2018, the three-month, six-month, and one-year Shibor interest rate centers have fallen sharply, 1.8, 1.6 and 1.23 percentage points lower than the end of 2017 and 1.65, 1.42, and 1.1 percentage points down from the same period of 2017 respectively.

In the context of the apparent decline of interest rate centers of the money market, the real interest rates of the credit market keep rising instead of going down, indicating the insufficiency of the strength of the monetary policy. In 2018, the weighted real interest rates of ordinary loans of financial institutions have continued to rise. Specifically, the weighted real interest rates of ordinary loans of financial institutions in the first, second and third quarters rose to 3.88 %, 4.15 % and 4.32 % respectively, an increase of 0.35, 0.62 and 0.79 percentage points over the end of 2017. In fact, the weighted real interest rates of ordinary loans of financial institutions have basically rebounded to the level of the third quarter of 2015 after economic recovery in three consecutive quarters. In spite of the extremely low-interest rates of the interbank market, those of the loan market are still rising, a sign of impeded transmission and channeling between the two markets. A review of the U.S. economy from 1929 to 1933 reveals that in addition to a sound growth rate of monetary base at that time, the U.S. nominal interest rate had dropped to a very low point, an indicator reflecting the strong intensity of the U.S. monetary policy. From a modern perspective, however, the policies of the Federal Reserve Board from 1929 to 1933 were not strong enough. This example shows that while measuring the intensity of monetary policy, we should consider both the interest rate of the interbank market and that of the credit market, of which the latter should be even given more attention. The real interest rates of private lending in Wenzhou have been on the rise recently, implying that the problem of difficult financing for small and medium-sized enterprises still exists.

In addition, funds from the money market haven't been channeled to the credit market and the real economy in an effective manner. In terms of aggregate amount, the balance of aggregate financing to the real economy has grown at a significantly lower rate. By the end of November 2018, it had fallen to a historical low of 9.9 %, a drop of 2.62 percentage points from the same period in 2017. The growth of M2 has also continued to be sluggish, declining to the lowest level of 8 % in history in October and November

2018. As for capital flow structure, the proportion of funds flowing to the real estate market has been on rise, while those flowing to the real economy have decreased. Only 39.6 % of new loans were channeled to the real estate market in the first three quarters of 2018. Despite a drop from the top level of 44.8 % in the fourth quarter of 2016, such a proportion was still relatively high and 0.1 percentage points higher than the same period of 2017. New loans going to the real estate sector have continuously accounted for a high proportion, resulting in a rising share of the balance of the loans flowing to the real estate sector. By the third quarter of 2018, the proportion of the loan balance in the real estate sector had risen to 28.1 %, 1.7 percentage points higher than the same period of 2017 and a record high since 2015.

The proportion of the loans flowing to industrial and service industries (without considering the real estate sector) and other physical sectors has slightly decreased rather than risen. Since the beginning of 2018, a downward trend has manifested concerning the proportion of the balance of medium and long-term loans flowing into the industrial and service industries in the balance of all loans of financial institutions, dropping from 31.35 % in the first quarter to 31.09 % in the second quarter and 30.91 % in the third quarter and a relatively low level since 2010. Moreover, the proportion of the balance of medium and long-term loans in the service industry has shown a downward tendency, an obvious difference from the situation in 2017.

Why can't the relatively abundant funds in the money market be effectively channeled to the credit market? It is because of the supply contraction and the cooling demands for credit funds. In terms of credit supply, in order to promote structural deleveraging, especially to cut down the debts of state-owned enterprises and the hidden debts of local governments, financial supervision has been dramatically strengthened since the beginning of 2018, which has restricted the off-balance-sheet credit of financial institutions. As for credit demands, under the influence of adverse factors such as the deteriorating international environment, sharply rising domestic macro tax burdens, reduction of overcapacity, and restricted production for environmental protection, enterprises are faced with difficulties of poor operating environment and decreasing profitability, leading to the drop of their credit demands. According to the survey data of the central bank, the index of overall loan demand was 70.9 % in the first quarter of 2018 but fell sharply to 66.7 % and 65.2 % in the second and third quarters respectively.

Monetary policy is aggregate amount-oriented, but too much emphasis on "structural adjustment" would cause the efficiency of monetary policy to decline. In order to create a favorable financing environment for small and micro enterprises and enterprises associated with agriculture, countryside and farmers, especially private enterprises, the central bank has introduced a good number of measures since the beginning of 2018: firstly, the cuts to required reserve ratio are carried out to mainly bring benefits to small and micro enterprises and enterprises associated with agriculture, countryside and farmers; secondly, place small and micro bonds, green bonds and bonds associated with agriculture, countryside and farmers with a rating of no less than AA as well as high-quality small and micro loans, private-enterprise loans and green loans under the central bank's Eligible Credit Support; thirdly, increase the amount of re-lending and lower the re-lending interest rate; and finally, set up bond financing support tools for private enterprises, through which the central bank can offer credit enhancement support for the development of private enterprises via re-lending. However, the effect of monetary policy on "structural adjustment" is not prominent.

Theoretically, monetary policy should focus on overall economic stability, finance should rely on macro-prudential supervision, and structural issues should be adjusted mainly through structural reforms or fiscal policies. After the subprime mortgage crisis in 2008, many countries around the world have started to adopt structural monetary policies. With more severe structural problems, China has, more or less, placed its focus on monetary policy in this regard, which fits the international practices in general and China's national conditions over the past decade. From the perspective of economic principles, however, the efficiency of monetary policy regulation will weaken, and the funds will not flow into the most efficient sectors if the focus of monetary policy is placed on structure. Therefore, structural problems should be solved with the help of other structural policies. According to Tinbergen's Rule, the number of macro-regulation tools shall be in line with the number of the goals of macro regulation whereas the monetary policy tools shall mainly focus on the objective of economic stability. We cannot count on a single tool for its regulation of multiple goals at the same time because it cannot satisfy all the purposes simultaneously and will eventually affect the outcome and efficiency of the policy.

The Fiscal Policy

Fiscal policies mainly lie in the following two aspects:

> Firstly, the weakening of fiscal expenditure. In terms of general public budget expenditure, its growth slowed down in 2018 with a cumulative year-on-year growth rate of 6.8 % from January to November, 3.4 and 1.0 percentage points lower than the same period of 2016 and

2017 respectively. As for governmental fund expenditure, according to the data released by the Ministry of Finance, it has grown at a dramatically faster rate in 2018 with a cumulative year-on-year growth rate of 38.2 % from January to November, an increase of 7 percentage points over the same period of 2017 and the record high in the same period of the past five years. It should be noted that the reason behind the rapid growth of governmental fund expenditure is the rapid increase of revenue from land leasing, accompanied by increased cost expenditures such as financial compensation for land acquisition and demolition, development before land leasing, and subsidies for land-expropriated farmers at the same time. The cost expenditure in governmental fund expenditure cannot be treated as a kind of financial expenditure in the true sense but as an "equivalent exchange" with land-expropriated farmers or relocatees. With cost expenditures deducted, the growth of governmental fund expenditure from January to November 2018 would drop to 29.5 %.

The strength of fiscal policy may be better measured by combining the growth rate of the two indicators mentioned above. In 2018, the sum of general public budget expenditure and governmental fund expenditure (excluding cost expenditure) has grown at a lower rate than that in the same period of 2017. From January to November 2018, the sum of the two types of fiscal expenditures grew at 8.5 %, in contrast to the rate of 9.2 % in the same period of 2017.

China's economic problems cannot be solved by macro policy alone; but only when a relaxed economic environment is created through macro policy can a valuable time window be created to further deepen the reform and opening up. This is the strategic significance of the macro policy. In this perspective, China's macro policy is relatively weak.

And secondly, the substantially weakened strength of various "quasi-fiscal" expenditures. We usually believe that expenditures with quasi-government credit and investments in infrastructure-related fields can be regarded as "quasi-fiscal" expenditures, which mainly cover spending related to urban investment bonds, financial bonds of policy banks, and bonds of government-backed institutions (including railway construction bonds). Since there are no official statistics on such expenditures, the approximate value of the net financing amount of various types of bonds is usually adopted as the substitute. In addition, the PPP (public-private partnership) projects usually focus on the fields of infrastructure construction such as transportation, municipal engineering, comprehensive urban development, and ecological construction, which happen to be the key driving force for conventional fiscal policies to realize "steady growth". As a result, they can also be regarded as "quasi-fiscal" expenditures to a certain extent. In the past, "quasi-fiscal" expenditures were a crucial and powerful supplement to fiscal policies—the strength of local fiscal policies mainly relied on the support of "quasi-fiscal" expenditures in particular.

Firstly, although the amount of bonds financed by government-backed institutions in 2018 is basically the same as that in 2017, the net financing amount of urban investment bonds and policy-bank financial bonds has decreased dramatically. The sum of the two types of bonds, exceeding ¥2 trillion each year between 2014 and 2016, fell to ¥1.69 trillion in 2017 and has continued to drop in 2018, with the total net financing amount reaching only ¥1.15 trillion from January to November. The total amount of the three "quasi-fiscal" expenditures hit ¥1.31 trillion in the January-November period of 2018, a significant decrease compared with ¥1.87 trillion in 2017 and a drop by more than half in comparison to ¥3.03 trillion in 2016.

Secondly, the real financing amount of PPP projects has diminished sharply due to the central government's strict rectification and clean-up. The PPP projects had gone through rapid development between 2016 and 2017. Since the end of 2017, the central government and the Ministry of Finance have released a good number of documents for strict review and concentrated rectification of PPP projects, resulting in a substantial slowdown in their development. On the one hand, the amount of PPP projects implemented has been continuously cut down, as evidenced by a dramatic slowdown presented by ¥904.4 billion, ¥488.4 billion, and ¥313.5 billion in the first three quarters of 2018 respectively; on the other hand, a large number of PPP projects have been cleaned up—a total of 2,554 PPP projects, with a total amount exceeding ¥3 trillion, had been cleansed between the end of November 2017 and the end of the third quarter of 2018. Moreover, PPP projects in various areas have been required to be rectified. Clean-up is, of course, necessarily conducive to the resolution of financial risks arising from local debts as well as structural deleveraging.

And finally, the dramatically rising macro tax burden has further weakened the strength of proactive fiscal policy. Macro tax burden has three kinds of calibers, with the proportion of tax revenue to GDP—a common method overseas—as the smallest one. But there is a large amount of non-tax revenue in China, so it is improper to make a comparison between China and foreign countries based on the proportion of tax revenue to GDP. Instead, the proportion of total government revenue to GDP stands as a more appropriate indicator. According to the newly revised *Budget Law of the People's Republic of China*, after excluding the overlapping parts covered in the sum of the four sections of total government revenue, China's macro tax burden would reach 35.7 % in 2018, a significant increase of 1.9 percentage points compared with 2017. Judging from international practices, the macro tax burden should be drastically reduced to play the role of an automatic stabilizer, if the economy is under downward pressure. However, the characteristics of the Chinese tax system—a low proportion of direct taxes but a high proportion of indirect taxes—have restrained it from functioning as an automatic stabilizer. Direct taxes, such as individual income tax, account for a high proportion in the United States. When the economy is under downward pressure, individual income tax will automatically decrease significantly due to a progressive tax rate. Then the macro tax burden will drop as a result, which means automatic implementation of expansionary fiscal policy. The macro tax burden in China is rising too fast at present, which is an inappropriate phenomenon in need of correction.

In a nutshell, both monetary policy and fiscal policy in China are insufficient. Its economy may have a better performance if both of them can be strengthened.

Suggestions about the Policy

For the problems mentioned above, several suggestions are listed below.

Strengthening of the Macro Policy

Quantitative measurement should be carried out as regards to what extent the macro policy should be strengthened. It should abide by the principle of counter-cyclical adjustment, instead of being relaxed, at least when the GDP is on a downward trend. This is the most basic rule for sure.

Strengthening of Macro-policy Coordination

Firstly, reinforce the coordination between monetary policy, fiscal policy and financial supervision.

From a macro-theoretical perspective, strengthening policy coordination will help improve the effectiveness of policies and better achieve economic and financial stability. In the context of the coexistence of economic downward pressure and increasing financial instability, macro-policy coordination is more necessary. Therefore, not only relaxed monetary and fiscal policies are required to cope with continued economic downward pressure, but also the implementation of tightened macro-prudential policies and strengthened financial supervision are needed to address increased financial instability.

Traditional macroeconomic theory believes that monetary policy and fiscal policy should not be in coordination and cooperation because it will lead to the loss of independence of the central bank. According to modern macroeconomics and contemporary international practices, however, strengthened coordination between monetary policy and fiscal policy during the period of economic downturn will help realize economic stability at a faster speed without necessarily harming the independence of the central bank, which will not be undermined especially when the two types of policies coordinate and cooperate under a framework safeguarding its independence.

Secondly, strengthen the coordination between macro policy and long-term growth policy.

Both Keynesianism and Monetarism believe that the roles of monetary policy and fiscal policy are prominent, so macro policy alone is capable enough of stabilizing the economy and subsequently boosting it in the long run. According to New Classical Macroeconomics, however, the long-term effect of short-term macro policy is limited and thus of little practical significance; as a result, policymakers should pay greater attention to the accumulation of factors, the growth of productivity and the improvement of basic factors of the former two during the long-term growth. Keynesianism and New Classical Macroeconomics, two major schools of macroeconomics, focus on and analyze short-term and long-term issues respectively. But it is a fact that the running of the economy is indeed in need of coordination and cooperation, so appropriate economic measures should go beyond such sectarianism and narrow-minded academic opinions from different schools of macroeconomics. Targeted at short-term economic and financial stability, macro policy is not conducive to long-term growth. Take monetary policy as an example. Due to price stickiness, monetary policy does have a short-term and significant effect because interest rate cuts can influence aggregate demand by adjusting real interest rates. So it is radical to uphold that monetary policy is useless at all. In the long run, however, the nominal dichotomy and the quantity theory of money are valid, and more money will definitely translate into a higher price level. Therefore, the currency has no real effect in the long run. Whether there are real effects of fiscal policy seems very clear in theory, but an empirical research consensus is not yet solid.

As is shown by macroeconomic practices, macropolicy is of great significance because of the importance of short-term economic and financial stability. Short-term financial instability will lead to financial crises and subsequently economic collapse. The Great Depression of the United States from 1929 to 1933 occurred because people had a low level of understanding of the importance of short-term economic stability while focusing too much on market clearing—it was believed that the companies and banks able to pull through the crisis would be of high quality and efficient and could facilitate better economic development. However, economists at that time did not expect that it would be unwise to directly apply the principles of marketing and market clearing in macroeconomics. From a modern point of view, this will cause debt deflation as well as the trap of a vicious circle. Consequently, short-term problems will worsen in the long term and eventually cause economic collapse.

For China, a relaxed macroeconomic environment must be created through macro policy to win a valuable time window for supply-side reform.

Then how should the long-term growth policy be implemented? Three major factors will affect the economic growth of a country from the perspective of macroeconomic theory: firstly, the accumulation of capital, labor, human capital and other factors; secondly, the improvement of productivity; and finally, the exertion of the functions of fundamental factors. Since China's reform has entered the deep-water zone, better economic performance and resource allocation can be achieved only when the reform and opening up and the market-oriented reform are furthered on the one hand and the government plays a better role on the other hand.

The above analysis reveals that although the economic and financial situations in the short term are controllable, we must also be aware of some prominent risks. As long as appropriate countermeasures are conducted with proper strength, it is unnecessary to worry about the risks. The keys of the countermeasures are listed as follows: first of all, intensify the strength of macro policy to achieve economic and financial stability; and secondly, strengthen macro-policy coordination to realize economic stability at the minimum policy cost. Optimal policy portfolios should be adopted in a macroscopic perspective to take into consideration short-term economic stability as well as long-term growth and high-quality development. Only such policy portfolios can help cope with the difficulties and even predicaments at present.

(This article is compiled and edited based on Professor Chen Yanbin's lecture, part of the RDCY Master Series Lectures, on December 20, 2018.)

14. *Disputes of Individual Income Tax Reform and the Solutions*

Lv Bingyang

The reform of individual income tax has a profound influence on the whole society. It is not only an economic issue embodied in the protection of the real interests of the people, but also a legal issue manifesting the will of the people; moreover, it is also a social issue reflected in the promotion of harmonious and orderly social development by means of tax reforms as well as an issue of national governance presented in the enhancement of national governance capabilities via tax reforms. It can be seen that individual income tax is given a variety of expectations. But how can it carry so many expectations?

Key Points of the Reform of Individual Income Tax

"Tesuji" (smart move) and "tsuke" (vital point) are two terms of Go (or Weiqi). Go is intricate, so is the individual income tax in nature. In a complicated situation, we should deploy a tesuji aimed at key points, after which a tsuke will appear. Then it is time to conduct a series of countermeasures.

There are several key points of the reform of individual income tax this time.

> Firstly, comprehensive income taxation for parts of labor incomes. In the Fourth Session of the Eighth National People's Congress held in 1996, the establishment of an individual income tax system that combines both classification and comprehensive taxation covering all types of individual incomes was proposed in the *Ninth Five-Year Plan for National Economic and Social Development and the Long-range Objectives through the Year 2010 of the People's Republic of China.* But

individual income tax is still levied based on tax classification although more than two decades have passed. The reform of individual income tax this time is the first step towards comprehensive income taxation. Specifically, four types of labor incomes—wages and salaries, remuneration for personal services, incomes from authors' remuneration, and incomes from royalties—have been included in the scope of taxation in this reform. However, whether the income from royalties is part of the property income or labor income remains prominently controversial.

Secondly, optimization and adjustment of the tax rate structure. Based on the current income tax rate of wages and salaries, the monthly taxable income has been adjusted to an amount calculated on a yearly basis, along with the optimization and adjustment of the rating ranges concerning some tax rates. The specific measures are listed as follows: the rating ranges as regards the three levels of low tax rate, namely, the rate of 3 %, 10 % and 20 %, have been widened, with that for the rate of 3 % doubled and parts of the incomes currently levied at the rate of 10 % seeing a rate cut to 3 %; the rating range for the rate of 10 % has been expanded significantly; and parts of the incomes currently collected at the rate of 25 % have had a rate cut to 20 %.

Thirdly, higher basic deduction standards for comprehensive income taxes. The basic deduction standards have been raised from ¥3,500 per month to ¥5,000 per month, which has become the greatest concern of society.

Fourthly, the set-up of special individual income tax deductions. Expenditures closely associated with the people, namely the spending on children's education, continuing education, health treatment for serious diseases and housing loan interests and rents, are stipulated as the special individual income tax deductions.

And finally, the newly added provision of combating tax avoidance. For individuals who avoid taxation by transferring property in violation of the arm's length principle, avoiding taxation in overseas tax havens, conducting unreasonable commercial arrangements, obtaining improper tax benefits and other tax avoidance behaviors, tax authorities are entrusted with the right to carry out tax adjustments in a reasonable manner. In consideration of recent hot news in show business, this move is conducted with a particular purpose. As a mild provision, it does not specifically stipulate that individuals with serious violations shall be turned over to the judicial organs.

Controversies of the Reform of Individual Income Tax

Though aimed at reinforcing the role of individual income tax in adjusting income distribution, the draft of the reform has given rise to numerous social controversies, which mainly center on the following areas:

> Firstly, is it reasonable to set the amount of tax exemption at ¥5,000? What is the ground for it? Some members of the National People's Congress of the People's Republic of China even proposed to raise the amount of tax exemption to ¥10,000. Since the living cost is extremely high in cities like Beijing, Shanghai and Guangzhou, it is very necessary to raise it to a higher standard; in the central and western regions where the living cost is comparatively low, however, is it still appropriate to use the same standard?
>
> Secondly, should the top marginal rate be maintained at 45 %? Currently, the world is facing a wave of tax cuts. The U.S. marginal rate for individual income tax is set at 39.6 %, significantly lower than that of China. Some countries have tried high tax rates. For example, the French Hollande administration once levied the Reichensteuer (tax on the rich), causing a large number of rich people to change their nationalities. To attract high-net-worth individuals in the midst of intensifying global competition, is it still necessary to maintain the tax rate at 45 %?
>
> Thirdly, should the tax be collected based on individuals or families? Given taxation based on individuals, who should bear the taxes if some of the spending is borne by the whole family instead of any individuals, such as the costs of house purchase in the name of a family and those borne by the couple altogether for child-rearing? If the tax is levied based on families, then how should a family be defined? The people registered under the same household register cannot be considered to be part of the same family because the information on the household register can be changed at any time.
>
> Fourthly, will the newly added special individual income-tax deduction for housing loan interests and rents affect the real estate market dramatically? The U.S. tax reform in 1986, which was extremely influential, allowed housing loan interests to be deducted as an expense from the individual income tax. As a result, the real estate market was boosted by leaps and bounds. The implementation of the policy in China has actually cut down the housing costs of the people, which may stimulate investment in the real estate market.

Fifthly, should other special individual income tax deductions (such as elderly care) be supplemented?

Sixthly, should regional differences be taken into consideration? Since the living cost differs in different regions, should a differentiated cost deduction standard be set for different regions or a uniform benchmark be applied nationwide?

And finally, the three concerns from the perspective of tax authorities, namely the three problems of "what should we do". Professor Yang Bin of Xiamen University put forward long ago that three problems should be solved in terms of taxation of natural persons: firstly, what should we do if taxpayers do not declare taxes? The taxpayers may not declare taxes when they feel it is a burden. But can tax authorities find out about it when the people refuse to declare taxes? Secondly, what should we do if the taxpayers make false tax declarations? For instance, if the taxable income is ¥10,000, will tax authorities find out it if an amount of only ¥5,000 is declared? Finally, what should we do if the taxpayers cannot afford to pay after the declaration? Can tax authorities adopt compulsory taxation measures when the taxpayers refuse to pay taxes on the grounds of financial constraint?

Constraints of the Reform of Individual Income Tax

The reform is carried out for the initial purpose of strengthening the role of individual income tax in adjusting income distribution. Constrained by two key inherent factors, the effect of individual income tax on adjusting income distribution cannot be fully exerted.

Firstly, a small number of taxpayers. To measure the adjustment of individual income tax in adjusting income distribution, the difference between the Gini coefficients before and after taxation is the key. If the Gini coefficient drops dramatically after taxation, it indicates that individual income tax substantially influences the adjustment of income distribution. The effect of individual income tax on adjusting income distribution relies on the following two points: taxation progressivity (the design of progressive tax rate) and average tax rate (the ratio of the taxes paid by all the people to the incomes of all the people). Even if taxation progressivity is at a high level—the top marginal tax rate is set at 100 %, for instance—the role of individual income tax in adjusting income distribution is also limited due to a small number of taxpayers. At present, there is not a large amount individual taxpayers in China—half of the farmers do not need to pay taxes at least.

> Secondly, it is difficult to impose comprehensive taxation and progressive tax rates on capital earnings under the individual income tax system. Is it feasible to impose comprehensive taxation and progressive tax rates on capital earnings? It is a pity that it is infeasible even worldwide. Because capital has strong mobility and there are diversified ways to allocate capital in the era of globalization, taxation shouldn't intervene in the allocation of capital factors unduly, nor is it appropriate to implement an excessive progressive tax rate. Therefore, the effect of individual income tax on adjusting income distribution is inherently restricted. Judging from the actual conditions of China, the share of labor distribution is diminishing while that of capital distribution is rising, which is in line with the global trend.

Constrained by the two factors mentioned above, the role of individual income tax in adjusting income distribution is actually not as significant as we imagine.

Then what is the focus of the adjustment of income distribution currently? The report of the Nineteenth National Congress of the CPC pointed out that the principal contradiction we are facing is the contradiction between unbalanced and inadequate development and the people's ever-growing needs for a better life. The unbalanced and inadequate development between regions has a great impact on income distribution, which is the very key point of the reform or the area where the reform can play a role. Policies of the reform of social security system, poverty alleviation, the narrowing of regional and urban-rural gaps, etc. all play a key role in the adjustment of income distribution.

It Is Hard for the Reform of Individual Income Tax to Adjust Income Distribution

Generally speaking, the following rational awareness should be mentioned when it comes to the adjustment of income distribution through the reform of individual income tax:

> First of all, although it is difficult to reach a consensus on the reform of individual income tax, everybody believes in the role of individual income tax in adjusting income distribution. The scientific nature of such a "consensus" requires an in-depth analysis.

various departments is required. A comprehensive tax code system should be established in the first place to render each taxpayer his or her own tax code, which could either be an ID number or a social security number. As the only lifetime tax account of taxpayers, it even includes their tax evasion information. Secondly, the full implementation of a real-name registration system for personal assets will help monitor the capital income of taxpayers. Thirdly, the adoption of a cash management system. In order to prevent tax evasion, a bank transfer is required other than cash if remuneration exceeds a certain amount. Finally, the construction of a networked individual income tax-related information platform nationwide because individuals may earn remunerations for their labor services across the whole country. To effectively combat tax evasion, comprehensive management requires the tax, banking, public security, social security and other departments to cooperate, thus getting unified with tax authorities as the core.

And secondly, give play to the initiative of local authorities. Comprehensive management is infeasible if the central government is counted on alone. China is such a big country with so many taxpayers that the initiative of local authorities should be brought into play. Therefore, individual income tax can be regarded as the main tax of provincial governments. Provincial governments in China have a large area under jurisdiction—the areas of most provinces in China are equivalent to those of a medium-sized country. Under such circumstances, it will be advantageous if individual income tax is treated as provincial local tax from the perspective of convenient tax collection and management and taxation incentives.

The Greatest Significance of the Reform of Individual Income Tax

In summary of the analysis above, the current reform of individual income tax is meaningful in the following aspects:

> First of all, the reform of individual income tax is a way to awaken the taxpayer's consciousness. Taxpayer consciousness includes not only taxpayer obligation but also taxpayer rights awareness. Since the current tax system mainly targets enterprises for taxation, it is hard to stimulate the taxpayer consciousness. After the draft of the reform was announced, it immediately awakened everyone's taxpayer consciousness.
>
> Secondly, the reform of individual income tax has forcefully introduced a dramatic change in the tax collection and management mechanism,

which will in turn promote the modernization of tax collection and management.

And finally, the enhancement of national governance capabilities has been accelerated. The comprehensive taxation of individual income tax will deepen the government's penetration into society on the one hand and simulate the taxpayers' awareness of their obligations and rights on the other hand. The outcomes of the interaction between the two types of progress will enable the government to better respond to the needs of taxpayers and the taxpayers to better understand some of the government's measures, which will eventually accelerate the enhancement of national governance capabilities. This is the greatest significance of the reform of individual income tax.

(This article is compiled and edited based on Professor Lu Bingyang's lecture, part of the RDCY Master Series Lectures, on June 25, 2018)

15. *New Government-enterprise Relationship: A Decisive Factor for China's Economy to Grow at a Medium-to-high Speed*

Nie Huihua

The unprecedented anti-corruption campaign since the Eighteenth National Congress of the CPC had shattered the former long-lasting government-enterprise relationship. With this campaign as a mark, a new stage was ushered in to reshape the government-enterprise relationship. The process could be briefly summarized as follows: "Conspiracy is risky and cooperation lacks motivation; it is safer to become separated though harms are inevitable." The separation of government administration from enterprise management coexisted with the mutual harm between the government and the enterprise. With the proposal of establishing a "close" and "clean" government-enterprise relationship, put forward by General Secretary Xi during the Fourth Session of the Twelfth Chinese People's Political Consultative Conference National Committee, a new type of government-enterprise relationship is taking shape.

This article is about my summary of and thoughts on the government-enterprise relationship in China since the reform and opening up.

The Government-enterprise Relationship: The Most Important Economic and Social Relationship in China

Why should we study the government-enterprise relationship? To answer why the government-enterprise relationship is an urgent issue currently, three events should be mentioned.

Firstly, the complaint of Mao Zhenhua, chairman of CCX Group, in front of the camera at the Yabuli ski resort in Heilongjiang Province against the unreasonable management of the local management committee, which was mainly because of the committee's occupation of the land purchased by CCX Group. The event had attracted wide attention.

Secondly, the real-name reporting by Huang Ming, chairman of Himin Group, of the administrative omission of the Secretary of the Dezhou Municipal Committee of the Communist Party of China, Shandong Province. This was mainly because the government had failed to fulfill its promise of granting a plot of land to Huang Ming for his construction of the Solar Valley (a characteristic town in today's words), which he had undertaken at the invitation of the local government ten years ago. With the rising of the land prices, he would only have a slimmer chance of getting the promised land.

And finally, the posting of a video and an open real-name letter by Zhang Fangcheng, head of Shandong Linyi Golden Phoenix Real Estate Co. Ltd., on the Internet to accuse the director of the local management committee of "being a deadbeat", a dispute also rising from the land transfer.

The three events had drawn much attention. Such things were unimaginable in the past because the most important thing for businessmen is to maintain a good relationship with the local government, who would not sour such a relationship unless they had no other choices. Nowadays, the intensive and frequent petitions and complaints of entrepreneurs within a short period indicate the sensitivity and fragility of the current government-enterprise relationship.

The government-enterprise relationship is the most important economic and social relationship in China. The relationship between the government and the market is of great significance in economic performance. To be precise, it is the relationship between the government and the enterprise that is of great importance because the enterprise plays a crucial role in the market. This can be illustrated by the following three aspects:

First of all, the government-enterprise relationship is one of the institutional environments influential in economic development. The government-enterprise relationship shapes the property rights system and the contracting system. A sound government-enterprise relationship will protect the contractual relationship or agreement between the government and the enterprise in the first place, and will also safeguard the relationship between enterprises, but a bad government-enterprise relationship would only result in opposite results. The two systems are two key elements for measuring the quality of the business environment.

Secondly, the government-enterprise relationship has everything to do with the immediate interests of officials and businessmen. Theoretically, the officials would have a higher prospect of promotion if a sound local government-enterprise relationship is maintained and the economy grows at a fast rate; a distorted one, however, would lead the enterprises to a dilemma of development. Therefore, all entrepreneurs are concerned about how to improve the government-enterprise relationship.

And finally, China is facing a critical period of reshaping the government-enterprise relationship. Currently, the central government has attached great importance to it. A seminar on the business environment was carried out at the first executive meeting of the State Council in 2018. It was decided that a mechanism of business environment platform would be soon established under the leadership of the National Development and Reform Commission and would be gradually put into place across the country. Therefore, the study of the government-enterprise relationship has become an urgent need at present.

Four Types of Government-enterprise Relationship

Then how should we study the government-enterprise relationship?

To have an in-depth study in this regard, we need to review and evaluate the situations or characteristics of the government-enterprise relationship over the past 40 years. Before that, however, it is necessary to generalize and distinguish such concepts as what the government-enterprise relationship is and what types are included, based on which in-depth discussion can be conducted in the circle of media and academia.

The government-enterprise relationship is a kind of interaction model formed in the game in which the government contends with the enterprises under its jurisdiction through a variety of policies. As is shown by the model of the government-enterprise relationship in the West, there is a mutual influence between the government and enterprises. The government influences the enterprises through the following four channels: firstly, the law; secondly, special regulatory agencies like the National Medical Products Administration; thirdly, financial regulatory institutions; and finally, the trade policy—the Trump administration has exerted great influence upon government-enterprise relationship through trade policy. Enterprises affect the government in turn through various channels: firstly, individual lobbying; secondly, labor unions, trade associations and industry associations, which influence the government through institutionalization; thirdly, the so-called political actions; and finally, the investment. When Cao Dewang went to the

United States for investment, both President Trump and the governors had a meeting with him, which shows the government-enterprise relationship. From this perspective, there is not much difference between the government-enterprise relationship in the West and that in China because they both manifest the mutual influence between the government and entrepreneurs.

Based on clear definitions, the government-enterprise relationship can be categorized into four types on two dimensions: government-enterprise cooperation, separation of government administration from enterprise management, mutual harm between the government and the enterprise, and government-enterprise conspiracy (see Table 15.1). The two dimensions for classification are: whether the government interferes in the economic activities of the enterprise and whether the interactions between the government and the enterprise are legal.

Firstly, the government-enterprise cooperation. The government has a close relationship with enterprises. For instance, the government takes major responsibility for helping the enterprises develop by granting them subsidies to some degree and with other preferential policies and cooperating with them in some projects in line with laws and regulations.

Second, the separation of government administration from enterprise management. Similar to the model prevailing in Europe and the United States, this type of relationship requires a certain distance between the government and enterprises. In other words, the government is not allowed to intervene in the micro activities of enterprises, and enterprises are also forbidden to participate in politics for no reason. This is a state of relative independent management, which is called the separation of government administration from enterprise management.

Thirdly, mutual harm between the government and the enterprise. Behaving like landlords in pursuit of rents, some local governments may treat

Table 15.1. Four types of government-enterprise relationship

Whether the interactions between the government and the enterprise are legal	Yes	government-enterprise cooperation	separation of government administration from enterprise management
	No	government-enterprise conspiracy	mutual harm between the government and the enterprise
		Yes	No

Whether the government intervenes in the economic activities of enterprises

enterprises as gooses that lay golden eggs and would go all out to exploit them—they harm the enterprises through rent-seeking behaviors; enterprises may also coerce and harm the government by making use of their influence—for instance, some enterprises would cheat for governmental subsidies whenever it is possible and would disappear with a large sum of money after dishonest activities. Both two situations are considered the mutual harm between the government and the enterprise.

And finally, the government-enterprise conspiracy. This model features a very close government-enterprise relationship with most conduct between them being illegal such as the government's cover-up of the frauds and environmental pollution caused by enterprises.

More detailed subdivisions can be made based on the four types of relationships. For example, different models of government-enterprise cooperation can be categorized according to how close they are. The combination of government administration and enterprise management is a way for the government and the enterprise to cooperate, while the governance represented by non-interference is a state of separating government administration from enterprise management. According to the degree of conspiracy, the government-enterprise conspiracy can also be categorized into different levels.

Only by categorizing the government-enterprise relationship in this way can in-depth research be carried out. Without such concepts, we would not be able to study how to deal with and discern the government-enterprise relationship.

Three Stages of the Development of the Chinese Government-enterprise Relationship

We can sort out the Chinese government-enterprise relationship over the past 40 years under a theoretical framework.

Through an in-depth study, I've concluded that the development of private enterprises or the relationship between the government and the enterprise in China doesn't remain unchallenged as they seem to; instead, they have undergone various ups and downs.

The Chinese government-enterprise relationship has gone through the following three stages:

> Firstly, the stage of integration of the government and the enterprise from 1949 to 1978. Back then, there were no private enterprises but only state-owned enterprises. As part of the government, state-owned enterprises had a simple relationship with the government, which

could be considered the integration of the government and the enterprise. During this stage, the enterprises were completely affiliated to the government without being independent existence. As "workshops" of the government, state-owned enterprises had no autonomy at all, with most of them under the direct management of the central government.

Secondly, the stage of coexistence of government-enterprise cooperation and government-enterprise conspiracy from 1978 to 2012. The two forms were interwoven with each other as a key feature of this stage. The focus has been shifted to economic development after 1978. Sharing common interest demands, both enterprises and the government aimed for the boost of the economy, which would allow the government to obtain more fiscal appropriations, the officials to have more promotion opportunities and the enterprises to earn more profits—a win-win result for both sides. During this stage, both the government and the enterprise had the motivation to make the "pie" of economic development bigger. Therefore, there were both open and fair government-enterprise cooperation, as well as underhanded government-enterprise conspiracy.

Since the reform and opening up starting in 1978, China has maintained economic growth at a medium-to-high rate, in which government-enterprise cooperation has played a key role. Township and village enterprises came into being as the product of government-enterprise cooperation in the process of regional competition. Although there are basically no township and village enterprises at present, they could be said to be the major driving force of the private economy in that era, evidenced by numerous individual and private enterprises affiliated to the township government. This is a kind of cooperation.

"Attracting enterprises and investment from overseas" is one of the features in China's development, for which a good many of local governments have made painstaking efforts. In the southeast coastal and other regions, local governments have adopted "white plus black", "5+2" and other preferential industrial policies to attract enterprises and investment from overseas, all of which are manifested through government-enterprise cooperation and play as the driving force behind China's economic growth.

And thirdly, the stage since 2013. This stage is comparatively complicated because the separation of government administration from enterprise management—the government and the enterprise have become independent—intertwines with the mutual harm between the government and the enterprise. However, the government-enterprise relationship tends to develop toward a new type of government-enterprise cooperation, which has not yet taken shape.

The unprecedented anti-corruption campaign since the Eighteenth National Congress of the CPC had shattered the former long-lasting government-enterprise relationship. With this as a mark, a new stage was ushered in to reshape the government-enterprise relationship. The process could be briefly summarized as follows: "Conspiracy is risky and cooperation lacks motivation; it is safer to become separated though harms are inevitable." The separation of government administration from enterprise management coexisted with the mutual harm between the government and the enterprise. With the proposal of establishing a "close" and "clean" government-enterprise relationship, put forward by General Secretary Xi during the Fourth Session of the Twelfth Chinese People's Political Consultative Conference National Committee, a new type of government-enterprise relationship is taking shape.

Why Is It Difficult to Establish a "Close" and "Clean" Government-enterprise Relationship

How should a new type of "close" and "clean" government-enterprise relationship be established?

What measures should be taken is a hot issue that everyone cares about. The government-enterprise relationship has become a topic of discussion because of its difficult nature—it is so difficult that President Xi Jinping has to guide the solution for it in person. He talked about how to establish a "close" and "clean" government-enterprise relationship when the National People's Congress and the Chinese Political Consultative Conference were convened in 2016. The repeated mention of this topic in newspapers and other media indicated the difficulty in solving this issue. Why is the government-enterprise relationship so difficult to establish? What is the critical problem? We can analyze it from the following four aspects:

> Firstly, too much intervention of the government in microeconomic activities. As Wu Jinglian said, "China is a market economy under public surveillance."
>
> Secondly, a lack of guarantees for the personal safety and property rights of entrepreneurs. Among the enterprises surveyed, policy risks, rather than market risks, are the greatest concern of a considerable number of Chinese entrepreneurs. China is a developing country, so

its laws and regulations are still not completely perfect. To build a country based on the rule of law, we still have a long way to go. In addition to "stabilizing employment, finance, foreign trade, foreign investment, investment and expected growth", "stabilizing morale" is also of great importance.

Thirdly, unequal status between officials and businessmen. "Scholars, farmers, artisans and merchants" had embodied the order of social status in China since ancient times. Although such an order is not valued today, unequal status still exists between officials and businessmen in nature. Shanxi merchants are outstanding representatives of traditional Chinese business culture—Shanxi people had the habit of purchasing an official rank for their parents and even deceased grandfathers if they had made a big fortune, a way to glorify their ancestors. In other words, merchants will never enjoy a high status. Under such circumstances, it is difficult to establish a relationship that is "close" and "clean".

And finally, the long-existing ideology. Obstacles to the development of the private economy have always been there since the reform and opening up—ideological obstructions existed even in the 1980s, the golden era for the private economy.

Eight Suggestions for the Construction of a New Type of Government-enterprise Relationship

Next, how to build up a "close" and "clean" or a new type of government-enterprise relationship will be discussed based on the previous analysis, especially on the part about the critical problem of the government-enterprise relationship.

Firstly, strengthen the supervision of power to reduce the government's intervention in microeconomic activities. "The decisive role of the market" should be truly realized in the allocation of resources, with "the government playing a better role" as a supplementary measure.

Secondly, vigorously develop the private economy to advance the principle of "competitive neutrality". Studies have shown that where there is a relatively sound government-enterprise relationship, private enterprises would develop at a faster rate and the economy would have a better performance; as a result, the governments of relevant areas would be more inclined to create a better business environment for enterprises. On the contrary, where the government-enterprise relationship is poor, the number of private enterprises would be relatively small; coupled with strict supervision and the behaviors of "killing the goose that lays the golden eggs", the business environment would turn from bad to worse.

Thirdly, effectively protect the legitimate rights and interests of entrepreneurs to eliminate the presumption of guilt. Do not criminalize economic cases in a rash manner. In general, the market economy should be run based on civil law. In other words, let the market play the role if things can be solved through the means of the market, and hold the use of public power as much as possible. The intervention of public power will easily lead to corruption.

Fourthly, advance the standardization and transparency of policies.

Fifthly, enhance government-enterprise interaction in the process of policy-making. This can be considered a way to make the implementation of policies possible and enhance their feasibility. In the meanwhile, reinforce media supervision to curb government-enterprise conspiracy.

Sixthly, cultivate a sense of equality and strengthen the spirit of contract. A favorable business environment is forged on the basis of equality. In addition, the phenomenon of "problems in the past ignored by newly appointed officials" should be eliminated to strengthen the construction of the government's spirit of contract.

Seventhly, eliminate the influence of bad habits on the traditional official and business culture.

Finally, emancipate the mind to re-comprehend the basic issues of governance.

President Xi Jinping once expressed his opinions about the "two unswerving endeavors" that have contributed to a "close" and "clean" government-enterprise relationship—unswervingly consolidate and develop the public sector of the economy and unswervingly encourage, support and guide the development of the non-public sector of the economy. Allowing private entrepreneurs to join the CPC is a way to build a solid governance foundation. It is believed that solving the status issue of private enterprises ideologically will be conducive to the long-term stability of China.

(This article is compiled and edited based on Professor Nie Huihua's lecture, part of the RDCY Master Series Lectures, on December 19, 2018.)

16. *China's Environmental Governance over the Past 40 Years*

WANG HUA

The past 40 years have witnessed a rapid economic growth in China from 1978 to 2018, a proud achievement attracting attention all over the world. Since the reform and opening up in 1978, environmental problems in China have, emerging from zero, become increasingly prominent. During the past several years, although some environmental problems have been alleviated to some degree thanks to comprehensive national governance, the improvement is only confined to certain areas.

The changes in the field of environment in China over the past 40 years (1978–2018) will firstly be discussed, with a focus on the environmental institutional construction. Then, what I have pursued over the past 20 years (1998–2018) will be expounded in the latter part.

The Changes over the Past 40 Years

The changes in China's economy and environment can be summarized as follows: first of all, sustained rapid economic growth and proud achievements attracting worldwide attention; secondly, unbearable deteriorating environmental problems that have risen from scratch; and finally, eased environmental problems in some areas in recent years, ushering in the advent of the inflection point and hopes for the people.

Although the past several years have witnessed the decrease of some environmental problems to some degree due to national comprehensive governance, the improvement is only confined to certain areas. Figure 16.1 shows the environmental cost during economic development: neither pollution nor environmental problems existed when no economic development was underway; with economic development, however, environmental pollutants increased; after the economy has become developed, the inflection point in the environment is emerging as there is a need for environmental improvement. The Kuznets Curve is an inverted U-shaped curve that starts to fall after reaching the vertex, which is the so-called inflection point (see Figure 16.2). According to the actual situations of various countries, the inflection point appears when the per capita GDP reaches around \$8,000, a piece of proof that the inflection point in China is about to emerge. It is promising that the inflection point for some pollutants in China has already appeared, evidenced by their declined emissions.

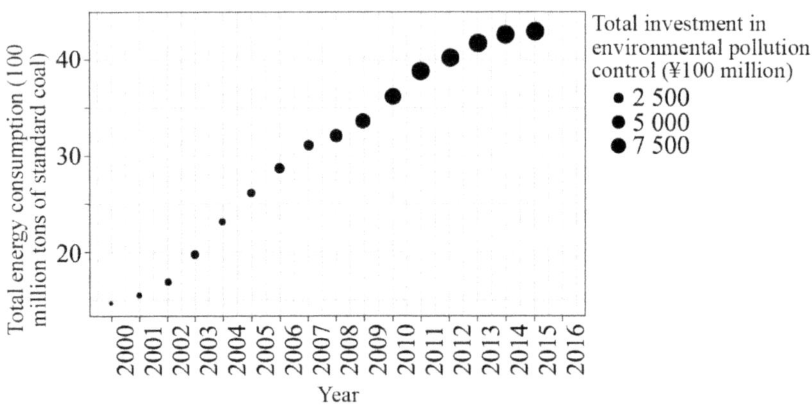

Figure 16.1. Environmental cost during economic development

Data source: National Bureau of Statistics

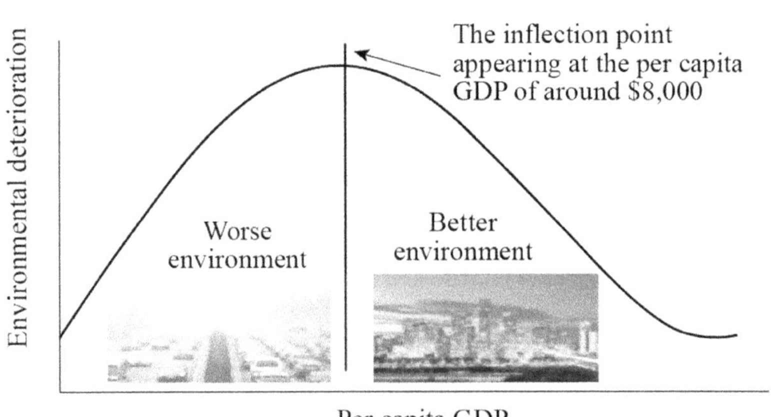

Figure 16.2. Environmental Kuznets Curve

The changes in environmental institutional construction can also be summarized as follows: firstly, both concepts and methods in this regard have been developed from scratch and continuously strengthened to reach the global advanced level; secondly, in comparison to the rapid economic development, the institutional construction has lagged with various problems emerging thick and fast; and finally, based on international experience, China performs better than developed countries in institutional construction for the second-mover advantage it enjoys.

Currently, the concepts and level of environmental governance in China have reached the global advanced standard. In spite of some areas not being as good as those in developed countries of Europe and the United States, the overall governing system and even related concepts are at an advanced level. The concepts of ecological civilization of China have even driven international sustainable development. Institutional construction is slower in China because it is always carried out after problems occur. China has witnessed an excessively fast development over the past 40 years (1978–2018), during which various problems have kept rising too fast. So it is impossible to foresee all the problems when the institutional construction is conducted. In fact, however, China is implementing its institutional construction at a faster rate and enjoys a second-mover advantage to some extent because we can learn from the current achievements of some developed countries. For example, the standards of the *U.S. Environmental Protection Law* were borrowed when the *Environmental Protection Law of the People's Republic of China* was formulated. China's institutional construction is at an advanced level if compared with those at the same level of development. Moreover, Chinese environmental management organs are also under constant reforms with their capabilities continuously strengthened. There was only one leading group in environment in 1974. In 1982, the Environmental Protection Administration was set up under the leadership of the Ministry of Urban and Rural Construction and Environmental Protection, which later became the State Environmental Protection Administration in 1984 and evolved into the State Environmental Protection Administration at the deputy ministerial level in 1988 and the State Environmental Protection Administration at the ministerial level in 1998. The Ministry of Environmental Protection was established in 2008, which was later renamed the Ministry of Ecology and Environment in 2018. The construction of China's environmental institution can be divided into four stages: firstly, the stage focusing on the development of heavy industry between 1953 and 1978; secondly, the preliminary construction stage between 1979 and 1991; thirdly, the stage of active response between 1992 and 2012; and finally, the stage of ecological civilization construction from 2012 to present.

Specific policies and tools adopted by China in environmental protection mainly cover those of command and control, economic incentive, and persuasion and encouragement. Command and control policy tools are used to formulate standards with clear requirements and prohibitions, which include the environmental impact assessment mechanism, the Three Simultaneous System, the pollution discharge permit mechanism, and the environmental standard system. Economic incentive policy tools are conducted for the goal of adjustment by means of market taxes, fees and transactions, which, costing less than governmental control methods, cover the pollution charging system, the tradable permit system, etc.; persuasion and encouragement policy tools include environmental information disclosure policies, environmental certification policies, the environmental hearings and public participation system, etc. In addition, there are also information and social policy tools. In China, information and social policy tools are not weaker than control and economic ones and are expected to be stronger than them in many cases. In some places without control or economic policy tools in the world, social and information policy tools still play an important role.

The changes in environmental protection policy tools over the past 40 years present the following characteristics: firstly, governmental control policy tools play a leading role, with high efficiency as well as a high cost; secondly, the failure to abide by laws and slack law enforcement, significantly prominent in the past, have been eased in recent years; thirdly, economic and social policy tools have not been fully utilized in spite of their remarkable effect; and finally, the institutional system is in need of reform and transformation to realize the modernization of the environmental governance system and governance capabilities.

What I Have Pursued over the Past 20 Years

Next, innovations and development of some policies I have taken part in over the past 20 years (1998–2018) will be shared, which mainly consist of environmental information disclosure, environmental round-table dialogues and environmental social governance.

Environmental Information Disclosure

I came to realize that environmental information disclosure should be vigorously carried out in China when I joined the World Bank in 1995. My opinion is based on two reasons: firstly, from the perspective of constructing a society under the rule of law, information disclosure is the only way to guarantee people's legal rights to know, participate, supervise things, and claim compensation related to them. Secondly, from the perspective of institutional construction, environmental information disclosure is a feasible and effective policy tool for environmental management, which parallels other policy tools like pollution charges and environmental standards. Based on what I had learned at that time, I planned to promote the implementation of environmental information disclosure in China and subsequently held several lectures in China to publicize the benefits of environmental information disclosure.

Before 1998, since all environmental information in China was confidential, almost everyone at that time questioned the disclosure of environmental information. With my efforts, environmental information disclosure was piloted in enterprises in Zhenjiang and Hohhot from 1998 to 2000. It was found that information disclosure, instead of arousing a strong sense of revulsion in society, would gradually drive enterprises to become better (see Figure 16.3). Environmental information disclosure was then promoted in Jiangsu from 2000 to 2002. In 2002, I published the *Environmental Information Disclosure: Concepts and Practices.* A pilot program for environmental information disclosure was conducted from 2002 to 2005. From 2005 to 2007, I organized and formulated the draft proposal for China's *Environmental Information Disclosure Management Measures*, and proposed to and urged the government to establish a formal mechanism in this regard. The *Environmental Information Disclosure Measures (Trial)* was passed in 2007 and came into effect on May 1, 2008. From 2008 to 2018, I have continued to promote the implementation, training, forum activities, evaluation, and revision of the measures.

Figure 16.3. Environmental information disclosure drives enterprises to improve

At present, China's environmental information disclosure is relatively advanced in terms of institutional construction but still needs improvement in specific measures. The current major weaknesses of environmental information disclosure mainly lie in the following aspects: incompleteness, inaccuracy, untimeliness, unsustainability, and unfriendliness to users. Therefore, it is recommended to strengthen the leadership of government departments, internal coordination, platform construction, and database construction.

Environmental Roundtable Dialogues

I came up with the method of roundtable dialogue to promote the improvement of the environment, eliminate social conflicts, and drive the development of a wide range and large number of small businesses. Most of the environment-related contradictions involve multiple parties, which cannot be resolved through negotiation, adjustment, arbitration, judicial litigation and other conventional measures. Through roundtable dialogues, however, stakeholders, responsible parties, and even independent third parties and fourth parties can sit together for a roundtable meeting, which has later evolved into the model of environmental roundtable dialogue. Environmental roundtable dialogue is a form of meeting in which various stakeholders can engage in equal consultation and dialogues (including government departments, representatives of enterprises and residents and environmental experts, environmental non-governmental organizations and media, etc.) to solve environmental problems. Despite a dim prospect for this idea when I first proposed it in 2000, I have never given up my exploration and practices of it. My exploration in this regard mainly includes township report meetings, county-level institutional arrangements, pilot projects in Jiangsu and Chongqing, national green community construction, questionnaire surveys, community roundtable dialogues, etc. Through my exploration and practices, I believe that it is feasible, effective and low-cost. The key to the next step is how to promote it.

Environmental Social Governance

The environmental governance system can be categorized based on three dimensions: firstly, it is government-related; secondly, it is market-related; and finally, it is society-related. Environmental social governance refers to the realization of environmental protection by mobilizing all social forces through means of social governance concepts and methods, thus eliminating social conflicts caused by environmental problems. Environmental social governance has two major goals: mobilize social forces to put forward environmental protection and prevent and eliminate social conflicts. My suggestions for China's Fourteenth Five-Year Plan cover environmental institutional reforms, environmental institutional construction, construction of the environmental-social interaction mechanism, construction of the social supervision platform, and local pilot demonstration programs.

The concept and significance of the construction of an environmental governance mechanism is to promote the construction of a sustainable development system through a bottom-up approach, and to supplement the current public management manners with abundant and diversified measures of social governance, thus promoting environmental protection, preventing and eliminating social conflicts and improving the public management system.

(This article is compiled and edited based on Professor Wang Hua's lecture, part of the RDCY Master Series Lectures, on December 5, 2018.)

List of Contributors

Lv Bingyang
Professor, doctoral supervisor and director of the School of Finance, Renmin University of China.

Fang Changping
Vice dean and doctoral supervisor of the School of International Studies, Renmin University of China.

Yang Guangbin
Dean of the School of International Studies, Renmin University of China.

Wang Hua
Former dean and overseas distinguished professor of environmental and resource economics of the School of Environment and Natural Resources, Renmin University of China.

Nie Huihua
Executive vice president of the National Academy of Development and Strategy and professor and doctoral supervisor of the School of Economics, Renmin University of China.

Bao Jianyun
Professor and doctoral supervisor of world economics of the School of International Relations and director of the Research Center for International Political Economy, Renmin University of China.

Song Lifang
Vice dean of the Institute of Belt and Road Economic Research and professor of the School of Economics, Renmin University of China

Yang Shu
Former vice president of Lanzhou University and director of the Institute for Central Asian Studies, Lanzhou University.

Zhao Suisheng
Tenured professor of the Josef Korbel School of International Studies and director of the Center for China-U.S. Cooperation, University of Denver, USA.

He Weiwen
Former Economic and Commercial Counselor of the Consulate General of China in San Francisco and New York and senior researcher at the Chongyang Institute for Financial Studies, Renmin University of China.

Wu Xiaoqiu
Vice president of Renmin University of China and director of the Institute of Finance, RUC.

Dong Ximiao
Senior researcher of the Chongyang Institute for Financial Studies, Renmin University of China.

Zheng Xinli
Former deputy director of the Policy Research Office of the CPC Central Committee and executive chairman of the China Association of Policy Science.

Chen Yanbin
Distinguished "Outstanding Scholar" professor of Renmin University of China.

Chen Yaoguo
Professor of the School of Information, Renmin University of China.

Shi Yinhong
Second-level professor of the School of International Studies and director of the Center for American Studies of Renmin University of China.

www.ingramcontent.com/pod-product-compliance
Ingram Content Group UK Ltd.
Pitfield, Milton Keynes, MK11 3LW, UK
UKHW021838100926
8556IPUK00004B/410

9 781433 185908